COMPARATIVE AND INTERNATIONAL

Volume 8

The International Education
of the
Development Consultant

Communicating with
Peasants and Princes

COMPARATIVE AND INTERNATIONAL EDUCATION

Series Editor: PHILIP G. ALTBACH, State University of New York at Buffalo, USA

Editorial Advisory Board:
SUMA CHITNIS, Tata Institute of Social Sciences, Bombay, India

S. GOPINATHAN, Institute of Education, Singapore

GAIL P. KELLY, State University of New York at Buffalo, USA

KAZAYUKI KITAMURA, Research Institute for Higher Education, Hiroshima, Japan

THOMAS LA BELLE, University of Pittsburgh, USA

GUY NEAVE, Institute of Education, University of London, UK

Volume 1   WAGNER: The Future of Literacy in a Changing World

Volume 2   EISEMON: Benefiting from Basic Education, School Quality and Functional Literacy in Kenya

Volume 3   TARROW: Human Rights and Education

Volume 4   THOMAS & KOBAYASHI: Educational Technology—Its Creation, Development, and Cross-Cultural Transfer

Volume 5   BRAY with LILLIS: Community Financing of Education: Issues and Policy Implications in Less Developed Countries

Volume 6   LAUGLO & LILLIS: Vocationalizing Education: An International Perspective

Volume 7   CUMMINGS, GOPINATHAN & TOMODA: The Revival of Values: Education in Asia and the West

Volume 8   FRY & THURBER: The International Education of the Development Consultant

The International Education of the Development Consultant

Communicating with Peasants and Princes

GERALD W. FRY

and

CLARENCE E. THURBER

University of Oregon

PERGAMON PRESS

OXFORD · NEW YORK · BEIJING · FRANKFURT
SÃO PAULO · SYDNEY · TOKYO · TORONTO

UK	Pergamon Press plc, Headington Hill Hall, Oxford OX3 0BW, England
USA	Pergamon Press, Inc., Maxwell House, Fairview Park, Elmsford, New York 10523, USA
PEOPLE'S REPUBLIC OF CHINA	Pergamon Press, Room 4037, Qianmen Hotel, Beijing, People's Republic of China
FEDERAL REPUBLIC OF GERMANY	Pergamon Press GmbH, Hammerweg 6, D-6242 Kronberg, Federal Republic of Germany
BRAZIL	Pergamon Editora Ltda, Rua Eça de Queiros, 346, CEP 04011, Paraiso, São Paulo, Brazil
AUSTRALIA	Pergamon Press Australia Pty Ltd., P.O. Box 544, Potts Point; N.S.W. 2011, Australia
JAPAN	Pergamon Press, 5th Floor, Matsuoka Central Building, 1-7-1 Nishishinjuku, Shinjuku-ku, Tokyo 160, Japan
CANADA	Pergamon Press Canada Ltd., Suite No. 271, 253 College Street, Toronto, Ontario, Canada M5T 1R5

First edition 1989

Library of Congress Cataloging in Publication Data
Fry, Gerald.
The International Education of the Development
Consultant: Communicating with Peasants and
Princes./Gerald W. Fry and Clarence E. Thurber. — 1st ed.
p. cm. — (Comparative and international education series;
v. 8)
Bibliography: p.
1. Technical assistance. 2. Technical assistance —
Anthropological aspects. 3. Consultants. 4. Intercultural
communication.
I. Thurber, Clarence E. II. Title. III. Series.
HC60.F82   1989
658.4'6 — dc19   88-36929

British Library Cataloguing in Publication Data
Fry, Gerald W., *1942–*
The international education of the development
consultant: communicating with peasants and princes.
(Comparative and international education series; v.8)
1. Foreign assistance. Consultants
I. Title II. Thurber, Clarence E. III. Series   338.91

ISBN 0-08-035847-0 Hardcover
ISBN 0-08-035846-2 Flexicover

Printed in Great Britain by A. Wheaton & Co. Ltd. Exeter

Introduction to Series

The Comparative and International Education Series is dedicated to inquiry and analysis on educational issues in an interdisciplinary cross-national framework. As education affects larger populations and educational issues are increasingly complex and, at the same time, international in scope, this series presents research and analysis aimed at understanding contemporary educational issues. The series brings the best scholarship to topics which have direct relevance to educators, policymakers and scholars, in a format that stresses the international links among educational issues. Comparative education not only focuses on the development of educational systems and policies around the world, but also stresses the relevance of an international understanding of the particular problems and dilemmas that face educational systems in individual countries.

Interdisciplinarity is a hallmark of comparative education and this series will feature studies based on a variety of disciplinary, methodological and ideological underpinnings. Our concern is for relevance and the best in scholarship.

The series will combine careful monographic studies that will help policymakers and others obtain a needed depth for enlightened analysis with wider-ranging volumes that may be useful to educators and students in a variety of contexts. Books in the series will reflect on policy and practice in a range of educational settings from pre-primary to post-secondary. In addition, we are concerned with non-formal education and with the societal impact of educational policies and practices. In short, the scope of the Comparative and International Education Series is interdisciplinary and contemporary.

I wish to thank the assistance of a distinguished editorial advisory board including:

Professor Suma Chitnis, Tata University of Social Sciences, Bombay, India.

Professor Kazayuki Kitamura, Research Institute of Higher Education, Hiroshima University, Japan.

Professor Gail P. Kelly, State University of New York at Buffalo, USA.

Dean Thomas La Belle, University of Pittsburgh, USA.

Dr S. Gopinathan, Institute of Education, Singapore.

Professor Guy Neave, Institute of Education, London.

PHILIP G. ALTBACH

Contents

vii

Foreword

Technical assistance cannot be exported; it can only be imported

In a single sentence Paul Hoffman, the man who converted the Marshall Plan from a good idea into a huge success and later served as first administrator of the United Nations Development Programme, thus captured the essence of international consulting.

Clarence Thurber and Gerald Fry rightly describe it as an art. They should know. As reflective practitioners they have learned from their own experience, and as scholars of practice they have studied cross-cultural advising and learned much from the experience of others.

In four decades of postwar trial and error we have all learned that the transfer of technology is not the efficient delivery of magic machines, or even the successful transmission of useful facts and ideas. It's a meeting of minds. This wise and comprehensive book is about that encounter—a daily experience for one-third of a million men and women who visit, live and work away from their own homes, trying to stir together the insights of science and technology with the workways of several hundred local cultures around the world.

US readers may be surprised, as I was, to learn from this book that only 10 percent of the advisers and consultants working in other people's countries are from the United States. Professors Thurber and Fry have wisely chosen to study the whole canvas, not just the US corner of it. In doing so they reveal that the cross-cultural complexities of international consulting are common to the human race, and that we all have much to learn from our common experience.

The dilemma of this ubiquitous encounter is all too clear. Consultants think they know what others need to know, and that the problem is to get it across by breaking down barriers of ignorance and apathy. But the people who need that special knowledge know much more about their own special conditions and traditions than the hired or volunteer visitors can ever learn.

Although I have managed programs of technical aid and advice, I have learned most about consulting from being a client, a consumer of advice from consultants. Few of the consultants I have worked with in my executive life came to me saying, 'Let's start with the proposition that you know more than I do about what puzzles you or holds you back from what you want to do.' If they had, I would have hired them on the spot.

Usually, consultants have tried to convince me that they have a corner on some snake oil with mysterious properties, that they have mastered some arcane discipline that is plainly beyond my depth, that they have invented a tested all-purpose formula, developed a canned training format, written a solvent piece of computer software that I couldn't possibly decipher by myself, so I need help.

The French, as usual, have a succinct way to describe such behavior: *épater les paysans* (or, in American slang, 'snow the peasants').

But what I've learned as a client is that you never get out more than you, the client, put into the consultant. The information you put into the consulting machine is processed with a new perspective combined with different knowledge to produce a uniquely appropriate idea about what you (not the consultant, who will soon be gone) should do next.

Whether this mutual meeting of minds is valuable, to you as the receiver of outside advice, depends on whether the minds really do meet. If the visiting adviser comes up with some prefabricated strategy, designed to fit some superficially similar case, send the visitor quietly away. A fresh angle of vision, a new insight, an innovative use of appropriate technology, applied to a problem you have been living with for too long, can be worth a hundred times what you (or an aid agency or corporation or World Bank) paid for it. But only if the outside consultant has taken the trouble to understand your special cultural context and is working on your unique perplexity.

The outsiders also have to do something even more difficult: refrain from taking credit for what the insiders have been able to accomplish with outside help. Technology transfer works best when it doesn't show—and especially when it doesn't show off.

The errors of theory and practice from which we have learned run like a *leit-motif* through this scholarly yet readable book. The errors are inherent in this most difficult of human relationships: in the 1960s I studied the Soviets' experience with bilateral 'foreign aid,' and found that they made the same mistakes our US programs made, in the same order in which we had made them.

Three of these mistakes stand out: the temptation to push economic growth without worrying enough about fairness, the narrow compartmentalization of knowledge transferred, and the too-chronic failures of cultural empathy.

In every developing country the burgeoning beginnings of modernization have produced a triple collision in which the imperatives of economic growth collide simultaneously with resentments about fairness and resentments about the perceived rape of cultural identity. Consultants and advisers who enter this conflictual arena need to take all three forces into account. If they measure their success only by calculating the changes in per capita gross national product—a measure which teaches us that an increase in food production and an increase in drug addiction both are positive signs—they are bound to be misled, as the generation preceding them were misled, by mistaking economics for society.

Scholars and scientists are catching on to what development practitioners have long known by instinct: that no real-world problem can be tackled by one or another discipline. But the disciplines into which we have divided the life of the mind need to be melded into interdisciplinary wisdom as a basis for policy decisions about what to do next. In the sixth century BC Lao Tse said it: 'To pretend to know what you do not is a disease.'

A wider view of development, and a broader sense of the interconnections among the formal fields of knowledge, are teachable skills. And so is cultural empathy—a 'feel' for cultural difference, a preference for cultural diversity, a willingness to mingle as equals with people who wouldn't feel comfortable in the 'golden ghettos' in which too many international advisers and consultants have dwelt.

Early in my life, when working in Southeast Asia, I heard a story which helped me cope with diversity. An old Malay and a British colonial administrator named Sir Hugh Clifford were arguing about whether it was best to eat with one's fingers or with Western knives, forks, and spoons. The old Malay ended the conversation with an unanswerable comment: 'What you don't understand, Sir Hugh,' he said, 'is that my fingers haven't been in anybody else's mouth, but I'm not so sure about your spoons.'

The authors of this book make a strong case for a mode of international consultation that promotes 'creativity, respect, cooperation and harmony.' We have tried everything else. We would do well to take their advice for the 1990s and beyond.

HARLAN CLEVELAND

Hubert H. Humphrey Institute of Public Affairs
University of Minnesota
August 1988

Preface

This book is the product of many journeys. It is about those who travel beyond their own national borders to share their skills, thoughts, and energies with others who are working to liberate themselves from poverty, hunger, and disease. A special concern is the nature of their cross-cultural encounters and their 'cultural collisions.'

The title of our book is somewhat reminiscent of *The Education of Henry Adams,* probably the best known autobiography ever written in the English language. After he graduated from Harvard in 1858, Adams took the 'grand tour' of Europe and experienced the joys of inter-cultural exploration. In European culture he found a whole new world out there. In the middle of the 20th century, large numbers of American and other western technical consultants 'discovered' the Third World. Many of them claimed that the experience fundamentally changed their lives and their world views. Adams' book might be considered an exemplar of what today we call both experiential education and lifelong education. The ability to engage in both are essential qualities for the successful technical assistant. Thus, Adams' life may be seen to carry important lessons for the modern development consultant.

It would probably be a mistake to draw the parallels too closely. Many would consider Adams a somewhat effete intellectual who rejected his own youthful and turbulent culture in favor of an older, more stable, and perhaps a more cynical one. Still there are some striking similarities. In *The Education,* Adams as a historian of the medieval period, tried to come to understand and cope with the explosion of science and technology that occurred in the 20th century. This created a pluralistic, or as he might have written, a multiplistic society. In this, as opposed to the unified vision of medieval religion, Adams saw a new Godhead: the dynamics of modern individualistic values and energies. Here, relative value instead of ancient verities predominate. In a somewhat analogous manner, modern development consultants are engaged in assisting Third World nations to make the transition into a rapidly changing information age where the benefits of science and technology can be made more widely available. Both Adams and the development consultant have tended to be concerned with, if not obsessed by, the processes of change. Adams in the end came to believe that society as a whole had retrogressed, i.e., that the accumulation of changes had been for the worse. On the contrary, development consultants probably remain optimistic that change is necessary, desirable, and can be progressive.

xiii

During the past three decades perhaps as many as several million individuals have worked in foreign countries as development assistance personnel; serving as administrators, advisers, consultants, experts, and volunteers. As indicated by our bibliography, there is an extensive literature on the experiences of such individuals, including both empirical surveys and popular novels. Drawing on the literature this research, experience, and conferences represent, we feel that it is an appropriate time to reflect on the important and changing process of cross-cultural advising and consulting. We are interested in both notable successes and the undoubted failures; as well as in future trends, such as the increased emphasis on technical cooperation among developing countries.

In a type of qualitative 'metaresearch' we draw heavily on the extensive and diverse existing literature on technical assistance personnel overseas. This research began approximately 35 years ago with Sayre and Thurber's *Training for Specialized Mission Personnel*, to be followed by Harlan Cleveland's important book, *The Overseas Americans*. We have since then had countless discussions, both formal and informal, in various nations about the work of development assistance personnel. We ourselves have served as consultants and advisers in a number of diverse cultural settings. Thus, in approaching our topic, we rely on *multiple* sources of data, such as documents, various surveys, and our own extensive participant observation and interviews.

One major gap in the literature remains unfilled. To our knowledge, there has not been a rigorous quantitative study of the correlates of successful international advising and consulting which would identify clearly the key background factors accounting for success in these types of roles. Given the importance of context and the complex interaction between varying contexts and individual traits and capacities, such a study would be extremely difficult and costly. For those interested in such a challenge, our study may help to define the key variables essential for such analyses.

Given the extensive literature concerning technical assistance work abroad, some may see our study as *deja vu*. We, however, feel that our book presents a new perspective on 'old issues' in several respects. Unlike most of the literature which views this topic from the perspective of a single nation-state, we take an international perspective with concern for the overseas technical assistance personnel of all nations, including socialist societies such as China. We also draw on a wide range of international research sources.

An interdisciplinary approach also characterizes our work on international advising and consulting. In our analyses we draw on perspectives from disciplines such as political science, public administration, sociology, anthropology, economics, and also the humanities.

Unlike much of the literature which tends to be rather reductionist in overstressing the traits of the single individual, we attempt to utilize an ecological perspective that reflects the interaction between context and the individual personality.

We have tried as well to identify as explicitly as possible criteria for judging success in international advising and consulting. Finally, and perhaps most importantly, we postulate the knowledge base and ethical foundations to define a profession for international advisers and development assistance personnel.

Central to our approach is an emphasis on communication and a participative orientation towards development. This perspective is reflected in our subtitle: 'Communicating with Peasants and Princes.' We see such communication, particularly a genuine dialogue with peasants, as central to the development process.

Unlike most of the existing literature which sees advising as a one-way process, we view advising and consulting as a two-way or three-way process. We view returned overseas technical assistance personnel as potentially influential educational, cultural, and political forces in the rich industrial societies.

The basic assumption underlying our book is that the human being will continue to be central to the process of intellectual exchange and technology transfer. We anticipate that the process of international advising and consulting will become even more diverse and international. Thus, we hope that our study may be helpful to the following groups of individuals:

1. Professionals sent abroad by international organizations, bilateral technical assistance agencies, private voluntary organizations, and nongovernmental organizations.
2. Volunteers sent abroad under various bilateral, international, or private auspices.
3. Private businessmen and government officials with short-term or long-term assignments abroad.
4. Those engaged in technical cooperation among developing countries.
5. Those working with minorities within a single nation-state.

With reference to the development process, our focus on international consultants and advisers in this volume could be misinterpreted. Our view is that all external aid is and must be marginal to efforts made internally, and this includes expert advisers. We see international advisers and related technical assistance as only one of *many* factors involved in the development process. Obviously both important internal and external forces are at work that determine developmental prospects and results. However, in this volume we limit our focus to one important dimension of external forces: the role of international advisers and consultants.

The Scope of the Study

This study is comprised of six parts. Part I provides background for the study, including a statement of research objectives and methodology used. Part II consists of five chapters which cover the following major issues: the multiple roles of advisers, the use and abuse of foreign languages, the political role of advisers, the economic role of advisers, and in-service local training. In Part III we present specific criteria for assessing the effectiveness of international advisers and consultants. Part IV consists of case studies, both exemplary and anonymous, of individual advisers having served overseas. Included are both notable successes and distinctive failures, from which we hope important lessons may be learned. Part V presents issues related to the question of professionalism in international advising and consulting. Foundations for a profession are made explicit, including a code of ethics (included as an appendix) and a specific knowledge base. In Part VI future trends in advising and consulting are considered with special emphasis on the internationalization of the advising and consulting profession. This is followed by an appendix which provides a detailed statistical profile of international advisers and consultants. This profile presents information on the numbers of advisers, where they come from, where they go, and what they do. The final part of the study is an extensive analytical bibliography on international advising and consulting, which we hope will prove useful to other scholars and practitioners concerned with improving the practice and conduct of international advising and consulting.

Value Premises Underlying the Study

Gunnar Myrdal in his important but, we think, neglected work, *Objectivity in Social Research*, argues that it is naive to think that the social sciences are value-free. All social science research is influenced by underlying but often unstated value premises. Myrdal, thus advocates that social scientists state in the very beginning their basic values which influence their research and thinking. In an attempt to be responsive to Myrdal's concerns, we will make explicit the basic value premises underlying this study. They can be briefly summarized as follows:

1. We believe in the fundamental worth and value of cultural, scientific, technical and educational exchanges. Overall we feel that such movement of individuals across national boundaries has helped to improve the human condition and prospects for peace and international understanding. There have been, to be sure, some notable failures and some adverse effects associated with such activities, and these are discussed in this volume. But also described are many examples of technical assistance provided by international advisers that have resulted in positive enhancements of the human condition. We believe that consultants who describe and analyze their experiences in writing contribute to the educational process by which some of the former (failures) may be transformed into some of the latter (successes). We also believe that technical assistance represents an important element in the development process.

2. Since we believe that the social sciences are inherently value-laden, we also view the international advising process as inherently political. The term, 'technical' assistance was apparently invented to mask this underlying reality. In Chapter 4 we discuss the political dimensions of international advising and consulting. In that chapter we present two opposing views with respect to the politics of advising. From the perspective of the individual consultant, the most political aspect of advising is the initial decision to accept an assignment to assist a given government. That decision should be based on a match of values between the host government and the potential adviser. Once the decision has been made to advise a government or ministry, our basic orientation stresses that advisers should adopt a service role and not try to impose their own personal values and solutions on a host government. Instead they should dedicate themselves to helping their hosts achieve

the goals they have determined for themselves. Often, helping the host government or agency better to define the problem, so that alternative solutions are clarified, is the most important contribution an adviser can make. Among the competing loyalties faced by consultants we believe that the commitment to helping the host agency is foremost. Thus, we postulate the ideal of the consultant who accepts the limited advisory role and deplores direct political interventions which may impinge on other nations' basic sovereignty.

3. The international consulting process involves important ethical and normative dimensions. There are ambiguities and difficulties inherent in such activities. Unfortunately, violations of professional standards have occurred and will probably continue to occur. For these reasons we include a special appendix which includes an explicit statement of professional standards for international advising and consulting. In many ways this statement, we recognize, also reflects values that we share.

4. Although much of the literature portrays advising as a one-way process involving individuals from 'rich' countries going to help those in 'poor' nations, we view the advising process as more complex, exemplifying a two-dimensional or even a three- or four-dimensional phenomenon. Thus we consider advising that takes place under the auspices of technical cooperation among developing countries (TCDC) as particularly important, because the context of development in both the donor and the host may be similar, and progress in the one may more easily be transferred to the other. Such South–South exchanges have considerable potential.

5. We also believe that the international advising and consulting process has had important consequences in terms of reverse communications for the rich nations. The experiences of international advisers has provided, for example, a rich knowledge base for international development. Sir Arthur Lewis, the Nobel laureate in development economics from Saint Lucia, certainly enriched his understanding of development problems while serving in advisory capacities in Africa; and this is but one of many such examples. International advising and consulting represents an important form of life-long learning and an important presence in the field of development education. For example, the presence of former Peace Corps volunteers from the Philippines in the US polity no doubt helped the US to understand the change from Marcos to Aquino.

6. International consulting and advising is thus an important form of international communication by which we have learned much about the syndrome of development problems associated with what we now characterize as the 'Third World.' But as L. S. Stavrianos so graphically illustrates in his major work, *Global Rift,* the industrialized countries are now coming to recognize that the 'Thirld World' exists at home as well as abroad.

7. Throughout this work, we have an important concern for *praxis*. Since a significant portion of technical assistance involves advising and consulting, it is important to evaluate rigorously the effectiveness of such individuals as well as the organizational contexts which condition their opportunities for both success and failure. The formulation of relevant criteria for such evaluations is an important task. This type of evaluation is essential if we are to improve the practice of international advising and consulting. In this sense our book perhaps fits the genre of what Chris Argyris terms action science in his work on methodology, *The Inner Contradictions* of *Rigorous Research*. Thus, it is our goal in this work to link scholarly research and analysis with practical concerns related to improving the quality of international advising so as to enhance its role in improving the human condition.

8. While material changes are an inevitable part of the development process, human beings must be central and represent the first priority in terms of development strategies. Basic human needs, individual empowerment, human rights, self-fulfillment, and reverence for life are fundamental values integral to humanistic development.

9. Despite our stress in this volume on international advising and consulting, we recognize that outside aid is *marginal* to the development process. Development can be assisted, but it cannot be produced, as if by injection, from abroad.

10. We believe that much can be learned from both success and failure. We also feel that too much of social science is preoccupied with discovering the representative case. Anomalies and extreme cases can contribute significantly to the development of insight and understanding. Much of the development literature tends to be too optimistic or too pessimistic. By examining both successes and failures, we hope to present a balanced perspective.

Acknowledgments

Our thinking about, and interest in, the roles of international advisers and consultants have been influenced by many individuals. Among those most significant and deserving of mention are the following whom Fry would like to recognize: Paul Baran, John Bock, Martin Carnoy, William Fuller, Reuben Frodin, Peter Geithner, Fred Harbison, Sir Arthur Lewis, James March, Joseph Mestenhauser, Robert Textor, Hans Weiler, and Peter Weldon. Thurber would like to recognize Roger Churnside, Harlan Cleveland, Milton Esman, John Ferguson, John Gange, John Howard, John Montgomery, Rogerio Pinto, and Robert Walker. Both authors would like to indicate special thanks to Richard Hill, former Provost of the University of Oregon, for his important support and encouragement of our efforts to strengthen International Studies at the University of Oregon, which facilitated completion of this research project.

We would also like to thank the many individuals who were willing to spend time sharing, in often extremely candid terms, their thoughts about international advisers and consultants. Particularly valuable were interviews with Dr Sippanondha Ketudat, President, Petrochemical Authority of Thailand; Dr Herbert Bisno of La Trobe University, Australia; Mr Ken Aspinall, Department of Foreign Affairs, ADAB, Australia; Mr Paul Bartel, former AID adviser in Morocco; Mr Jessie Brandt, currently an adviser in Bangladesh; and Ms Jackie Eckman of USIA. We also owe an important debt to the many officials of CIDA and IDRC who granted helpful interviews during Clarence Thurber's research in Ottawa during the summer of 1984.

Also valuable were informal discussions with colleagues such as Michael Moravcsik, Institute of Theoretical Science, University of Oregon (UO); Norman Sundberg, Department of Psychology, UO; George Zaninovich, Department of Political Science, UO; Ed Comstock, Peace Corps director, Pakistan; and Galen Martin, Research Associate, UO. We also appreciate the critical comments of Nelly Stromquist, a Peruvian formerly with IDRC, on an earlier draft of the manuscript.

With respect to research assistance, we are grateful to Sununthorn Setboonsarng, who helped with the quantitative analyses of the study; Tatsanee Setboonsarng, who assisted in bibliographical work; Yukiko Morikawa, who assisted in updating our quantitative material; and Mustafa Mohamed Mustafa, Ministry of Foreign Affairs, the Sudan, for help related to African materials used in the study. Terry Fry also helped in the preparation of graphs and figures.

Khun Kannika Mahawat, a reference librarian at ESCAP in Bangkok, was extremely helpful during fieldwork in Thailand.

We would like to thank Tasanee Fry, Maggie O'Grady, Maryann Cole, Camilla Pratt, and Linda King for their dedicated assistance in manuscript preparation and typing.

This work, a genuinely collaborative effort dating back to 1969, has our names as authors listed alphabetically. It is our hope that the whole is greater than the sum of the individual parts we have contributed. Without such collaboration the blend of qualitative and quantitative research approaches used would not have been possible. Each author has influenced the other in ways too numerous to mention, critically assessing the role of advisers and consultants.

Finally, we would like to thank our wives, Tasanee and Louise for their continuing support and encouragement.

We are deeply grateful to the individuals mentioned above for their contributions to this study. The authors, however, are responsible for the views and interpretations expressed here.

GERALD W. FRY
CLARENCE E. THURBER

Eugene, Oregon
August 1988

Glossary of Acronyms

ADAB	Australian Development Assistance Bureau (Canberra)
AID	(US) Agency for International Development
AIT	Asian Institute of Technology (Thailand)
ANU	The Australian National University
Aramco	Arabian American Oil Company
ASPA	American Society for Public Administration
AUFS	American Universities Field Staff
CGIAR	Consultative Group on International Agricultural Research
CIASP	Conference on Inter-American Student Projects (Cuernavaca, Mexico)
CIDA	Canadian International Development Agency (Ottawa)
CIMMYT	Centro International de Majoramiento de Maize y Trigo (International Maize and Wheat Improvement Center), (Mexico)
CIP	International Potato Centre (Lima, Peru)
CUSO	Canadian University Service Overseas
DAC	Development Assistance Committee of OECD
DTCP	Development Training and Communication Planning (UN)
ECDC	Economic Cooperation among Developing Countries
ESCAP	Economic and Social Commission for Asia and the Pacific (Bangkok)
FAO	Food and Agricultural Organization of the United Nations (Rome)
GVS	German Voluntary Service
HIID	Harvard Institute for International Development
ICA	Institute of Cultural Affairs (Chicago)
ICAO	International Civil Aviation Organization
ICARDA	International Centre for Agricultural Research in Dry Areas (Aleppo, Syria)
ICRISAT	International Crop Research Institute for the Semi-Arid Tropics (Hyderabad, India)
IDRC	International Development Research Centre (Ottawa, Canada)
IESC	International Executive Service Corps
IHB	International Health Board
IIE	Institute of International Education (New York)
IIEP	International Institute for Educational Planning (Paris)

IIST	Institute for International Studies and Training (Japan)
ILO	International Labour Organization (Geneva)
IRRI	International Rice Research Institute (Los Baños, Philippines)
JCRR	Joint Committee on Rural Reconstruction (Taiwan)
JICA	Japan International Cooperation Agency
JOCV	Japanese Overseas Cooperation Volunteers
JUSE	Union of Japanese Scientists and Engineers
LDC	Less-developed Country
MEM	Mass Education Movement
NGOs	Nongovernmental organisations
NIDA	National Institute of Development Administration (Thailand)
NSV	National Service Volunteers (France)
OECD	Organization for Economic Cooperation and Development (Paris)
PRC	People's Republic of China
PUMC	Peking Union Medical College
PVOs	Private voluntary organisations
SFID	Study Fellowships for International Development
SID	Society for International Development
SIETAR	Society for Intercultural Education, Training and Research
TAC	Technical Advisory Committee
TAICH	Technical Assistance Information Clearing House
TCDC	Technical cooperation among developing countries
UNDP	United Nations Development Programme
UNEP	United Nations Environmental Programme (Nairobi)
Unesco	United Nations Educational, Scientific, and Cultural Organization (Paris)
UNFPA	United Nations Fund for Population Activities
UNIDO	United Nations Industrial Development Organization (Vienna, Austria)
UNITAR	United Nations Institute for Training and Research
UNU	United Nations University (Tokyo, Japan)
UNV	United Nations Volunteers
UPU	Universal Postal Union
VDC	Volunteer Development Corps
VITA	Volunteers for International Technical Assistance
VSA	New Zealand Voluntary Service Abroad
VSO	Voluntary Service Overseas (United Kingdom)

PART I

Background

CHAPTER 1

Introduction

Opportunities for technical cooperation are abundant, not the tutelage
relationship of technological transfer, but applied research and learning that link researchers with practitioners and local with foreign
specialists . . . the methods and skills required, however, are more
akin to mutual learning than to the conventional transfer of known
technology from donor to recipient (Milton Esman).[1]

According to Lynn T. White, a specialist in the history of technical innovation at UCLA, the earliest form of 'official' technical assistance occurred as
early as 1400 BC when the ruling monarch of Macedonia sent aid to the King
of Egypt. Although the surface motive was diplomatic (friendship), the
underlying one was to promote military cooperation. In ancient China the
common word for 'to wander' or 'to travel' in Confucian circles meant 'to go
from Court to Court as peripatetic counsellor.'[2] Also the Ottoman Empire
made extensive use of foreign technical personnel after the fall of Constan-
tinople in 1453. Prior to the contemporary era this was apparently the
largest-scale utilization of foreigners for political, administrative, and military service.[3] Also in early Southeast Asian history, Brahmin advisers from
India strongly influenced the royal courts of that region.[4]

Ever since these early forms of technical assistance, there have been
serious difficulties as well as some impressive examples of success. The
popular literature both in the United States and abroad has tended to stress
the failures as illustrated by such well-known titles as *The Ugly American,*
The Ugly Russian and *Japan Unmasked* (the Japanese version of the ugly
American).[5] In contrast, a popular song of the Kingston Trio and a feature
film made Tom Dooley, who provided medical assistance to Laos, a youth
hero.[6]

Despite the long history of technical assistance, the subject remains
ridden with controversy. Writers such as Illich, Roberts, and Arnove are
highly critical of the role played by international consultants and advisers.[7]
Despite such criticism, international agencies and foundations continue to
employ consultants and advisers in large numbers.

The period since World War II has seen a vast expansion in the number of
people who live, work, study, or travel in other nations. During the past 30
years there has been approximately an eightfold increase worldwide in the
number of individuals opting for foreign study alone.[8] The most recent data

3

from the US Bureau of the Census indicate that the number of US citizens (excluding federal employees) residing abroad increased 26 percent between 1960 and 1970.[9] Between 1960 and 1980, US federal employees (excluding military personnel) working abroad increased 25 percent. During the past decade, 1970–80, the number of foreign born in the US increased by 46 percent. These data show a dramatic increase in the movement of individuals across national boundaries in recent decades. The *Times Atlas of World History* calls ours the Age of Global Civilization.

It will come as no surprise, then, that these marked increases in the transnational exchange of persons are similarly reflected in trends related to the provision of international advisers and consultants. We estimate the number of individuals serving abroad as technical advisers, consultants, or volunteers to be approximately 370,000 (see Table 1.1, which presents these data in a worldwide profile of international advisers).[10] The largest number, 107,300, are technical assistance personnel provided by communist nations to non-communist LDCs.[11] The bilateral aid programs of the various OECD nations provide the second-largest number of advisers, 82,900 in 1985.[12] There were also 12,200 advisers and experts working under the multilateral auspices of the United Nations and 11,152 under the Colombo Plan.[13]

TABLE 1.1.   *Types and Numbers of International Advisers and Volunteers*

Type of adviser or consultant	Number	Percentage of total
Publicly financed under OECD bilateral programs	82,900	22.5
Communist economic technicians serving in non-communist LDCs	107,300	29.1
World Bank consultants	5,000	1.4
United Nations experts	12,200	3.3
Colombo Plan experts	11,152	3.0
Experts of Commonwealth Secretariat	330	0.1
Experts provided by OPEC nations	328	0.1
Experts of NGOs and PVOs	58,290	15.8
Volunteers of NGOs and PVOs	89,532	24.3
Colombo Plan volunteers	1,307	0.4
Total	368,339	100.0

Sources:
Development Co-operation, OECD, Paris, 1987, p.243.
Communist Aid Activities in Non-Communist Less Developed Countries, 1979 and 1954–79: A Research Paper, CIA, Washington, DC, 1980, p.21.
Yearbook of the United Nations 1980, United Nations, New York, vol. 34, 1983, pp.604–5.
The Colombo Plan Annual Report 1986, Colombo Plan Bureau, Colombo, Sri Lanka, 1986, p.15.
Report of the Commonwealth Secretary-General, Commonwealth Secretariat, London, 1979.
Aid from OPEC Countries, OECD, Paris, 1983.
Directory of Non-Governmental Organizations of OECD Member Countries Active in Development Co-operation, OECD, Paris, 1981.
Note: The data for NGOs and PVOs were aggregated from the country organization reports in the OECD Directory of Non-governmental Organizations active in development cooperation.

Payments for the services of experts accounted for more than half of the total UNDP expenditures for projects in 1979.[14] From 1962 to 1981 there was a remarkable 16.4-fold increase in the proportion of budget used for consultants by the various organizations of the United Nations system.[15] There are also a large number of advisers and consultants serving with various foundations, private voluntary organisations (PVOs), and nongovernmental organisations (NGOs).

Table 1.2 shows the growth in advisers provided by various OECD countries between 1970 and 1985. Clearly Japan's corps of overseas technical assistance personnel has grown the fastest, followed by the Netherlands, Italy, Australia, Austria, Denmark, Switzerland, and Canada. Appendix I provides detailed data for each OECD country with respect to trends in the provision of international advisers and consultants. It also includes detailed quantitative data on Colombo Plan experts, technical assistance personnel sent abroad by communist nations, and the extent of expertise provided under TCDC (technical cooperation among developing countries). An econometric analysis of the demand for and supply of United Nations experts is also provided in this appendix.

TABLE 1.2. *Shifts in the Provision of Technical Assistance Personnel by OECD Nations During the Period 1970–85*

Country	Percentage shift in the provision of technical assistance personnel
Japan	+447
Netherlands	+142
Italy	+ 97
Australia	+ 82
Austria	+ 56*
Denmark	+ 46
Switzerland	+ 41*
Canada	+ 40
Norway	+ 12
Belgium	− 8*
United States	− 11
Germany	− 13
Sweden	− 16
France	− 39*
New Zealand	− 55*
United Kingdom	− 69

* For France, data are for the period 1970–79.
  For Switzerland, data are for the period 1970–83.
  For New Zealand, data are for the period 1975–85.
  For Austria and Belgium, data are for the period 1970–84.
Sources:
  Development Co-operation, 1986 Report, OECD, Paris, 1987, p.243.
  Development Co-operation, 1981 Review, OECD, Paris, 1981, p.223.

Consistent with the data above, a major study of the US Agency for International Development (AID) maintains that the adviser–counterpart relationship still forms the core of the technical assistance process.[16] Denis Goulet similarly recognizes the pivotal role played by consultants in the complex and controversial area of technology transfer.[17] Goulet views such consultants, however, as 'one-eyed giants' who too often fail to appreciate non-scientific modes of rationality.[18]

Thus, the major focus of this study is the provision of advisers and consultants from one nation to another, an international and cross-cultural process that is still inadequately understood. This topic, for example, was the subject of an extensive and detailed discussion at a meeting of the Society for Intercultural Education, Training and Research (SIETAR), held in March 1981, in Vancouver, Canada. The World Bank is also devoting considerable attention to this issue.[19]

There is also a lack of a clear definition of 'experts,' 'consultants,' and 'advisers.'[20] For purposes of this volume we define international advisers and consultants as those individuals who cross national boundaries to share information, skills, knowledge, or expertise with individuals of other nations and cultures for the purpose of development. Usually, financial fees are associated with such sharing of knowledge, though we also include in our definition those who undertake such assignments on a voluntary basis (e.g. United Nations Volunteers, US Peace Corps, and International Executive Service Corps). Since teachers and professors are often engaged in sharing expertise and providing advice on the development of academic or training programs abroad, they are included in our definition.[21] The term 'expert' is also frequently used in this volume. We use this term with its conventional meaning of 'one whose special knowledge or skills causes him/her to be an authority.[22]

Our basic concern in the study is to develop a deeper understanding of the complex process of providing technical expertise across national and cultural boundaries. While there is a consideration of attributes needed by individuals for technical assistance abroad, the major thrust is to understand the intricate links among role, behavior, political-bureaucratic environment, cultural context, and organizational development, all of which affect an adviser's potential for constructive impact.

The study is intended for the sizeable and growing number of individuals involved in cross-cultural advising and consulting. This would include, for example, an adviser of the People's Republic of China working in Tanzania or Western Samoa; a German on a World Bank mission to Thailand; an American AID adviser working in Morocco; or a Swedish volunteer working in Africa.

Although the study's major focus is on the various international roles suggested above, it also has relevance to two other audiences. First, many businessmen working in other countries and cultures become involved in complex adviser–counterpart relations. As the distinction between the private and public sector continues to blur, increasingly private sector personnel working abroad need to be sensitive to many of the same issues we discuss in this study.[23] For example, when Nike, Inc., the running-shoe company, opened factories in the People's Republic of China, it sent six Nike executives to serve as counterparts to six Chinese managers, providing them technical assistance on how to produce high-quality running shoes for the world market.[24]

Second, within countries which are culturally heterogeneous, many individuals are involved in working with minority groups. For example, in Thailand, Central Thais are now doing development work with hill tribes in Northern Thailand under a major AID project. Projects of this type involve complex adviser–counterpart relations among host country nationals and minorities of different cultures and languages within their own country. The same situation exists for the Hispanic Peruvian working with Aymaras in the rural areas of that country. Thus, many of the concerns of this study are of considerable relevance to professionals doing development work with members of other cultures within the boundaries of their own nation-states.

Shifting Trends in Cross-cultural Advising and Consulting

The style and form of cross-cultural advising and consulting have changed dramatically in recent years. In the 1950s and 1960s it was common to find large teams of advisers working in developing countries. Individuals would sometimes work for as many as 5–10 years in such advisory positions. Large teams and long extended stays are now less common. One recent major AID project in Northern Africa specifies a 3-week period as an ideal contract period for outside consultants. There are many reasons for this shift away from large teams and long tours of duty. The major factor is, of course, the increasingly prohibitive cost of funding such efforts. A second factor relates to the strengthening of local technical capacity, thereby reducing the need for large teams of outsiders for lengthy stays. Finally, there is the serious and inherent 'golden ghetto' syndrome associated with such teams, and its tendency to diminish contact and interaction with host country nationals.

A major new trend affecting cross-cultural advising and consulting is technical cooperation among developing countries (TCDC), a term developed by the UN. Both the UN and countries such as Sweden, Switzerland, New Zealand, and the Federal Republic of Germany are actively supporting TCDC.[25] The basic principle is that 'project inputs such as expertise should be provided entirely, or to the largest extent possible, by the partner developing countries themselves.' Already there is concrete evidence of the TCDC approach being implemented. Experts from the People's Republic of China helped Western Samoa prepare for the recent South Oceania Games. China has also sent technical development experts to help in African nations such as Tanzania and Rwanda. Also in Asia, India has provided experts to Burma to help in fertilizer marketing, and Thai experts are helping the Philippines in the area of cassava processing.[26] Philippine experts have assisted in Latin America, where Colombia has also provided experts to Paraguay to participate in a program for the development of indigenous arts and crafts. Experts working under TCDC arrangements face a number of problems similar to those encountered by Japanese, European or US advisers working in developing countries. Fortunately, TCDC experts can draw on the decades of extensive experience of others as they undertake challenging opportunities in a wide range of cross-cultural settings.

A second trend, suggested above, is the move toward shorter consultancies.[27] Short-term consultants are employed on contracts by aid-granting agencies or foreign governments to deliver specific technical services to host countries. To stretch technical assistance dollars farther, the bulk of technical consulting is done by those who are engaged for shorter and shorter periods in which to transmit their advice.

A third and highly significant trend is a shift toward a greater emphasis on human capacity-building as a strategy of technical assistance and an integral part of development. In this connection the World Bank has been criticized for overemphasizing hardware and neglecting 'software,' (the human capacity-building and cultural aspects of development). As the Bank moves toward a greater balance between hardware and software, it will need to provide funding for more training in a wide range of technical areas.

Finally, given the high costs of formal education overseas, there appears to be a growing interest in providing intensive in-country training courses of short duration as a cost-effective alternative to sending large numbers abroad for formal study. This strategy, for example, is being emphasized by AID–Thailand. Numerous American experts have been engaged to come to Thailand as short-term consultants to assist in-country training projects.

Objectives of the Study

This study has several major objectives. The first objective is to present and discuss major issues in cross-cultural advising and consulting. Although there is an extensive literature on overseas advising and consulting, it is highly segmented and fragmented.[28] Much of the literature is polemical.[29] Other literature tends to be preoccupied with listing the characteristics of the 'ideal adviser.'[30] Thus, it is our hope to present a balanced, integrated, and comprehensive discussion covering the following major issues:

1. The evolving multiple roles of advisers—alternative typologies and some major polarities.
2. The tongue-tied adviser: the question of foreign languages and communication.

3. Problems of adjustment: cultural differences affecting advising, consulting roles.
4. The politics of advising and consulting.
5. The economics of advising and consulting.
6. Involvement of experts in intensive in-country training programs.

A second objective of the study is to develop criteria for assessing effectiveness in cross-cultural advising and consulting. This is an important but neglected area. Though advisers work in different environments, each calling for distinctive patterns of behavior, there is nevertheless a need to specify criteria for evaluating effectiveness. The criteria developed in the book derive from a critical analysis of the extensive empirical data now available on the experiences of various advisers and consultants during the past several decades.

Our third objective derives directly from the second, and involves the development of practical guidelines for professional advising and consulting in cross-cultural settings. We propose a specific code of professional ethics, oriented toward excellence and integrity. Anne Winslow has eloquently stated the case for professionalism:

> The intricate process of effecting social change, of translating into workable terms knowledge and experience from one culture to another, of communicating across boundaries is not an occupation for amateurs.[31]

Fortunately, given the data presently available, there exists a solid empirical foundation for the specification of professional standards and guidelines.

Methodology and Data Collection

David Tyack emphasizes that there are many ways of knowing and seeing.[32] In this book we rely on multiple data sources and research methods. A first data source is a wide range of previous related research which we attempt to synthesize. It includes the works of writers such as Robert Arnove, Harlan Cleveland, Paulo Freire, Denis Goulet, Ivan Illich, and many others who have directed attention to the issue of international consultants and advisers.[33]

The direct experiences of such advisers constitute a second rich data source. The late Paul Hanna at Stanford University, for example, developed a special archive containing considerable material of this type.[34] It includes the papers and documents of a number of former international advisers and consultants. For example, the collection includes the papers of individuals such as Arthur Young, financial adviser to China, 1929–46; Russell Davis, Harvard adviser to many foreign governments, 1967–79; Eddie Smith, Peace Corps Volunteer in Ghana, 1963–64; Philip C. McConnell, Vice

IEDC—C

President, Arabian American Oil, 1937–63; and many others having served overseas as technical consultants or advisers. Also the World Bank has published a special volume on the life work of Wolf Ladejinsky, an inspirational example of excellence in foreign advising and consulting.[35] Another useful source for data is provided by William Mangin, who recently published his thoughts on 24 years of work in Peru on the Vicos Project.[36]

A third source of data consists of formal and informal interview surveys of foreign advisers and their host country counterparts. We have conducted approximately 300 interviews of this type in Indonesia, India, Japan, Thailand, Pakistan, and Lebanon.[37] Also Meredith Minkler's report on his interviews of 50 AID and Ford advisers in India and 43 of their local counterparts provide a valuable source of data.[38] Interview surveys by Denyse Harari[39] and Francis Byrnes[40] similarly provide useful information.

Though valuable, data based on the direct interview of former advisers of those currently serving in such roles, have certain inherent limitations. There is a tendency for advisers themselves to report favorably on their activities and to minimize the reporting of failures or behavior which proved to be culturally inappropriate. To obtain data on these less favorable aspects of cross-cultural advising, we rely on 'significant others,' who have observed the *actual* (not reported) behavior of advisers and consultants working internationally.[41] These 'significant others' are a wide range of individuals met during our own overseas experiences in various settings. We ourselves are among this group of 'significant others' who have had the opportunity to observe the behavior and actions of countless advisers and consultants serving internationally in a wide variety of settings.

These observations have occurred over a period of approximately 30 years. Such observations provide the basis for most of our anonymous case studies.

Thus, a fourth source of data is direct participant observation represented by our own experience with organizations such as the Ford Foundation, AID, the Peace Corps, World Education and the United Nations. We have worked in countries such as Honduras, Indonesia, Peru, Guatemala, India, Costa Rica, and Thailand. Over the years we have known personally, and worked with, a wide range of international advisers and consultants. We ourselves have served as both short-term and long-term advisers during our careers in several cultural settings.

With respect to the methodology of the study, three concepts have influenced considerably our approach and orientation. The first concept is that of polarity emphasized by Ernest Becker.[42] Polarities are not dualities but a complex interdependence of opposites, which complement one another in a kind of creative tension.[43] The concept of polarity is particularly useful as we consider the individual personality attributes needed by international advisers and consultants. Many relevant traits can be represented by key polarities. Examples of important polarities introduced later in the book are arrogant–humble, etic–emic, power–service, and superior–colleague.

A second concept is that of anomaly. Physical scientists often emphasize the careful study of anomalies as a means to gain insight and understanding. In contrast, social scientists tend to emphasize the representative case. In this study, we emphasize such anomalies in our various case studies presented in Part IV. By looking at advisers who have been exceptionally capable, and at others who have had serious problems, we can develop a deeper understanding of the essence of effective cross-cultural advising and consulting.

A third concept derives from Robert Lifton's book, *Boundaries,* which introduces the notion of the protean character.[44] Also in literature Jack London, Saul Bellow, Günter Grass, and Eugene Burdick have portrayed this type of flexible individual. Protean individuals have an impressive talent for adapting themselves to divergent social worlds. They do not commit themselves to a single form, and instead engage in an interminable series of experiments and explorations.[45] As we discuss in the second chapter the many multiple roles which advisers play, the need for protean adaptability among international advisers should become increasingly salient and significant.

Notes

1. M. J. ESMAN, Developmental assistance in public administration: requiem or renewal, *Public Administration Review,* **40**, 430 (1980).
2. A. WALEY, *Three Ways of Thought in Ancient China,* Allen & Unwin, London, 1939; cited by H. Goldhamer, *The Adviser,* Elsevier, New York, 1978, p.77.
3. H. GOLDHAMER, p.82.
4. D. R. SARDESAI, *Southeast Asia: Past and Present,* Vikas, Delhi, 1983, p.17.
5. W. J. LEDERER and E. BURDICK, *The Ugly American,* Norton, New York, 1958; V. LASKY, *The Ugly Russian,* New York, Trident, 1965; I. KAWASAKI, *Japan Unmasked,* Tuttle, Rutland, Vermont, 1969. Advisers in overseas settings are also the subject of considerable 'fiction.' See, for example, A. BURGESS, *The Malayan Trilogy,* Pan Books, London, 1964; A. BURGESS, *The Devil of a State,* Ballantine, New York, 1968. The latter work describes the complex and difficult role of a UN adviser, Mr Tomlin, in the hypothetical nation of Dunia (actually Brunei). Burgess served as a colonial officer in both Malaya and Brunei. A Canadian example is provided by the novel written by T. KEENLEYSIDE, *Common Touch,* Doubleday, Toronto, 1977. This work examines the consequences of using career diplomats to manage development aid programs. Several South Pacific novelists, using striking satire, have also commented on foreign advisers. See E. HAU'OFA, *Tales of the Tikongs,* Longman Paul, Auckland, 1983 and E. HAU'OFA, Old wine in new bottles, in A. WENDT (editor), *Lali: a Pacific Anthology,* Longman Paul, Auckland, 1980, pp.225–30.
6. T. DOOLEY, *Dr. Tom Dooley's Three Great Books,* Farrar, Straus & Cudahy, New York, 1960.
7. I. ILLICH, To hell with good intentions. Address delivered at the Conference on Inter-American Student Projects (CIASP), Cuernavaca, Mexico, 20 April 1968; G. ROBERTS, 'Volunteers and neo-colonialism; an inquiry into the role of foreign volunteers in the Third World,' mimeo, US Peace Corps, 1968? R. ARNOVE (editor), *Philanthropy and Cultural Imperialism: Foundations at Home and Abroad,* Indiana University Press, Bloomington, Indiana, 1982.

8. E. BARBER, P. ALTBACH, and R. MYERS (editors), *Bridges to Knowledge: Foreign Students in Comparative Perspective,* University of Chicago Press, Chicago, Illinois, 1984, p.1.

9. *Statistical Abstract of the United States 1987,* US Bureau of the Census, Washington, DC, 1987, p.9.

10. This figure is based on an aggregation of data from the OECD, the United Nations, CIA, The Colombo Plan Bureau, and the Commonwealth Secretariat (see Table 1.1). Chesanow also notes that over 100,000 US business executives and their families are overseas on extended assignments, N. CHESANOW, *World-Class Executive,* Rawson, New York, 1985, p.46.

11. *Communist Aid Activities in Non-Communist Less Developed Countries, 1979 and 1954–79: A Research Paper,* National Foreign Assessment Center, CIA, Washington, DC, 1980, p.21.

12. *Development Co-operation: Efforts and Policies of the Members of the Development Assistance Committee,* 1986 Report, OECD, Paris, 1987, p.243.

13. *Colombo Plan Annual Report 1986,* Colombo Plan Bureau, Colombo, Sri Lanka, 1986, p.84.

14. J. L. WOODS, Suggested framework for determining roles of international advisers/consultants, Note for Project Formulators, no. 506, UNDP, DTCP, Bangkok, 1980, p.1

15. *Yearbook of the United Nations 1982,* United Nations, New York, 1986, p.1487.

16. *The Technical Assistance Process: an Introductory Bibliography,* US AID, Washington, DC, AID Bibliographic Series: Technical Assistance Methodology, no. 3, 1974, p.1. See F. LETHEM and L. COOPER, *Managing Project-related Technical Assistance,* World Bank, Washington, DC, Management and Development Series, no. 13, 1983.

17. D. GOULET, *The Uncertain Promise: Value Conflicts in Technology Transfer,* IDOC, New York, 1977, p.67.

18. D. GOULET, Development experts; the one-eyed giants, *World Development* **8,** 481–9 (1980).

19. *Report on the Progress Made in Implementing the Tasks Entrusted to the United Nations Development System by the Buenos Aires Plan of Action for Promoting and Implementing Technical Co-operation among Developing Countries,* TCDC/2/5, United Nations, New York, 3 March 1981, p.23. See also F. LETHEM and L. COOPER.

20. *Yearbook of the United Nations 1982,* United Nations, New York, 1986, p.1487.

21. See S. A. GARRETT, *Bangkok Journal: a Fulbright Year in Thailand,* University of Southern Illinois Press, Carbondale, Illinois, 1986.

22. J. D. HARGREAVES, Introductory note, in J. C. STONE (editor), *Experts in Africa: Proceedings of a Colloquium at the University of Aberdeen,* Aberdeen, 1980.

23. H. CLEVELAND, Frontiers of public administration. Plenary address at the American Society for Public Administration National Conference, Honolulu, Hawaii, 21–25 March 1982.

24. S. CARTER, Nike looks toward future in dealing with Chinese, *The Oregonian* (Portland, Oregon) 22 October 1984, D-8.

25. *Some Information on the Activities of Governments in Technical Cooperation among Developing Countries,* TCDC/2/7, United Nations, New York, 3 March 1981, pp.15–16; *The Role and Potential of Technical Co-operation among Developing Countries in Rural Development,* TCDC/2/8, United Nations, New York, 6 March 1981, p.3.

26. *Some Information on the Activities of Governments in Technical Cooperation among Developing Countries,* p.5.

27. R. PINTO, Consultant orientations and client system perception: styles of cross-cultural consultation, in R. LIPPITT and C. LIPPITT (editors), *Systems Thinking—A Resource for Organization Diagnosis and Intervention,* International Consultants Foundation, Washington, DC, 1981, pp.57–74.

28. See *The Technical Assistance Process: an Introductory Bibliography.*

29. G. ROBERTS, Volunteers and neo-colonialism: an inquiry into the role of foreign volunteers in the Third World; I. ILLICH, To hell with good intentions.

30. P. SCHWARZ, *Selecting Effective Leaders of Technical Assistance Teams,* Bureau for Technical Assistance, US AID, Washington, DC, March 1973.

31. A. WINSLOW, The technical assistance expert, *International Development Review,* **4,** 17 (1962).

32. D. TYACK, Ways of seeing—essay on history of compulsory schooling, *Harvard Educational Review*, **46**, 355–89 (1976).
33. R. ARNOVE, *Philanthropy and Cultural Imperialism;* H. CLEVELAND, G. MANGONE, and J. ADAMS, *The Overseas Americans*, McGraw-Hill, New York, 1960; P. FREIRE, The people speak their word: learning to read and write in São Tomé and Príncipe, *Harvard Educational Review* **51**, 28 (1981); D. GOULET, *The Uncertain Promise;* I. ILLICH, To hell with good intentions; I. T. SANDERS, *Interprofessional Training Goals for Technical Assistance Personnel Abroad; Report,* Council on Social Work Relations, New York, 1959.
34. F. MOUSSAVI, *Guide to the Hanna Collection and Related Archival Materials at the Hoover Institution on War, Revolution, and Peace on the Role of Education in Twentieth Century Society,* Hoover Institution, Stanford, California, 1982.
35. L. J. WALINSKY (editor), *The Selected Papers of Wolf Ladejinsky: Agrarian Reform as Unfinished Business,* Oxford University Press, New York, 1977.
36. W. MANGIN, Thoughts on twenty-four years of work in Peru: the Vicos Project and me, in G. FOSTER *et al.* (editors), *Long-term Field Research in Social Anthropology,* Academic Press, New York, 1979, pp.65–84.
37. C. E. THURBER, The problem of training Americans for service abroad in U.S. government technical assistance programs. Unpublished doctoral dissertation, Stanford University, *Dissertation Abstracts,* **22**, 1704 (1961).
38. M. MINKLER, Consultants or colleagues—role of United States population advisors in India, *Population Development Review,* **3**, 403–19 (1977).
39. D. HARARI, *The Role of the Technical Assistance Expert,* OECD, Paris, 1974.
40. F. C. BYRNES, *Americans in Technical Assistance: A Study of Attitudes and Responses to Their Role Abroad,* Praeger, New York, 1965.
41. Ibid., p.117.
42. E. BECKER, *The Birth and Death of Meaning; an Interdisciplinary Perspective on the Problem of Man,* 2nd edn, Free Press, New York, 1971; *Escape from Evil,* Free Press, New York, 1975.
43. D. ZIMNY, Polarity and political wisdom: the human science of Ernest Becker. Paper presented at the Western Social Science Association Annual Conference, Denver, Colorado, 24 April 1982.
44. R. J. LIFTON, *Boundaries; Psychological Man in Revolution,* Random House, New York, 1970.
45. Ibid., p.44.

PART II

Major Issues

CHAPTER 2

The Consultant's Paradox: The Multiple Roles of International Advisers

There are a number of reasons why advisers/consultants do not operate effectively. Some of the problems which may reduce their effectiveness are related to the design of the technical assistance project, failure of the government to specify what it wants the adviser to do, conflicting instructions from the international agency employing the adviser, and a lack of clear understanding by the adviser of what is his role.

It is the opinion of the author that many consultants, however dedicated they may be, do not fully understand the role they are to perform (John L. Woods).[1]

There are many different roles for the technical consultant or adviser working in another country. Of the many aspects of advising and consulting abroad, the issue of role is perhaps the most complex, confusing, and controversial. Pessimists such as Ivan Illich would have US nationals, for example, go abroad only as learners and not as 'helpers.'[2] In his research on advisers in India, Minkler found that many Indians prefer individuals who go beyond merely advising and aren't 'afraid of pitching in and getting their hands dirty.'[3] Others argue that consultants should avoid operational and action-oriented roles.

The patron saint of technocrats, Saint Simon, argued for the neutral, apolitical role of expertise.[4] Some scholars such as Freire of Brazil see consulting and advising as inherently political. Thus there tends to be an inevitable ambiguity related to the role of international advisers and consultants. Given such ambiguity and the multidimensional nature of advising and consulting roles, the relevance of Lifton's concept of the protean individual is clear. Needed are persons who have polymorphous versatility, who can adapt themselves to diverse situations and contexts.[5]

Major Roles of Advisers and Consultants

Table 2.1 provides a summary of the many diverse roles discussed in this chapter. These roles are broken down into six major categories: (1) analytical, (2) political, (3) economic, (4) operational, (5) informational, and (6) cultural.

TABLE 2.1.   *The Multiple Roles of Advisers*
and Consultants

Analytical roles	*Operational roles*
Expert	Operator or 'doer'
Third eye	Institution builder
Discussant	Builder of research capacity
Evaluator	Change agent
Editor/translator	Entrepreneur
	Talent scout
Political roles	*Informational roles*
Charterer (legitimator)	Educator
Broker	Messenger (networking)
Diplomat	
Ornament	
Economic role	*Cultural roles*
Fund raiser	Evangelist for Western values
	Colleague

Analytical Roles

The Consultant as Expert

Since advisers and consultants are ostensibly engaged to provide expertise, we should perhaps first consider their role as experts. In his discussion of educational advisers, Jerome Bruner makes the useful distinction between micro- and macroexpertise.[6] With respect to microexpertise, consultants derive the advice they give from a body of theory about known situations. Macroexpertise involves a more complex situation in which the advice given is to meet special situations often of a 'crisis' nature without any implications that its application shall become universal. Macroexpertise implies the kind of flexibility and versatility stressed by both Lifton and Pinto. While microexpertise may suffice for advising and consulting within an individual's own cultural boundaries, it will frequently be inadequate for complex situations in other cultures or societies.

For scholars concerned with cross-cultural communication and understanding it is tempting to downplay the role of expertise. In fact this was one of the major problems encountered by the Peace Corps, particularly during its initial phase. Many volunteers had wonderful enthusiasm and sensitive cross-cultural skills, but unfortunately had limited, if any, real technical expertise. In a book on cultural shock, JoAnn Craig stresses that the knowledge of cultural differences should definitely not be at the expense of professional expertise.[7] Later in this book we present a case study of Wolf Ladejinsky, a renowned consultant who spent many years in Asia working for the US government, the Ford Foundation, and the World Bank. It is said that Ladejinsky probably knew more about agrarian reform than anyone else.[8] He possessed exceptional expertise in an area of demonstrated need.

Since the provision of technical consultants has become increasingly expensive, governments and agencies expect to receive genuine expertise. Also in recent decades, many Third World countries such as Mexico, Brazil, Thailand, and the Philippines, have greatly strengthened their own local expertise. Thus their expectations with repect to foreign expertise are higher than ever before.

In the past, degrees were often used to indicate relevant expertise.[9] With the growing criticism of degreeism and the 'diploma disease' there is increasing skepticism about overreliance on degrees as a symbol of expertise or capability. Ladejinsky had no doctorate, but he did have remarkable expertise on agrarian reform and relevant Asian experiences in this area. Unfortunately, many individuals fail to keep up in their fields or to continue research after obtaining their final degrees. Such individuals suffer from serious professional obsolescence and are not capable of playing the role of expert. This problem applies to 'experts' coming from both rich and/or poor countries.[10]

A second problem relates to experts who are unable to share or disseminate their expertise. This is primarily a problem of poor communications skills.

A third and final problem related to the role of expert is the tendency to equate expertise with status superiority. It is easy to assume falsely that expertise is the basis for status in all societies. This is certainly not the case, and it is important for experts to show appropriate humility when necessary and not to flaunt their expertise and *individual* accomplishments.

The Consultant as Third Eye

Given certain complex problems it is often useful to have a new or different perspective brought to bear on an issue. This does not necessarily mean that advisers provide the solution to a problem as such, but that their ideas or perspectives may, in a catalytic way, stimulate local colleagues to come to their own creative answers consistent with the local context and culture.

The Consultant as Discussant

Another important role of the adviser is to provide a sounding-board for new ideas and thoughts. In societies with a strong emphasis on face-saving, local nationals may be reluctant to present new ideas or thoughts to superiors, for fear they might appear ridiculous or naive. Since advisers' bureaucratic roles are often ambiguous, the local national may feel more comfortable initially sounding out ideas with them. After having discussed an idea with an adviser, local nationals may have greater confidence in disseminating their ideas more broadly.

The Consultant as Evaluator

Consultants are frequently expected to perform either an implicit or explicit evaluation role. In some cases consultants are engaged specifically to evaluate a project funded by an international agency. In other cases the evaluation role remains subtle and implicit. As consultants perform their normal duties they may also be expected to observe implementation of various funding projects, and submit evaluation reports from time to time. This is an awkward role in that the consultant in a sense becomes a 'spy' or 'investigator' looking for evidence of corruption or inefficiency. There is also the serious problem of whitewash. Consultants may desire to portray projects as being highly successful (regardless of the reality) to please hosts, the international funding agency, and to ensure their continued employment as a consultant for the project in question. This evaluation role, of course, raises serious issues of ethics and professional practice, which we consider in detail later in the study.

The Consultant as Editor/Translator

Another role for advisers, particularly in countries where English is not the national language, is that of editor and/or translator. It is quite common for an adviser, particularly on a long-term assignment, to be asked to edit materials such as research reports, letters, fellowship applications, and funding proposals. The careful editing of research articles may, for example, significantly facilitate publication by host country nationals in prestigious international journals. Since this role is not particularly exciting and may, in fact, be rather tedious, it requires that the adviser have considerable patience. Also if advisers are fluent in the local language, they may be asked as well to do translation work from time to time.

Political Roles

The Consultant as Charterer (Legitimator)

In considering the role of schooling in society, the sociologist John Meyer has introduced the concept of the social charter.[11] The same concept could be applied to another important role of the adviser. To gain acceptance and implementation, ideas may need to be chartered. A bright young woman in a host country may have an excellent and creative idea, but finds it difficult to attain a hearing for her perspective. If a 'high-status' foreign expert can be persuaded to support or 'charter' the idea as well, chances of adoption or implementation may be considerably enhanced. The chartering role may be particularly important in promoting the ideas of the less powerful, such as women and minorities. It is a rather tragic irony that the powers of strangers may 'inspire greater confidence than those of one's own people.'[12]

Related to this same role, but often with quite different political implications, is the legitimating role emphasized by Benveniste and others.[13] The role of the outside adviser may be primarily to legitimate a particular government policy or program. Should the program or policy result in any negative outcomes which were unanticipated, the consultant can later become a convenient 'goat' to take the blame for the errant policy.

The Consultant as Broker

Another important potential role of the consultant is that of broker. Three types of 'brokering' are common: horizontal, vertical, and transnational. In many societies with fairly rigid status hierarchies, outside consultants with status ambiguity can move easily among diverse individuals and bureaucracies. They thus can facilitate important informal horizontal linkages among and within complex organizations and institutions. Such 'brokering' can contribute significantly to a new program or project development.

Vertical brokering can also be of considerable significance. This refers to communicating intimately with powerless individuals at the local level, and then later transmitting their ideas to high-ranking policy-makers and decision-makers of a society. A peasant in a remote area would have little opportunity to communicate directly with a high-ranking government official. Again we would like to cite the inspiring example of Wolf Ladejinsky, who had a remarkable ability to relate to both peasants and princes. He thus played the role of the vertical broker, contributing to bottom-up communications and feedback.

The consultant can also play an important role in dealing with a wide variety of international organizations on behalf of local colleagues and institutions. This we refer to as transnational brokering.

The Consultant as Diplomat

Jonathan Bingham, in his book *Shirtsleeve Diplomacy,* emphasizes the often neglected diplomatic role of the technical consultant.[14] Whether formally employed by their own government or not, consultants are frequently perceived as 'representatives' of their countries of origin or their international agency. The cultures of many Third World countries also place considerable emphasis on politeness and smooth interpersonal relations. Criticizing without offending is perhaps the diplomatic art most needed by foreign consultants. A failure to recognize the diplomatic role can easily limit the effectivenesss of a consultant. There is also, however, the danger of excessive diplomacy, i.e. the consultants who in their effort to avoid all criticism negate other important roles and functions. The latter consultants may be popular but ineffective. Alan Waters is particularly critical of pusillanimous advisers who have a career invested in being able to return to various African nations.[15] Such individuals, he argues, avoid any type of tough policy dialogue which would induce genuine change.

The Consultant as Ornament

In many developing countries, consultants by virtue of their being a foreigner or Westerner have relatively high status. This definitely represents a negative residue of colonialism and dependency. It is, nevertheless, a reality in many contexts. Thus the mere presence (even if the consultant were to make no substantive contribution) would add significance to a meeting, workshop or conference. The presence of the consultant may greatly facilitate involvement of local policy-makers or high-ranking officials in planned activities. Thus consultants may be invited to participate in some activities entirely for symbolic or ritualistic reasons. This represents the ornamental role of the foreign adviser.

Economic Role

The Consultant as Fund-raiser

Denis Goulet, in his thought-provoking book on technology transfer, emphasizes the role of consultants in raising funds for their clients.[16] In interviews with several Latin American government officials, Goulet found that the main reason these agencies contracted US consultants was not to obtain expertise, which was often available locally, but instead to draw on the consultants' access to development funding and their special understanding of how to prepare funding proposals to organizations such as the World Bank, the International Development Research Centre (IDRC), and other funding agencies. Goulet also mentions that consultants frequently enjoy the confidence of key transnational corporations from the US, Europe, or Japan. The endorsements of such consultants may lead to sizeable and significant foreign investments. Numerous advisers playing this role have assisted their clients to attain major international funding of such magnitude to repay their salaries many times over. With respect to this role, Goulet predicts that good consultants can expect considerable institutional longevity in the international area.

Operational Roles

The extent to which consultants should become involved in actual operational roles is an issue riddled with controversy. In some cases the consultant is explicitly engaged in an operational role. For example, a consultant could be asked to install a new computer system as a specific task. In other cases there may be considerable ambiguity. To avoid completely any operational or doer role is risky, in that it leads to the perception that the consultants are above getting their hands dirty and pitching in to help. It is best, however, to perform the operational or doer role as a *subordinate* in response to host country directives. Most problems arise when the international consultant is perceived as the 'boss' directing and ordering host country nationals to perform tasks. Even if foreign consultants have excellent administrative and human relations skills, they are still likely to be resented for playing a 'colonial' role. This role should thus be avoided, unless the consultant has been specifically engaged to carry out an operational task. Whalen forcefully articulates the view that outsiders must avoid decision-making roles:

> Nevertheless, it is essential for anyone from the outside who is asked to help, even if he is not told, to repeat to himself a dozen times a day that his role must always be an advisory and not a decision-making one.[17]

Many foreign consultants, particularly those from the US or Europe, do not easily accept the mere role of being a consultant or adviser. Thus they seek opportunities to assume control of projects and to become involved in operational tasks. As our case studies in the latter part of the book vividly illustrate, the consultant–operator polarity represents a major problem area of ambiguity and difficulty for international advisers.

The Consultant as Institution-builder

This role of the consultant has been emphasized by foundations such as Ford and Rockefeller. The essence of this concept is that, whatever field technical consultants may be working in, their principal job is to help build a viable bureaucratic and social institution which will carry out its functions with excellence, quality, and responsiveness. This role commonly involves the following major dimensions:

1. Assistance in arranging formal training for key staff members.
2. Provision of extensive on-the-job and informal training of various staff members.
3. Stimulants of an organizational ecology and ethos oriented toward excellence and service.
4. Quality evaluation and feedback related to organizational performance, particularly with regard to outcomes (quality control function).
5. Helping in developing and strengthening organizational linkages, both nationally and internationally.
6. Fostering personnel procedures to enhance the retention of qualified staff.

This role is obviously a challenging one, involving long-term service of several years' duration. Given the extensive and impressive institution-building that has already taken place in many Third World countries in the 1960s and 1970s, this role in the future is likely to diminish, except perhaps in the poorest countries still lacking important institutional infrastructure. In such countries, consultants from Third World countries already having achieved significant institution-building would be particularly appropriate for such roles under the TCDC concept of the UN.

The Role of Consultants in Helping Strengthen Research and/or Technological Capacity

An important goal of many developing countries is to build up indigenous research and technological capacity as a means to reduce dependency and improve their international competitiveness in world markets. It is crucially important that fundamental skills underlying effective research and development be shared widely and broadly. Building up research capacity in fields such as biotechnology takes time, and requires long-term commitments and perspective.

Outside consultants can play important roles in helping strengthen such research and technological capabilities. As the qualitative case studies presented in Chapter 9 demonstrate, advisers working with organizations such as the International Maize and Wheat Improvement Center (CIMMYT) in Mexico and the International Rice Research Institute (IRRI) in the Philippines have contributed significantly to strengthening indigenous applied agricultural research. Organizations such as the United Nations University in Tokyo, the Asian Institute of Technology, and the International Development Research Centre (IDRC) are all committed to building up research capacity in LDCs.

Although consultants are frequently employed by either public or non-profit organizations, the private sector also utilizes such talent. The Nike Corporation, for example, has technical consultants in both China and Thailand helping those nations develop their capacity to produce world-class athletic footwear. In Thailand such consultants are not only helping to improve production technologies, but are also involved in local research and development efforts.

A major problem with respect to the consultants' role relates to the nature of skills and technologies being shared. A common criticism in LDCs is that the rich industrial countries are unwilling to share cutting-edge technologies. It is often difficult, moreover, to persuade high-level scientists and researchers to leave their laboratories and think-tanks to help build research capacity in nations where research facilities are likely to be more limited.

In contrast, the major benefit of building research capacity is that it does help to reduce international dependency. A pool of local research talent eventually does emerge, reducing the need for continuing the use of outside consultants. Such talent is also capable of producing new technologies for export. Scientists in the PRC and Thailand have, for example, developed new vaccines for helping to prevent hepatitis. Over the long term, countries such as Korea, China, Thailand, Singapore, and Brazil, to name only a few, which are investing in building research capacity, will certainly have special economic and technological advantages.

Strengthening local research capacity is only one of the many roles of international advisers. But it is one in which there have been some impressive successes, and where genuine mutual interests have been served.

The Consultant as Change Agent

This is a role emphasized by writers such as Arensberg, Niehoff, Benveniste, and Ilchman, as well as many firms engaged in providing consultants.[18] For example, Arthur D. Little states that it considers 'its principal business to be the management of change and the optimal blending of change with continuity.'[19] In many respects this role is analogous to the 'county agent demonstrator.' It represents a direct transfer of the American county agent role into the foreign environment. Consultants are engaged to work, particularly at local levels, with farmers and rural administrators. They demonstrate new techniques such as the inoculation of cattle and the introduction of new seed strains. By demonstrating new techniques, and working closely with local counterparts, consultants contribute to local improvements in agricultural productivity. William E. Warne, one of the early country directors for the Point IV program, describes how Dr Henry Bennett, the first Director of the Technical Cooperation Administration, saw this role:

> He saw it as a world wide extension service, a transmission belt to carry the results of research to farms, homes, and factories, where technical knowledge could be put to use in practical ways. It was the land grant idea grown up to world proportions.[20]

An extensive literature has developed focusing on the practical aspects of performing effectively the change agent role abroad.[21] Peace Corps-like organizations of various countries have strongly emphasized the change agent role. National volunteer organizations such as those in Nepal and Indonesia also emphasize this role.

The Consultant as Entrepreneur

This role in some respects is similar to that of the change agent discussed above. The consultant as entrepreneur, however, is involved in a 'macro' role and expected to stimulate the development of innovative projects which potentially can have national or international impact. Two concrete

IEDC—D

examples from Thailand may be helpful. In recent years Thailand has experienced a dramatic fertility decline resulting in excessively small rural schools. To deal with this 'problem' and opportunity, two innovative projects were launched as experiments. One project called biennial entry or 'alternate intake' involves the staggering of entry into primary schools, thereby doubling enrollments and reducing teaching staff needs by 50 percent. The other project involves the use of bicycles as a potentially cost-effective alternative to the construction of new upper primary school classroom and/or schools. An international consultant was involved in promoting both these projects, although the initial idea for both projects came from 'rice roots' sources. If successful, the projects have implications for many other countries likely to experience fertility declines in the years ahead.

A common issue related to this entrepreneurial role is the potential replicability at both the national and international level of projects undertaken. International consultants often encourage highly successful local projects, but which unfortunately are too special and costly to be replicable elsewhere, or to continue on their own once the adviser has left.

The Consultant as 'Talent Scout'

The concept, 'discovery of talent,' has been absent in the social science literature for some time.[22] It is, however, a highly germane role for many advisers and consultants. During the course of their work, advisers may become acquainted with a wide range of individuals and become rather familiar with their respective abilities. They may then encourage bright and creative individuals to apply for scholarships, fellowships, and other professional training opportunities. Numerous advisers have made remarkable contributions by identifying dedicated and committed talent, often of lower socioeconomic background, for further training opportunities. Such a role is particularly important in societies where formal school examinations emphasize achievement rather than aptitude, and which favor markedly those from higher socioeconomic backgrounds.

Informational Roles

The Consultant as Educator

In arriving at most airports the individual must fill out an immigration card which normally asks for name of occupation. One colleague who has frequently served as a short-term consultant abroad always indicates educator as his profession. In fact, as more countries and international organizations have come to emphasize human capacity-building as an integral part of development, this role of the consultant has become more prominent. The consultant as educator may be involved in both formal and informal training. This role includes three basic dimensions. First, the consultants must have needed and relevant expertise to transmit. Second, they need sensitivity in adapting their expertise to a different cultural, political, and bureaucratic setting. Third, and of particular importance, they must be able to transmit effectively this adapted expertise in a cross-cultural setting.

Teaching and training in an individual's own cultural setting is no easy task. Doing so in another society, where student–teacher relations and cultural forms such as humor may be quite different, represents a real challenge. In some situations, particularly in Latin America or in rural areas of Asia, it will be necessary for the outside consultant to teach and train in Spanish, or whatever the indigenous language may be. For the consultant as educator, cross-cultural communication skills are the crucial competency.

In recent years, study abroad in the US , UK, or Australia, has become considerably more expensive, and governments are increasingly reluctant to lose staff for long periods of study abroad. There are also unintended cultural effects of long-term study abroad. These are not always considered desirable or positive. Thus, short-term training within various developing countries is likely to increase, suggesting the continued importance of the role of consultant as educator.

The Consultant as Messenger (Networking)

As we enter the information era, the concept of networks becomes increasingly significant. This networking role is somewhat similar to the brokering one described above. International consultants can play a significant role in linking professionals in Third World countries to various transnational networks. A foreign consultant may, for example, be aware that a group in Costa Rica and one in Thailand are working on a similar problem or issue. The consultant can then arrange communications contacts between the two groups. One consultant, for example played an important role in bringing a major Nicaraguan educational innovation to Thailand. Normally, the two groups would never be aware of their mutual interests. Even within the same geographic region, such as West Africa or Southeast Asia, local professionals may be inadequately aware of what is happening in other neighboring countries. The consultant can also bring to the attention of host country professionals opportunities to participate in a wide range of transnational networks. This role is particluarly important, in overcoming the serious and common problem of professional obsolescence. Critics such as Arnove and others, however, see this type of networking role as furthering intellectual dependence on, and dominance by, the rich nations.[23]

Cultural Roles

The Consultant as an Evangelist for Western Values

Although this role is rarely made explicit, its presence continues as a major problem in advising and consulting. The following statement by Sinai illustrates certain basic attitudes held by some individuals working in technical assistance abroad:

> Before this new elite, however, can even begin to wrestle with the ponderous and sluggish social forces with which it will have to contend, it will have to absorb the spirit generated both by the Reformation and Enlightment. Without assimilating these Western values, emotions, virtues and drives, no development of any sort will be possible.[24]

Advisers playing this type of role become in a sense cultural missionaries. Wolcott in a perceptive critique of the village development project of the Institute of Cultural Affairs (ICA) in Malaysia, refers to project personnel as 'non-missionary missionaries.'[25] Though all consultants and advisers carry with them to some extent their cultural baggage, evangelists allow their own culture to permeate and dominate their consulting work.

The consultant as evangelist may tend to view development as a linear process, with every society going through the same basic stages. Thus, these consultants attempt to promote the imitation of systems and approaches present in their own society and culture. If advisers were Americans working in education, they might well argue for decentralized schooling controlled by elected school boards. A consultant working in the field of economic development might well promote a liberal free-enterprise economy, which would emphasize the consumption of many common Western luxuries.

The evangelist role is certainly among the least appreciated by host country nationals, especially if 'I know what's best for you' attitudes are conveyed. Such approaches also partially explain the highly negative attitude toward consultants held by individuals such as Illich. But even with greater emphasis on TCDC, the problem, while probably less severe, will continue to persist. It appears to be natural to assume that one's own society has the correct solutions to all problems. For example, in the early 1960s a US advisory team (the Litchfield Group) helped draw up a master plan for Bangkok which led to turning many of the city's lovely and functional canals into cement.[26] Based primarily on such external advice, Bangkok lost its image as 'Venice of the East' and became Automobile City, in many respects similar to its namesake Los Angeles (Bangkok in Thai means city of angels). Had these urban development advisers been Danish or Dutch, the Bangkok of today might be quite different.

As suggested above, it is almost impossible for consultants and advisers to eliminate totally their own cultural baggage. Even so, the role of the cultural missionary is no longer considered legitimate. The mass media, already dominated by the West, constitutes a massive 'cultural invasion' in many other societies. Consultants and advisers must actively avoid reinforcing this cultural impact. This issue has been one of major concern in the PRC, reflected by the term, 'spiritual pollution' and elegantly expressed in the title of a book, *Watch Out for the Foreign Guests*, by Schell.[27] Japan offers a hopeful example in this regard, however. Japan has provided some of the most impressive examples of the potential impact of international consulting and advising (see the case studies of W. Edwards Deming and Wolf Ladejinsky in Part IV). While Japan has effectively utilized numerous consultants and advisers, its ability to become technologically modern while retaining and even expanding the appreciation of traditional Japanese cultural forms is indeed impressive.[28] Its example may offer a real inspiration to other societies in their transition to 'modernization.'

The Consultant as Colleague

A common question that arises in personnel evaluations in many contexts is: how is Ms X or Mr Y as a colleague? Increasingly international advisers and consultants are expected to be good colleagues, in addition to possessing relevant expertise. What is needed is effective 'colleaguesmanship.' This involves a number of dimensions. Perhaps most important, good colleagues have to be relatively selfless. They are willing to make personal sacrifices for the benefit of their organization and their colleagues. Another important aspect of being a good colleague is the willingness to share credit. It is common for distinguished Western professionals to guard their time carefully. In other cultural settings such a preoccupation with protecting private time is frequently considered to be definitely noncollegial. Thus, the consultant as colleague must be willing to share both credit and time. Colleagues are also willing to accept the ideas of others. They do not blindly persist in pushing their own ideas or perspectives regardless of their acceptability. Good colleagues will also work hard to further the implementation of a colleague's idea, even though it may have won out over their own.[29] Finally, good colleagues are careful and reflective listeners. They are sincerely interested in the ideas and thoughts of others. Underlying all of these traits of the good colleague is a willingness to demonstrate a sincere degree of selflessness. The good colleague role is aptly described by Dudley Seers:

> What is important is the *style* of work—that one should limit one's role to that of a friend who can point to some considerations which may have been overlooked, rather than offering solutions, especially solutions based on European models.[30]

Summary

James March, a noted specialist on organizational theory, emphasizes ambiguity as an integral part of organizational life.[31] The multiple roles and multidimensional nature of foreign advising and consulting result in a context rampant with ambiguity. As Woods points out, a failure to recognize such ambiguity often explains why advisers and consultants fail to operate effectively. The ambiguity inherent in international advising and consulting cannot be eliminated. Nevertheless, it can be dealt with by making as explicit as possible which of the multiple roles are to be emphasized in each particular assignment. Also it is important to have prior mutual agreement among the host country, the international or donor agency, and the individual consultant with regard to a more explicit definition of roles to be performed.

We would like to conclude this chapter with two basic propositions. The first is that advisers will perform more effectively if they are provided an understanding of the multiple and diverse roles expected of them, with an explicit role definition for their particular assignment. The second proposition is that the protean multidimensional and multicultural individual has the potential to cope effectively and creatively with the multiple roles of the international consultant.

Notes

1. J. L. Woods, Suggested framework for determining roles of international advisers/consultants. Notes for Project Formulators, no. 506, UNDP, DTCP, Bangkok, Thailand, 1980, p.2.
2. I. Illich, To hell with good intentions. Address delivered at the Conference on Inter-American Student Projects (CIASP), Cuernavaca, Mexico, 20 April 1968, p.7.
3. M. Minkler, Consultants or colleagues—role of United States population advisers in India, *Population Development Review*, 3, 409 (1977).
4. J. Bruner, The role of the researcher as an adviser to the educational policy makers, *Oxford Review of Education*, 1, 83 (1975).
5. R. Lifton, *Boundaries: Psychological Man in Revolution*, Random House, New York, 1979, pp.44–5.
6. J. Bruner, pp.183–4.
7. J. Craig, *What Not To Do in Malaysia and Singapore, How and Why Not to Do It*, Times Books International, Singapore, 1980.
8. L. Walinsky, *The Selected Papers of Wolf Ladejinsky: Agrarian Reform as Unfinished Business*, Oxford University Press, New York, 1977, p.8.
9. R. Dore, *The Diploma Disease: Education, Qualification and Development*, University of California Press, Berkeley, California, 1976.
10. See H. J. Laski, *The Limitations of the Expert*, Fabian Society, London, 1931.
11. J. Meyer, The charter: conditions of diffuse socialization in schools, in W. R. Scott (editor), *Social Processes and Social Structure*, Holt, Rinehart, and Winston, 1970, pp.564–78.
12. H. Goldhamer, *The Adviser*, Elsevier, New York, 1978, p.81.
13. G. Benveniste, *The Politics of Expertise*, 2nd edn, Boyd & Fraser, San Francisco, California, 1977.
14. J. Bingham, *Shirt-sleeve Diplomacy. Point 4 in Action*, John Day, New York, 1954.

15. A. R. WATERS, African development and foreign aid, *Publications in Comparative Research*, **2**, 9 (1984).
16. D. GOULET, *The Uncertain Promise: Value Conflicts in Technology Transfer*, IDOC, New York, 1977, p.66.
17. D. J. WHALEN, Technical law and the outside expert, in P. G. SACK (editor), *Problem of Choice Land in Papua New Guinea's Future*, ANU Press, Canberra, 1974, p.97.
18. A. H. NIEHOFF and C. M. ARENSBERG, *Introducing Social Change; a Manual for Americans Overseas*, Aldine, Chicago, 1967; G. BENVENISTE and W. ILCHMAN (editors), *Agents of Change: Professionals in Developing Countries*, Praeger, New York, 1969.
19. D. GOULET, p.64.
20. W. E. WARNE, *Mission for Peace. Point 4 in Iran*, Bobbs–Merrill, Indianapolis, 1956, p.20.
21. See, for example, H. WOLCOTT, A Malay village that progress chose: Sungai Lui and the Institute of Cultural Affairs, *Human Organization*, **42**, 72–81 (1983); W. H. GOODENOUGH, *Cooperation in Change; an Anthropological Approach to Community Development*, Sage, New York, 1963; G. FOSTER, *Traditional Societies and Technological Changes*, Harper & Row, New York, 1973.
22. D. WOLFE, (editor), *The Discovery of Talent*, Harvard University Press, Cambridge, Massachusetts, 1969.
23. R. F. ARNOVE (editor), *Philanthropy and Cultural Imperialism: The Foundations at Home and Abroad*, Indiana University Press, Bloomington, Indiana, 1982.
24. For a disturbingly ethnocentric analysis of the non-Western World, see, for example, I. R. SINAI, *The Challenge of Modernization; the West's Impact on the non-Western World*. Norton, New York, 1964, p.219. Sinai (pp.161–2) is also highly critical of the Burmese for failing to utilize the expertise of their foreign advisers.
25. H. F. WOLCOTT, p.73.
26. M. BONGSADAT, Reflections on the city planning development of Bangkok: the past, present, and possible future, *Proceedings of the International Conference on Thai Studies, 3–6 July*, vol. 3, Research School of Pacific Studies, ANU, Canberra, 1987. In a remarkably insightful short story, Khamsing Srinawk warned of such unanticipated consequences of external 'assistance.' The peasant and the white man, in *The Politician and Other Stories*, Oxford University Press, London, 1973, pp.61–71.
27. O. SCHELL, *Watch Out for the Foreign Guests*, Pantheon, New York, 1980.
28. See V. KOBAYASHI, The sage in the child, tradition, modernization, education: the case of Japan. Paper presented at the annual meeting of the Comparative and International Education Society, Tallahassee, Florida, 18–21 March 1981.
29. Z. DOR-NER and P. SOLMAN, *The Colonel Comes to Japan*, videorecording, Learning Corporation of America, New York, 1981.
30. D. SEERS, The international context within which European experts work, in J. C. STONE (editor), *Experts in Africa: Proceedings of a Colloquium at the University of Aberdeen*, Aberdeen University African Studies Group, Aberdeen, 1980, p.156.
31. J. MARCH and J. P. OLSEN, *Ambiguity and Choice in Organizations*, Universitetsforlaget, Bergen, Norway, 1979.

CHAPTER 3

The Tongue-tied Adviser:
The Use, Abuse, and Disuse of
Foreign Languages

Although science and technology are wiring up and connecting the
global village by telecommunications, meaning and knowledge will not
come from the wires or the waves at the present levels of language
constraints and cacophony (Dr William O. Baker, Retired Chairman
of the Board, Bell Laboratories).[1]

A reasonable command of the local language and understanding of the
background of the country in which our people work open many doors.
Besides we consider it only common courtesy toward the country in
which our people are guests that they acquire such knowledge (Erik J.
Jansen, Personnel Officer, Det Ostasiatiske Kompagni, Scandanavia's
largest corporation).[2]

Background

For decades there has been controversy about the importance of foreign
language competence for technical assistance personnel. The Sputnik crisis
provided impetus for an increased emphasis in the United States on foreign
language study during the 1960s. With the establishment of the Peace Corps
during the same period, increasing numbers of Americans began working
overseas in technical assistance with some knowledge of the local language.
In the 1970s, however, there was a return to complacency about foreign
languages. President Carter's Commission on Foreign languages and International Studies found foreign language training in the US to be woefully
inadequate, and a 'national disaster.' President Carter himself was personally embarrassed while in Poland by an incompetent interpreter. More
recently Senator Paul Simon's *Tongue-Tied American* and Joseph Lurie's
'America globally, blind, deaf, and dumb,' provide devastating critiques of
the adverse effects of language incompetence on US economic, political,
and cultural activities abroad.[3]

As background for our discussion of foreign language use and abuse, we
would like to present a simple matrix showing four types of language
contexts characterizing adviser–counterpart relations (see Table 3.1). The
FF cell of the matrix represents the simplest case. Adviser and counterpart

TABLE 3.1.   *Four Types of Language Contexts*

FF	FS
Adviser and counterpart share same first language.	First language of adviser is a secondary language of counterpart.
SF	SS
Secondary language of adviser is first language of counterpart.	Adviser and counterpart share the same secondary language.

share the same first language. An example would be an adviser from Spain working in Costa Rica. Though there are certainly some differences among variants of Latin American and Castilian Spanish, basically in this type of context there is no foreign language problem. Unfortunately, the number of relationships occurring in the FF cell is rather small. In the SF cell a secondary language of the adviser is the first language of the counterpart. An example would be a French adviser speaking Thai with a Thai counterpart, or a German adviser speaking Arabic with a Saudi colleague. This is the typical relationship of technical assistance personnel from voluntary organizations such as the Peace Corps, CUSO (Canadian University Service Overseas), and NSV (National Service Volunteers, France). The third FS cell in the upper right corner represents the context where the first language of the adviser is a secondary language of the counterpart. An example would be a Nepalese counterpart using English with a British adviser. The relationships of this cell exemplify the conventional stereotype of expert advisers working in their own language. This relationship also necessarily characterizes many short-term consultancies in which there is inadequate time to develop competence in a relevant local language. The fourth cell, SS, represents the context where both adviser and counterpart are using secondary languages. An example would be a Filipino adviser working in English with Kenyan counterparts. Such cases are increasingly common with the growing emphasis on TCDC, technical cooperation among developing countries. Another interesing variant of the SS context is the adviser speaking Spanish with native Indians in many Latin American contexts. Both the Indians and the adviser are using a secondary language, Spanish. A similar situation occurs in Thailand where, for example, a Thai-speaking US AID expert uses Thai in communicating with the hill tribes of Thailand, for whom Thai is a secondary 'foreign' language.

Varying Language Contexts

The matrix in Table 3.2 provides a second conceptual framework adding a time dimension for analyzing the varying language contexts encountered by overseas advisers and consultants. Cells S_1, S_2, and S_3 are shown in Table 3.2 and represent the simplest situations. In such cases the foreign language

TABLE 3.2.   *Varying Language Contexts of Overseas Consultants*

Length of consultancy	Nature of official language of host country		
	Same language as consultant	A major international language but not the first language of the consultant	An 'exotic' language
Short-term: less than 6 months	S_1	S_2	S_3
Medium-term: 6 months to 2 years	M_1	M_2	M_3
Long-term: 2 years or longer	L_1	L_2	L_3

issue does not arise, unless the consultant is working with minority groups who do not speak the national or host country language. If that is the context, then the third column covering 'exotic' languages is the relevant one.

If the working language of the host country is an international language, then even short-term consultants should be prepared to work in that language. There is, of course, the definitional issue of what constitutes an international language. We define an international language as one that is the official language in at least five countries. Thus, English, French, Spanish, Arabic, and Portuguese are considered international languages. Russian and Burmese, for example, are not. Thus, an adviser or consultant serving in the Ivory Coast would be expected to be able to work professionally in French. Similarly an adviser serving in Brazil would be expected to know Portuguese, or an adviser serving in Peru would need to know Spanish. Some countries use several working languages and have multiple national languages. Examples would be Singapore (English, Malay, Mandarin Chinese, and Tamil) and the Cameroon (French and English). Also some of the Arab countries appear to use both Arabic and English in official contexts. In the Philippines, both English and Tagalog are used in government and business circles. In such cases, advisers and consultants can get by if they know at least one of the multiple languages used.

The most complex cases arise with respect to column three, involving the so-called 'exotic' languages. William Mangin, in reflecting on his many years of working on the Vicos project in Peru, states that his biggest regret was not putting more effort into learning Quechua.[4]

It is, of course, unrealistic to expect short-term consultants working in countries where the national language is not an international one, to know or to learn the local language. Nevertheless, they can develop some of the simpler competencies shown in Table 3.3, such as learning to pronounce

TABLE 3.3. *Levels of Foreign Language Ability*

1. Ability to pronounce names and places in the local language.
2. Knowledge of a small set of words for simple greetings and courtesies.
3. Ability to comprehend some of the foreign language.
4. Ability to write the script of a foreign language.
5. Ability to use the foreign language in everyday market situations but not professionally.
6. Professional level of listening comprehension (in one's technical field), but without an active command of the language.
7. Active command professionally (both listening and speaking) but inadequate for delicate and complex negotiations.
8. Oral command adequate for all professional activities including complex negotiations.
9. Ability to read fluently (in one's professional field).
10. Ability to write professionally (with perhaps some minor editing by a local national).

names, places, and basic phrases for purposes of common courtesy. For medium- or long-term consultancies it is essential that advisers know or learn the local language. This principle has been clearly articulated in guidelines set forth by the United Nations for consultants in developing countries:

> Successful management depends on a two-way communication throughout an organization. All key foreign personnel from superintendents to operators must therefore learn the national language in order that a sufficient degree of communication might be established.[5]

Frankly, we consider it alarming to find advisers or consultants having spent many years in a country without learning the national language. Not only is it culturally offensive, but we also consider it unprofessional. Fox, for example, reports that no British officials working in Melanesia learned local languages, a typical pattern in colonial settings.[6]

A Continuum of Foreign Language Abilities

In the West there is a tendency to think in binary terms. Westerners learn a language or they don't. We feel that such an orientation is extremely unfortunate, and leads to many lost opportunities for important foreign language learning. Our preference is to think instead of foreign language learning as a complex continuum involving a polarity and many potential levels of competency. As suggested by the simple matrix in Table 3.1, foreign language contexts vary widely, and thus the continuum concept allows for considerable flexibility. We propose a continuum involving ten basic levels of competency in foreign language acquisition. These competency levels are indicated in Table 3.3. The first level is simply learning how to pronounce names and places in the relevant local language. We know one expert from a major international organization who has excellent technical capabilities but tends to mispronounce badly names of places and persons in the countries where he frequently serves on missions. In contrast, President

Kennedy made the effort to learn to pronounce faultlessly difficult but charming Laotian names.[7] Of course, it will be impossible for foreign adults to learn to pronounce perfectly such names and places. Nevertheless, they should make an effort to pronounce names and places as nearly correctly as possible.

Ability to Use a Small Set of Words and Phrases to Express Common Courtesies in the Local Language

This is a competency level which should be within the reach of almost all overseas advisers and consultants. Even those on missions of less than a month in another country should try to attain this competency. This minimal level of competency shows a respect for the local culture and language. A colleague of ours who has had years of experience in the Middle East strongly recommends that all individuals planning work or professional visits there learn at least a small set of Arabic phrases. Necessary phrases would normally include the terms for 'thank you,' 'excuse me,' basic greetings and numbers, and other similar phrases used for simple courtesies. The phrases should be pronounced correctly. Adequate pronunciation should be attainable through the use of language tapes and/or brief encounters with a language informant. It is surprising, however, that few individuals make the effort even to attain this level of competency. Later in the chapter we discuss the many obstacles which deter overseas professionals from learning other languages.

Ability to Comprehend Limited Amounts of the National Language

Even a limited listening comprehension of the local language can be helpful. Without such ability it is easy to become totally oblivious to what is happening in a particular setting. A principal means to cultivate this ability is to listen frequently to radio or watch television and motion pictures in the local language. This can be done after a basic course in the language, or simultaneously while undergoing instruction in the local language. We have known professionals who have attained considerable listening comprehension in another language, even though their spoken abilities were severely limited. Tonal languages are a case in point. It is far easier for a Westerner to comprehend a tonal language than to produce correctly the proper tones. It is also far easier to achieve perfection in listening to another language than in speaking it.

Ability to Write the Notational Script of another Language

Globally, many different writing scripts are used. Countries such as Korea, Thailand, Burma, and Nepal have their own unique ways of writing. Since such scripts seem so different from Roman letters they may seem 'inscrutable' and complex. In reality, such writing scripts are much simpler than they seem. It is also possible for the foreigner to learn to reproduce the scripts perfectly, sometimes even more elegantly than the local nationals. With such knowledge individuals will be able to write their own names in the local language. This is frequently a simple but impressive gesture. It is possible to learn many seemingly 'complex' scripts such as Korean in a day or less. In several weeks it is possible to learn the basics of the Hiragana script. This could be most useful in traveling by subway or bus in Tokyo. Learning a new writing script also seems to stimulate an interest in the foreign language itself. Individuals begin to take interest in the many signs and displays of foreign language around them. Since many foreign languages incorporate a large number of words from English, they find that they can begin right away to make out some words in the other language. Many foreign scripts have an attractive aesthetic dimension. Learning them helps to develop an appreciation of the local culture.

Ability to Use the Local Language in Market and Everyday Situations but not Professionally

Though of no direct use professionally, this level of competency is still meaningful. Perhaps most significantly, it makes the sojourn of advisers and consultants (and their families if married) more pleasant and enjoyable. They are able to relate to, and communicate with, the ordinary citizens of the country they are serving.

Listening Ability at the Professional Level

Individuals with this level of competency are able to comprehend the local language in their particular professional fields, but do not have the ability to speak well. Though limited, this level of competency still has much value. Meetings involving the consultant can be held in the local language. Having to hold meetings in a non-national language such as English has many adverse effects. First, it places the local nationals at a disadvantage, since they will normally tend to be less articulate in a second language. Also local nationals will vary enormously in their command of the non-national language in question. This will give advantages to those with a strong command of English, for example, who may not be the individuals with the best or most creative ideas. Advisers with good listening comprehension in their field can thus participate in meetings conducted in the local language, though when speaking they may need to use English or another international language. This level of ability also enables them to attend speeches and presentations by local nationals in their field, and to listen to media programs relevant to their endeavors. Frequent exposure to radio and television media is also an excellent way to develop this particular form of foreign language competency.

Active Command of the Language Professionally (Speaking and Listening), but Inadequate Competency to Conduct Complex Negotiations

Consultants with this level of competency can use the local language in their field with ease, and can interrelate with host nationals in a wide variety of professional settings. Given such a level of competency it is easy to become overconfident, and to use the language in situations where it may not be appropriate. For example, this level of competency may not be adequate to conduct extremely complex financial negotiations or other types of contractual deliberations. In such cases, where the competency level in the local language is inadequate for such situations, either a professional interpreter or an international language should be used. Unfortunately there are cases where individuals will not admit that their foreign language competency is not adequate for such tasks. This we also consider unprofessional behavior.

Oral Command of a Local Language Adequate for All Professional Activities Including Complex Negotiations

Obviously, this is the most useful level of competency. A Vice-President of Nike, David Chang, has this level of competency which has greatly facilitated Nike's establishment of a major corporate presence in the People's Republic of China. Once, upon arriving in Beijing, a colleague at Nike asked Mr Chang to translate a banner written in Chinese. Chang with some embarrassment and humor admitted that he couldn't read Chinese. The Nike executive than exclaimed, 'what did we hire you for?' Actually Chang's oral command of Chinese was more than adequate for the task of negotiating Nike's activities in the PRC. Some languages such as Chinese, Japanese, and Thai are particularly hard to learn to read and to write. In such cases it is somewhat unfortunate that there is often an undue emphasis on learning to read and write the languages. As a result many students of these languages never develop an adequate oral command of the language to work professionally. They frequently give up study of the language because of the frustration of trying to learn to read the language.

Ability to Read the Language in One's Professional Field

Attainment of this ability has many pay-offs. Perhaps most importantly, local nationals do not have to waste inordinate amounts of time translating documents for foreign advisers and consultants. Such translation represents a rather expensive opportunity cost. Also this level of competency enables consultants to become much more aware of what the local nationals are doing with respect to their professional field. Though this level of attainment is rarely achieved in non-international languages, it is an objective which deserves high priority in the selection and training of consultants.

Ability to Write Professionally in a Local Language

This is the competency level most rarely attained. If attained, however, it can greatly multiply the impact and effectiveness of consultants. It can make their thoughts and ideas accessible to virtually the entire literate population of a nation. While only less than 1 percent of a population may be able to read a paper written in an international language, some 50–90 percent may be able to read a paper written in a local language. Also even for those host nationals who do read an international language, it is almost always a burden to read something written in another language. Thus, other things being equal, individuals are more likely to read first something written in their own language. Given that most professionals have far more to read than the time available, they may tend to neglect items written in a foreign language. Thus, many fine reports of advisers and consultants are underutilized because they are not written in the local language.

Foreign Languages for Special Purposes

Affecting all these levels of competency is the issue of foreign languages for special purposes. Consultants or advisers working in the field of agriculture, for example, will be primarily using a highly specialized set of language terms. It is not essential for them to know the local language used in classical literature, for example, or that used in the fine arts. Thus, to achieve the competencies outlined above with the most efficiency, training in foreign languages should emphasize the specialized vocabulary of the professional fields in which the advisers or consultants will be working. CUSO, the Canadian volunteer development organization, has successfully emphasized this efficient approach to foreign language learning.

The Importance of Knowing the Local Language

Given the criteria discussed, the need for local language ability varies with the particular context. French or English may be adequate for advising or consulting in West Africa, Singapore, or the Philippines, for example. In Latin America, most parts of Asia, the Middle East, and East Africa, knowledge of the local language is often of critical importance. There are many reasons for this, which we now outline in some detail.

Need for Knowledge and Awareness of Prior Development Efforts

A major weakness in technical assistance efforts is a common tendency to ignore previous related development efforts, whether by local nationals or international agencies. Knowledge of the local language, particularly a reading ability, can significantly facilitate acquisition of knowledge about previous efforts in the area in which the consultant is working. There is a need to know what has been tried and what has worked or not worked in the past. For example, in Thailand there seems to be the perpetual recommendation that rural teachers broaden their roles to become community developers as well.[8] Considerable empirical evidence exists which shows that this has not worked in the past, mainly because of adverse incentive systems affecting teachers' motivation. There is too little emphasis on the retention of institutional memory and learning from failure.[9] With a good command of the local language (oral and/or reading), consultants should be able to review more easily past developmental efforts related to their assignments.

Need to Broaden Contacts and to be Directly in Touch with Those Affected by Development Programs

Without knowledge of the local language, advisers will primarily be in contact with 'knights in air-conditioned offices.' Their contacts with non-elites will be non-existent or severely limited. They will be Mandarin, not Samurai, consultants. As Robert Chambers elegantly points out, they will lack opportunities to perceive real rural conditions.[10] Since the elites' perception of needs may differ markedly from those of villagers, it is necessary for consultants to have a balanced view of needs and the reactions of ordinary citizens to the development programs affecting them. The ordinary knowledge of villagers, which may be surprisingly profound, is an important source of information and new ideas.[11] To be able to communicate with both princes and peasants, knowledge of the local language is essential. Elites in many countries have little time to spend listening to the voices of villagers and ordinary citizens. Also frequently substantial status differences make such communication difficult, if not impossible. Outside consultants from other nations, but with a knowledge of the local language, can help build important communication bridges between peasants and princes. They can provide valuable feedback to elites. Since they are not career civil servants they can be more frank and open in relaying the voices of villagers to the elites.

Unlike the Mandarin consultants who have contacts only with elites in rarefied atmospheres, Samurai consultants with an adequate command of the local language thrive on 'spending time in the trenches.' They seek opportunties to perceive real needs and conditions in natural settings. Through extensive informal contacts with villagers, peasants, or workers they gain insights into how various development programs are working and affecting ordinary citizens. Senator Paul Simon eloquently argues for this type of bottom-up communication:

> But when we fail to learn to communicate with those who yearn for something better, we miss an opportunity to communicate with future leadership, and, more important, we fail to know the people of a nation.[12]

The World Bank has also now come to recognize the centrality of foreign language competency to the effectiveness of many projects, as illustrated by the following comment of a World Bank staff member:

> Even the most straightforward of engineering reports sometimes sit on shelves unread simply because they cannot be read easily by technical host-agency staff. Even where translated, follow-up is often delayed or misdirected because staff were unable to participate fully during report preparation, or simply because of translation difficulties. Language in the case of institutional technical assistance is of course a more serious issue. Projects designed with high-level clients—the kinds of people aid-agency staff meet on missions—often have to be carried out by lower-level staff lacking English skills.[13]

Expanding Training Opportunities for Counterparts

Training counterparts is often a major role of foreign consultants and advisers.[14] Without a knowledge of the local language, consultants are only able to share their skills and competencies with those counterparts speaking the international language of the consultant. Local nationals with a limited knowledge of English, for example, will hesitate to have contact with consultants not speaking their local language. They do not want to be embarrassed by making mistakes in speaking English. Thus, such advisers will have relatively few host-country counterparts. These colleagues will tend to be those who have already had extensive overseas training opportunities, and who are of higher socioeconomic background. Knowledge of the local language can dramatically multiply the number and diversity of counterparts and colleagues of a foreign consultant. This in turn can lead to a much greater impact in terms of the extent of informal training provided by consultants.

Language as a Vehicle for Understanding Culture

Much research has shown that language and culture are closely intertwined and interrelated.[15] It is difficult to acquire an in-depth understanding of another culture without knowledge of its language. For example, in the cultures of countries such as Thailand and Laos, much humor is based on the manipulation of tones in the tonal languages of Thai and Lao. It is virtually impossible to appreciate such humor without knowledge of the local language.

Another fascinating example of the language–culture linkage is the complex of heart-compound words found in Thai. There are a multitude of Thai compound words involving the base, 'heart.' These words mainly deal with complex affective feelings and emotions. A good understanding of these many heart compounds can provide considerable insight into the nuances of Thai culture which emphasizes social harmony, affect, and affiliation.[16] A number of these words such as *grengjai*, are extremely difficult to translate into English.[17] Without understanding the concept of *grengjai*, which permeates Thai culture, social relations, and organizations, it would be difficult to work effectively in Thailand.

Much technical assistance and many foreign consultants are concerned with the introduction of technological change. To ensure that such change improves the quality of life, and is consistent with local customs and traditions, consultants must be conversant with the local culture, and a command of the local language facilitates the development of such understanding. A major housing project in Iran failed because the foreign consultants located the bathrooms inappropriately with respect to Islamic traditions. From the extensive technical assistance literature there are countless examples of technical change which failed because of fundamental contradictions with the local culture. One of the greatest challenges facing consultants and advisers is to adapt appropriately and creatively new technologies to local conditions and cultures. Knowledge of the local language definitely enhances the potential for introducing and adapting technological change to meet genuine local needs.

Keeping Politically and Bureaucratically Informed

Americans working in Iran during the period of the Shah's rule were for the most part unaware of the extent of the anti-Shah feelings of many Iranians. Not knowing Farsi, most Americans could only learn about Iranian politics from elites speaking English, and from English-language publications. In many Third World countries the English-language press is moderate and reserved politically. Such countries are concerned about their image presented to outsiders.

In many Third World countries such as Indonesia or Thailand, formal communications tend to be extremely polite. In such contexts there is an emphasis on social harmony and avoidness of overt conflict. Nevertheless, in such contexts there is negative communication but it is often indirect and subtle. Without a knowledge of the local language it is easy to be unaware of negative communications.

Another form of informal communications are anonymous letters sent to high-ranking officials to register complaints or criticisms which in high-context cultures are difficult to express directly.[18] These letters normally appear in the local language. Although such letters represent an irresponsible form of communication, frequently involving libel and ugly rumor, they nevertheless may reveal subtle bureaucratic problems or antagonisms which may not appear on the surface. Since these letters are nearly always in the local language, foreign advisers are usually unaware of them.

In countries with rigid press and media control, informal underground newsletters and mimeographed material ('gray literature') provide an important source of information about bureaucratic and political realities, particularly critical feedback on governmental performance. These underground materials are almost always written in the local language.

In regimes with rather repressive control of the media, novels and short stories in the local language may provide considerable insight into the nature of local politics and government. In such contexts, 'fiction' may become non-fiction and 'non-fiction' materials may be actually fiction. In Brazil, for example, there is a rich indigenous literature dealing with fundamental development problems.[19]

If consultants must rely solely on communication in their own language, they will lack in-depth information on local bureaucratic and political phenomena. The local political and bureaucratic context may have a major influence on potential for technical change. Thus, in many cases it is essential for consultants to understand the local political and bureaucratic environment, if they are to be effective in introducing appropriately adapted innovations. A command of the local language can greatly facilitate the development of such understanding.

Foreign Language Use as a Public Relations Tool

The use of the host country language can be device for becoming friends and for convincing the host government and its people by showing the sincere desire to meet them on their own ground. Use of the host country language reflects respect for the local country and its culture. The effort to learn and use a second language definitely has public relations value, but it is important to emphasize that the effort must be continuing, and at least partly productive.

To accomplish their tasks, foreign consultants and advisers often need the goodwill of diverse groups within a country or culture. Use of the local language can greatly facilitate the building of warm and cordial relations with many local individuals and groups. Often a critical factor is the number and range of human contacts in the host country. Use of the local language enables consultants to multiply and diversify their professional contacts. Given the impermanence of politics in many developing countries, multiple contact points are particularly important. Influential friends today may easily be out of power tomorrow. Similarly, individuals or groups without power may suddenly move into positions of importance. Without a command of the local language, consultants will find it difficult to build goodwill among an adequately broad range of local groups and individuals. Even in former colonial societies where an international language is widely spoken, knowledge of a local language still has exceptional public relations value. In such contexts, colonial rulers, despite being in the country for long periods of time, often not only did not learn the local language but considered it beneath their dignity to study it.[20] A divergence from traditional colonial patterns of behavior can certainly improve the image of contemporary consultants and advisers.

Command of the Local Language as a Means to Enhance the Two-way Nature of Technical Assistance

Scholars such as Illich, Goulet, Hazzard, and the Paddocks all argue that the provision of foreign experts as part of technical assistance has been a failure and should cease.[21] To use the Paddocks' terminology, 'we don't know how to help,' or Illich, 'come not to help, but to learn.' Though we would be the first to admit that the effectiveness of foreign advisers and consultants has been certainly mixed with many notable failures, in other parts of this study we also argue that the provision of technical expertise can be effective and in some instances has been dramatically so. A basic assumption of our argument is that technical assistance is inherently at least a two-way process.[22] There is always an important dimension of cultural exchange. But without a command of the local language this two-way process is difficult to achieve.

The Inadequacy of Reliance on Translators and Interpreters

Dr Gordon S. Seagrave, an American surgeon serving in Burma for many years, describes an encounter with the famous Burmese political leader, U Nu. His reflections on this encounter indicate the inadequacy of reliance on translations.

> To enjoy one of U Nu's Burmese speeches a foreigner must stop thinking in his own language and think in Burmese, and thus absorb U Nu's language without translation. I tried that once when I was sitting almost at his feet, and it was very effective. The translation I read later was a crude reflection of what he had really said.[23]

Many of us have observed speeches or presentations being translated, and noticed that frequently the translation is considerably shorter than the original remarks, raising a curiosity about what has been omitted. We personally have had experience interpreting for individuals who did not know the local language. We found it extremely difficult to avoid *selective* interpreting. There were times when we were sure that we neglected to translate certain elements which we may have thought offensive, foolish, or inappropriate.

Also there is the fundamentally important question of deciding what to translate or interpret. Critically important material may never be translated, because certain individuals, whose skills may be primarily linguistic, do not realize the highly significant political or policy implications of various documents or materials in the local language. In some cases there may be an intentional desire not to have outsiders informed of certain internal developments. The government of the Shah in Iran, for example, wanted Westerners to think that the regime was held in high regard by Iranians. Thus, many impressive white papers (in English, of course!) were published to convince Westerners of the effectiveness of the Shah's various modernization programs. Much critical material in Farsi was probably never translated.

As illustrated by President Carter's problem in Poland, there is always the issue of quality control in relying on translations and interpreters. It is costly and time-consuming to check the reliability and validity of translations.

Misjudging Local Talent Because of a Reliance on the Adviser's Language

Ability to use English or other international language such as French often becomes a basis for judging local talent, particularly in those cases where advisers do not know the local language. While there may be some correlation between overall competence and ability to use an international language, reliance on this criterion alone will tend to favor those from higher socioeconomic backgrounds and with previous international experience. The British in Melanesia often selected headmen based on the latter's knowledge of pidgin. As a result they frequently made inappropriate appointments of individuals not respected in the local community.

Potential Abuse of Foreign Languages

We have mainly discussed the many positive implications of knowing and being able to use the local language. There are also numerous ways to abuse foreign languages, which we summarize below.

Overuse of a Limited Vocabulary for 'Public Relations' Purposes

Van Wagoner, a linguist who spent many years working for the Arabian American Oil Company, stresses that there is a tendency for some individuals to wear out a few expressions by overuse.[24] Use of a limited set of expressions, at worst mispronounced, can be rather tedious for local nationals exposed constantly to this type of low-level performance. Van Wagoner feels that this shallow type of 'public relations' is definitely counterproductive.

Improper Use of a Foreign Language

Most local nationals are tolerant of mistakes made by foreigners trying to speak their language. Outsiders can, however, be extremely crude and rude.

Many non-Western languages have complex and subtle nuances related to status differentials. Westerners frequently fail to appreciate these subtleties and in so doing can become rather offensive. Outsiders also often have difficulty distinguishing between proper and improper language. Language use appropriate for one context may be totally inappropriate for another. In his evaluation of missionary work in the South Seas, Gunson finds that the missionaries often were guilty of using words which gave offense. A Samoan chief who ceased to attend chapel complained:

> I ought to tell you that allusions to such matters, or even to death, before chiefs, are contrary to Samoan etiquette.[25]

Use of a Foreign Language to Express Criticism of Local Conditions

Among certain advisers and consultants there is a tendency to develop a syndrome of severely criticizing locals and local conditions. There are constant remarks about the problems of dealing with 'these people.' When this happens in English, relatively little harm results, since much of the criticism remains within the circles of the outsiders. Such criticism done in the local language, often harshly and impolitely, creates resentment and epitomizes the stereotypes known as the 'Ugly American,' 'Arrogant Russian,' or 'Unmasked Japanese.'

Insensitivity to Status Aspects of Foreign Language Use

In many developing countries, speaking English or a Western language is a sign of high social status and prestige.[26] Many high-ranking officials in such countries have previously studied abroad and enjoy speaking a Western language. Some consultants prefer to speak the local language with such officials, even when their command of the local language is inferior to the local official's command of a Western language. In such cases, one approach is to start communication in the Western language and then shift to the local language if the local national suggests such a preference. In one rather amusing case of this type the Westerner always spoke in the local language and the local national always communicated in English.

This problem usually does not arise in Latin America, where it is assumed that Spanish or Portuguese (in the case of Brazil) will be the language of interaction and communication, regardless of the status level of the host country national. Similarly in Francophone Africa, French is the normal language for official business.

Obstacles to Foreign Language Learning

Nearly all individuals of normal intelligence can learn foreign languages, but overseas Americans tend to have a rather poor record. The Japanese also, despite their performance in American English, do not have an outstanding record in other areas. To our knowledge the Scandinavians, the Dutch, and various Third World nationals (Singaporeans, Nepalese, Saudis, Indians, Ethiopians, and Egyptians, deserve high marks for having made impressive efforts to learn other languages).

We would now like to review the major obstacles to foreign language learning faced by overseas consultants and advisers.

False Stereotypes about Language Learning

Two common stereotypes exist about language learning which are both essentially false. Nevertheless, they have had serious adverse effects on language learning. The first stereotype is that an individual must be a genius or have an exceptional flair to learn other languages, particularly difficult ones like Chinese, Arabic, or Thai. Acceptance of this sterotype deters many individuals from even seriously considering the possibility of acquiring command of a second language. A second stereotype, the polar opposite of the first, is that learning another language is routine, rote learning. Given this perception, individuals see foreign language learning as below 'their intellectual dignity.' They don't want to 'waste their time' in boring rote learning routines.

The Perfectionist Syndrome

Some individuals have a strong perfectionist orientation. Such an attitude can have deleterious effects on learning another language. In speaking a second language it is difficult to avoid making mistakes of some type (word order, grammar, pronunciation, usage). As W. Somerset Maugham stated, 'unless you devote your whole life to it, you will never learn to speak the language of another country to perfection.'[27] Individuals, particularly those in rather high-status positions, usually want to avoid making mistakes in public. Speaking another language involves the risk of losing face. Also associated with this syndrome is a tendency to be extremely self-conscious about image and appearance. Such individuals do not like to be laughed at. Using and speaking another language requires a relaxed view of the self, a tolerance of looking foolish and being able to laugh at oneself. It is necessary not be sensitive to host nationals who more often than not are actually laughing *with* rather than at us, when mistakes are made. Though it is certainly important to try to speak another language as well as possible, a perfectionist attitude will normally lead to avoidance and disuse of the local language. Professionally we have encountered cases of this type in many overseas settings.

The Vicious Circle of Language Usage Opportunities

Some consultants may make considerable efforts to learn the local language, only to find their host country colleagues prefer to speak English. Their command of the local language is not yet adequate to communicate easily with their colleagues. Naturally, in such situations, there is a tendency to use the international language. Thus consultants find inadequate opportunities to practice the local language, even though it is important for at least some aspects of their work. The major solution to this problem is to use the language as extensively as possible with ordinary people outside the workplace who may not know English or an international language. Barbers and taxi-drivers, for example, can provide fascinating comments on the local political scene. Talking with children can also be a good avenue for practice of the second language.

The Problem of Language Teaching Methods

Organizations such as the Peace Corps have demonstrated that individuals can learn other languages quickly and with enjoyment. Nevertheless, language teaching methods currently in use are often dominated by traditional approaches. Such approaches emphasize the mechanical learning of grammatical principles and stress the simultaneous learning of reading, writing, and speaking. The teacher often does not even use the foreign language extensively in teaching. Rules and principles are explained in English. Frequently the learning process is boring and tedious, with little opportunity for playfulness and humor. Under such circumstances it is easy to understand why individuals fail to acquire command of a second language.

There are, however, some hopeful signs. Cornell University, for example, is pioneering an innovative approach to Japanese. This enables individuals to concentrate initially on the task of conversing in Japanese, without the need to invest enormous amounts of time in learning to read the language. Programs such as Volunteers in Asia, at Stanford University, have trained individuals to use language informants effectively. Learning a foreign language with a language informant can be an exciting and enjoyable way to acquire a working knowledge of another language.

Foreign Language Use as Information Exchange versus the Inducement of Cooperative Interaction

If the goal is solely information exchange, then translation of documents and the use of professional interpreters may in some respects suffice, despite the considerable economic costs of such services. In many aspects of technical assistance, however, consultants and advisers are professional agents of change. Communicative competence is central to their deeper purposes of inducing and achieving cooperative interaction. Consultants working within a single culture find that communication is an important dimension of their work. Surveys indicate that 70 percent of a consultant's time is devoted to communicating with others.[28] Thus we argue that both a command of the local language and an appreciation of the silent language (nonverbal communication) are crucial skills needed by consultants and advisers involved in the inducement of cooperative interaction to bring about constructive change or improvements.

We will consider in the next section the problem of developing 'cultural and social intelligence.' This is the ability to read and understand the subtle nuances of nonverbal communication in other cultures.

The Need for Social and Cultural Intelligence: Non-verbal Communication

> The open, direct and straightforward approach is seen as admirable to many Westerners. However, here in the East, if one opens oneself, it is thought to be a sign of weakness and/or cowardliness. It is seen as humiliating to reveal your inner being. The one who 'opens' is not to be trusted. He tells secrets! (JoAnn Craig)[29]

> Bacon reproached Aristotle for not having realized that the gestures of the body are comprehensible. (Herbert Goldhamer)[30]

The expertise provided by advisers and consultants is normally of an analytical or cognitive nature. Such analytical or cognitive expertise *per se* is not adequate. Advisers and consultants working cross-culturally must also have what Archer terms 'social intelligence' or what the anthropologist Hall has termed the 'silent language' or the 'hidden dimension.'[31] Empirical research by Birdwhistell and others provide support for the importance of developing social and cultural intelligence.[32] They found that at most only about 30 percent of what is communicated in a conversation is verbal. Thus, sensitivity to the nuances of nonverbal communication in diverse cultures is essential if advisers and consultants are to communicate their analytical expertise effectively. The development of such sensitivity is particularly difficult since nonverbal communication patterns vary significantly from one cultural setting to another. The following are major dimensions of social and cultural intelligence which advisers need to understand.

Paralanguage

This refers to speech rate, volume, pitch, and inflections. A major problem is the tendency for the Westerner to speak too loudly and forcefully. Gerald Fry admits that he has offended Latin Americans by speaking too loudly. Advisers whose native tongue is English find that they have a tendency to speak too quickly and with too much slang and/or academic jargon. Alternatively, some advisers slip into a form of pidgin in talking to locals. This can be quite offensive, particularly in countries such as Malaysia or Singapore where local officials and intellectuals often have an impressive command of English. Another disconcerting tendency is for some advisers to speak too softly so that locals have to strain to hear the adviser's comments. Such a pattern of language expression is sometimes considered to reflect a high power status.

The role of silence is another complex dimension of paralanguage. In American communication silence is to be avoided, and a sign that something is wrong. In many other cultures, such as the Japanese, silence can be quite normal and even highly functional. In Melanesia, silence can indicate gratitude for a gift received.[33] Westerners have often misinterpreted this silence to mean a lack of gratitude. Thus it is important for advisers and consultants to have a good understanding of the nuances of paralanguage in the cultures in which they are serving.

Touching Behavior

Touching behavior and taboos vary significantly from culture to culture. In many cultures it is absolutely *verboten* to touch across sexes in public. Even in dancing in such cultures, men and women will not touch. This can be a serious problem for Westerners accustomed to touching members of the opposite sex casually during conversation. In contrast, there are many cultures where it is common for members of the same sex to touch. First, the outsider has to learn that such behavior has no homosexual or lesbian implications. Second, outsiders may face situations in which they are expected to hold hands, for example with members of the same sex. In such situations it is easy to reject rudely the friendly and warm gesture of the local national who may be unaware of Western taboos against such touching behavior. This is normally not a problem in modernized urbanized capitals, but a more common problem in remote rural areas where there is less awareness of Western cultural norms.

Time Symbolism

Attitudes toward time vary enormously from culture to culture. Also different cultures may use different systems of organizing and calculating time. For example, in Thailand time is frequently divided into four segments of six hours each. Thus, a two o'clock appointment could mean eight in the morning, two in the afternoon, or possibly eight in the evening. The outsider must clarify which is meant, to avoid the possibility of not showing up at the appropriate time for a meeting.

In many Western societies there is a fairly clear segmentation of time between work and leisure. In East and Southeast Asia much important work eight to five. In many other cultures there is much less of a clear segmentation between work and leisure. in East and Southeast Asia much important work takes place 'after hours.' Lauchlin Currie, in discussing his advising experiences in Colombia, mentions that many of his important meetings with his advisory group took place after office hours.[34]

In Thailand the word *ngan* means both work and party (social gathering). As in Japan, there is no clear delineation between work and leisure, whether in rural or professional settings. In such cultural contexts, advisers desiring to retain their privacy after formal working hours will face serious difficulties. If they express reluctance to participate in weekend seminars or evening social–business engagements, they will be perceived as not fully committed to their work.

Individuals coming from cultures such as the US, Germany, and Singapore consider time to be of great value. They have a tendency to want to begin business immediately after meeting. In many cultures such a communication approach is considered inappropriate. Prior to discussing formal business it is essential to chat over tea and/or coffee, so that individuals can get to know each other and to begin to develop trust. Considerable investments of time in developing personal relations may be essential as a means to accomplish important tasks in the future.

Punctuality is another important dimension of time symbolism. Also it may be common to be kept waiting in certain cultures and bureaucratic contexts. In a number of countries social engagements begin considerably later than the time suggested on the invitation. The Westerner who arrives promptly at six in the evening may be embarrassed to be the only guest present, arriving much earlier than other guests who understand the local time symbolism.

Time delays may be another frustrating dimension of time symbolism. Mañana does not necessarily mean tomorrow. This phenomenon probably more than any other is irritating to Westerners serving in other cultures with different conceptions of time. There is no easy answer to this problem. Based on our own experience we feel that the best approach is polite and diplomatic persistence in the face of frequent time delays. In many cultural contexts, angry displays of emotion will be counter-productive and may make the time delays even longer. In many cultural settings it is essential for advisers and consultants to develop a more flexible and relaxed view of time. Excessive attachment to time can be a major source of frustration and depression in cross-cultural settings.

Uses of Hands and Feet

This is an area fraught with potential problems. In Muslim societies individuals must be careful to avoid using the left hand in eating and other social activities. Also there are many taboos in various cultures about where the hands should be placed during eating. The need to eat with the hands in some settings can also come as a shock to many advisers.

In many cultures there are taboos about pointing with various parts of the body. In Thailand it is considered extremely rude to point a foot at an individual's head. Thus, careful sitting posture is important so as to keep the feet on the floor. Also in Thailand there is a strong taboo against touching another person's head, particularly an adult. In Malaysia, making a fist and hitting against the open hand is considered impolite and rude.[35] The Australian hand gesture for 'drinking up' could be quite offensive to older Malays implying that 'God is evil.'[36] Soon after arriving in another cultural setting, advisers should seek out a well-informed local cultural informant to specify taboos associated with hand gestures and uses.

Interpersonal Distance (Proxemics)

Customs concerning proxemics and eye contact also vary significantly from culture to culture. In some cultures individuals are expected to be in close proximity, while in other cultures considerable physical distance must be maintained during conversation. If proxemic norms are violated, individuals will feel highly uncomfortable. In an experiment at Stanford University involving students from Latin American and Southeast Asian cultures, we found that Southeast Asian students had a tendency 'to retreat' because the Latin American students were seeking to be too close during conversation.

There are similar variations with respect to eye contact. In some cultural contexts direct eye contact is considered improper, while in other cultures avoidance of direct eye contact is thought to be impolite. What is considered 'staring' in one cultural context may be quite appropriate in another.

Tastes and Food

In many cultures there is a strong emphasis on local hospitality. In such cases it is common to be offered food and drinks of various types. The symbolism of food is often important in rural cultures, and rejection of the local food is synonymous with rejection of the people themselves. In one Southeast Asian country, Japanese sojourners are famous for taking box lunches with them in their visits to rural sites. For health reasons they prefer to avoid local meals. Although their behavior is reasonable from a health perspective, culturally it is extremely awkward. In Northeast Thailand the local people are extremely proud of delicacies such as small fried birds, monkey's blood, red ants, and frog skin. Both fish and birds are always served with heads in this area. In Southeast Asia the durian fruit is a great delicacy. Showing genuine fondness for this 'horrible-smelling' fruit is a sure way to win local friends. Sharing food with local inhabitants certainly helps to build important intercultural bonds. In Melanesia, 'to eat together is the great test of friendship.'[37]

With respect to either food or drink, it is important also not to partake of such until formally invited. We recall one instance in a Southeast Asian country where cool drinks were on the table. Only after about twenty minutes were we invited to have our drinks. This required considerable patience since we were extremely thirsty after a hot dusty ride in a Land-rover. Also in such settings, it is important to wait for the higher-status individual to drink or eat first.

In many Western cultures alcoholic beverages are commonly served. In most Muslim societies there is a strict taboo against alcohol. Even the smell of alcohol on the breath can be offensive. Recently one of Australia's highest-ranking diplomats was sent home by Saudi Arabia for having alcohol in his home. In Muslim societies it is also essential to be extremely careful in hosting local individuals to be sure that no pork is served, and that all meat and vegetables are prepared in a proper Muslim way. With respect to dinner parties and other social settings it is important that pets not be allowed to jump on and lick guests. In Malaysia such exposure to pets would be considered offensive and impolite.

When 'Yes' means No and 'No' means Yes

In many cultures, particularly in East and Southeast Asia, individuals are reluctant to say 'no' directly.[38] They may seek subtle, soft, and indirect ways of saying 'no.' Several years ago my co-author was involved in a meeting in Thailand involving both Westerners and Thais discussing in English a possible cooperative project. Upon leaving the meeting the Westerners felt extremely reassured that things had gone well. In fact they had misinterpreted the Thais' impressive politeness and hospitality to mean agreement for cooperation with respect to the proposed project. Later they were disappointed to find that no follow-up had occurred, and that the Thais did not appear to be seriously interested in the project.

Related to the yes–no problem, there was a certain Westerner working in Thailand who was extremely positive and polite. In a number of instances his verbal 'nos' were interpreted as 'yeses' since his nonverbal communication patterns were so remarkably positive and enthusiastic. This led to considerable misunderstanding later when individuals realized that the true message was 'no.'

Summary

The above are just samples of the many nuances of cultural and social intelligence. Condon and Yousef, for example, mention 24 different domains of nonverbal intercultural communication.[59] Since intercultural communication is so central to the advising and consulting process overseas, we would like to stress special importance on the need for all advisers working cross-culturally to enhance their cultural and social intelligence.[40] It is also extremely important for advisers to be conscious of the wide variations in nonverbal communication patterns from culture to culture.

To conclude, we would like to try to respond to a commonly asked question concerning the kind of language competence which can be reasonably expected of consultants. In thinking about the language capabilities needed by international consultants of the 1990s and the twenty-first century, we would stress two factors. First, there is the contextual factor and related guidelines elaborated in Table 3.2 (p. 34). Situations vary significantly with respect to language skills needed. Key dimensions are length of consultancy and the nature of the host country's own national language. Even within a single nation contexts may vary, depending, for example, on whether a consultant will be working in a cosmopolitan capital or a remote rural area. A second important factor is the evolving nature of the status of various world languages. Evidence indicates, for example, that the dominance of English as a world language is diminishing as an increasing proportion of the world's scientific and technical literature appears in 'emerging' languages such as Japanese, Chinese, Korean, and Portuguese.

To prepare themselves for the complexity of contexts related to international advising, consultants ideally need both considerable linguistic flexibility and versatile communication skills. Generally, a working knowledge of at least one recognized international language such as French or Spanish is highly desirable. Even more consulting opportunities and potential will exist with, in addition, a solid command of a second language, one of the 'emerging' world languages such as Arabic, Chinese, Korean, Portuguese, or Indonesian. Those nations preparing their young professionals in the latter languages will have distinct comparative advantages in the service sector of international consulting.

Notes

1. W. O. BAKER, Foreign language skills as factors in economic competency and world trade, in *Education and Economic Competitiveness Abroad*, Consortium of Social Science Associations, Washington, DC, 1983, p.20.
2. Cited in P. SIMON, *The Tongue-tied American: Confronting the Foreign Language Crisis*, Continuum, New York, 1980, p.28.
3. P. SIMON; J. LAURIE, *America, Globally Blind, Deaf, and Dumb: A Shocking Report of Our Incompetence, through Ignorance, in Dealing with Other Countries*, Adelphi University, Garden City, New York, 1981.
4. W. MANGIN, Thoughts on twenty-four years of work in Peru: the Vicos Project and me, p.72.
5. *Manual on the Use of Consultants in Developing Countries*, United Nations, New York, 1968, p.81.

6. C. E. Fox, *Kakamora,* Hodder and Stoughton, London, 1962, p.137.
7. J. K. Galbraith, *A Life in Our Times; Memoirs,* Houghton & Mifflin, Boston, Massachusetts, 1981, p.465.
8. R. Nairn, *International Aid to Thailand; the New Colonialism?,* Yale University Press, New Haven, Connecticut, 1966.
9. D. Korten, Community organization and rural development—a learning-process approach, *Public Administration Review,* **40,** 480–511 (1980).
10. R. Chambers, Rural poverty unperceived: problems and remedies, *World Development,* **9,** 1–19 (1981).
11. C. Geertz, *Local Knowledge: Further Essays in Interpretative Anthropology,* Basic Books, New York, 1983.
12. P. Simon, p.54.
13. F. Lethem and L. Cooper, *Managing Project-related Technical Assistance,* World Bank, Washington, DC, Management and Development Series, no. 13, 1983, p.58.
14. L. Currie, *The Role of Economic Advisers in Developing Countries,* Greenwood Press, Westport, Connecticut, 1981, p.80.
15. See, for example, R. W. Brislin, *Cross-cultural Encounters, Face-to-face Interaction,* Pergamon Press, New York, 1981, pp.30–4.
16. See C. K. Lee, Heart language, in *Proceedings of the International Conference on Thai Studies, 3–6 July 1987,* Research School of Pacific Studies, ANU, Canberra, vol. 2, 1987, pp.149–93.
17. *Grengjaj* implies a reluctance to impose on other persons. There is the connotation of awe and respect. See R. and N. Cooper, *Culture Shock! Thailand,* Times Books International, Singapore, 1982, pp.76 and 82–3.
18. See M. Imai, High context culture vs. low context culture, *Japanese Economic Journal,* 30 November 1982, p.12.
19. See, for example, the works of authors such as Gilberto Freyre, Jorge Amado, and Graciliano Ramos.
20. C. E. Fox, p.137.
21. W. and E. Paddock, *We Don't Know How,* Iowa State University Press, Ames, Iowa, 1973; S. Hazzard, *Defeat of an Ideal; a study of the self-destruction of the United Nations,* Little, Brown & Co., Boston, Massachusetts, 1973; S. Hazzard, *People in Glass Houses,* Penguin, Middlesex, 1983.
22. See B. Hayden, The ethics of development: aid—a two-way process? Speech by Mr Bill Hayden, Minister of Foreign Affairs, Australia, at the 17th Waigani Seminar, University of Papua New Guinea, Port Moresby, 10 September 1986; R. Chambers, Cognitive problems of experts in rural Africa, in J. C. Stone, *Experts in Africa,* p.101.
23. G. S. Seagrave, *My Hospital in the Hills,* W. W. Norton, New York, 1955, pp.102–3.
24. Private communication with Van Wagoner.
25. N. Gunson, *Messengers of Grace: Evangelical Missionaries in the South Seas 1797–1860,* Oxford University Press, Melbourne, 1978, p.265.
26. L. Winfield, *Living Overseas,* Public Affairs Press, Washington, DC, 1962, p.167.
27. W. S. Maugham, *Summing Up,* Penguin, Middlesex, 1978, p.69.
28. M. Kubr (editor), *Management Consulting: A Guide to the Profession,* ILO, Geneva, 1976, p.353.
29. J. Craig, *What Not to Do in Malaysia and Singapore,* p.7.
30. H. Goldhamer, p.106.
31. D. Archer, *How to Expand Your Social I.Q.,* M. Evans, New York, 1980; E. T. Hall, *The Silent Language,* Anchor Press, Garden City, New York, 1973; E. T. Hall, *The Hidden Dimension,* Doubleday, Garden City, New York, 1976.
32. R. L. Birdwhistell, *Kinesics and Context,* University of Pennsylvania Press, Philadelphia, Pennsylvania, 1970, p.125.
33. C. Fox, p.141.
34. L. Currie, p.50.
35. J. Craig, p.9.
36. Ibid., p.9.
37. C. Fox, p.125.

38. M. IMAI, *Never Take Yes for an Answer: an Inside Look at Japanese Business for Foreign Businessmen,* Simul Press, Tokyo, 1982.
39. J. C. CONDON and Y. YOUSEF, *An Introduction to Intercultural Communication,* Bobbs-Merrill, Indianapolis, 1981, pp.123–4.
40. A valuable volume using international fiction to enhance understanding of the process of cross-cultural adaptation is T. LEWIS and R. JUNGMAN (editors), *On Being Foreign: Culture Shock in Short Fiction: An International Anthology,* Intercultural Press, Yarmouth, Maine, 1986.

CHAPTER 4

The Political Role of Advisers

Perhaps I should say a word about how I understand my relationship as a consultant to a government that has requested my assistance. Neither my wife nor I regard a consultant as a cold, neutral, uncommitted figure, always disposed to offer technical advice to any problems presented. On the contrary, it seems to us that the consultant's work has political implications, whatever the field of expertise (Paulo Freire).[1]

Debate and controversy surround the so-called political role of advisers and consultants. This arises partly out of the diverse meanings of the word 'politics.' For example, in Spanish, the word '*politica*' means both party politics and *policy*, for example, the policy of government. Some believe that advisers must remain officially neutral and that such neutrality is indeed possible. The meaning is consistent with the term 'technical assistance,' emphasizing the non-political nature of the advisory role. Others state that the role carries with it inherently political implications in a broader sense, and that is is illusionary to think that foreign advisers and consultants can ever be totally politically neutral. Still others, while accepting the logic of the above, maintain that it's important for advisers to *act* as though they are objective, fair and politically neutral.

We have some sympathy for all of these perspectives. First, depending on the particular context and the consultant's own abilities to relate to 'princes,' an active policy-forming or policy-advisory role may be appropriate, if there is agreement all around that this is desirable. However, such a role is more likely to arise when the consultant is an 'old hand' in the country, or when the level of his prestige is so high and widely accepted as to warrant it, e.g., Edward Mason, Harvard–Pakistan Planning Board Project. Experience tends to demonstrate that an active political role maximizes *both* potential impact as well as to heighten the risks of failure.

The most important political dimension of the advisory role is probably the decision whether or not to accept a particular overseas assignment. Paulo Freire, a Brazilian with extensive consulting experience in both Latin America and Africa and cited above, will not work in a country unless the government is sincerely committed to the types of progressive changes that he seeks to promote. For reasons similar to Freire's a number of advisers and consultants probably would not work for the Pinochet regime in Chile. Some economists, however, of the Chicago school, such as Milton Friedman, have made the decision, which would appear to have political overtones, to use their expertise to assist this controversial regime. In contrast, Harry Wilhelm, then a Ford Foundation representative, was unwilling to continue to work in Brazil or Argentina under military regimes.

All actions and behavior of advisers may be seen to have political implications in the local milieu. An adviser with well-honed diplomatic skills may enhance the image of a certain political regime. Others through their advice may help to improve the performance of a regime and thus its legitimacy. But advisers with poor interpersonal skills or inappropriate behavior may bring discredit to a regime. Alternatively, advisers may serve as convenient 'scapegoats' when certain projects or policies prove ineffective, or fail. The foreign adviser may be rightly or wrongly blamed for such failures.

Benveniste highlights the *legitimation* function in his insightful study, *The Politics of Expertise*.[2] Benveniste states that a common role for outside advisers is to provide an overall rationale for decisions already made but not yet widely approved by the public. Or they may be used to test political reactions to a new idea or contemplated action. If the idea later proves unpopular or unworkable, the local politician does not suffer. Thus, it is convenient to use outsiders to test new ideas or approaches. For example when Clarence Thurber was in Guatemala it seemed that *all* innovations were being introduced under US AID, Israeli, West German aid, or United National Development Programme auspices to the extent that no one in government was assuming any risks for their success or failure.

At the same time, advisers may also provide a desired rationale for inaction by a local politician. Although it will probably never be formulated in a contract, outside advisers are frequently sought to perform this important legitimation function now widely recognized by scholars such as Cleveland, Benveniste, and Habermas.[3] In this sense the legitimation function involves the outside adviser in a direct political role, however direct or indirect it may be couched.

In this sense, although a role with political overtones is inevitable, experienced advisers respect certain caveats. First, they try to avoid becoming identified with certain partisan political factions. Instead they cultivate a broad range of diverse political contacts. There is a doctrine of developing contacts with 'the next' or potential alternative governments. The necessity for this was recognized when the Attlee government was elected in 1945. For a period of time the only person in the US Embassy in London with any knowledge of, or contacts with, the Labour Government was a relatively low-level official, Sam Berger, the Labor Attaché. For a critical period of time, almost all relations with the new government were handled through this 'channel.' As a result the doctrine of keeping open contacts with opposition parties and factions became apparent, a doctrine that tended later to be forgotten during the Shah's regime in Teheran, Somoza's regime in Nicaragua, and elsewhere. The point is that technical consultants can often be useful in developing such communications. Given the 'impermanence of politics' in many developing countries, close identification with political groups or factions, which may fall from power, may leave advisers in an exposed and highly awkward position. Their effectiveness then becomes minimal.

Experienced advisers also try to avoid becoming embroiled in *bureaucratic* politics. Here again, factions may play an important role. As with national politics, identification with any particular faction in a bureaucratic setting carries high risks, ones which have to be carefully assessed.

Advisers in another country should not, in our opinion, participate in partisan activities such as political rallies, demonstrations, or political fund-raising dinners. 'Political castration' of this type may be frustrating, but it is essential to maintaining an official position of neutrality while serving in a foreign country.

Contacts with the local military or police officials are also to be avoided unless the advising role has a direct military, defense, or intelligence aspect. This is true despite the political power which the military may exercise in a number of countries. Such contacts can be easily perceived as inappropriate political interference on the part of outside foreigners.

Occasionally, foreign advisers have played a 'guru' role for young political activists. They seek to raise political consciousness concerning social injustices and inequities. While such advisers often have impressive moral commitments, such behavior is considered offensive by many host governments. There are also certain ethical considerations related to responsibility after the adviser's departure. If such activists later suffer unintended harm, who is ultimately responsible? William Sewell, a much-beloved University of Wisconsin sociologist visiting at Delhi University, inculcated US-style 'participative roles' in his seminar. After he left some of his students suffered at the hands of local professors, and many were later dismissed under Indian professors who did not utilize his methods. He apparently failed on Cleveland's 'art of the possible.'

Adam Curle[4] describes common aspiration of advisers to be an *eminence grise* entering the corridors of influence to 'speak truth to power.'[5] This vision of the role of the adviser may once have been appropriate, when a developing country may have lacked well-trained leaders, and when a colonial mentality prevailed in many parts of the world.

The case studies of John Grant, Wolf Ladejinsky and Lauchlin Currie indicate that such individuals multiplied their policy impact by developing close personal relations with powerful and influential governmental leaders. In the 1980s and 1990s this type of advisory role is likely to become increasingly uncommon. Many developing nations now have large cadres of technically sophisticated officials, educated at some of the world's best universities. They do not seek the *policy* advice of outside experts. They are capable of making their own decisions, and normally have a much better sense of local politics than most outsiders. They may still utilize foreign expertise, but basically as technicians to assist, for example, in developing local research capacity in biotechnology, computer science, or satellite communications.

Some experienced foreign advisers serving in the 1980s fail to recognize that local conditions have dramatically changed. They assume they can advise in the same manner they did 20 or 30 years ago. They strive to influence policy, and to be directive, without realizing that, in the current decade and beyond, outside advisers must play a collegial and subordinate role.

Harlan Cleveland, in his classic work *The Overseas Americans*, stressed the need for a sense of politics.[6] In this respect he meant 'the art of the possible' or a sense of realism. Guy Benveniste similarly argues that, to be effective, an adviser must have some degree of political *savoire faire*.[7] This is difficult, given the increasing complexity of the political scene. Political contexts vary dramatically from one nation to another. What may be the appropriate behavior in one polity may be unacceptable in another. Thus, advisers must have the protean flexibility to adapt their behavior with respect to political role according to both historical changes and particular national contexts. It would be naive to prescribe fixed general rules with respect to the political role of foreign advisers.

The Politics of Advising—an Alternative Perspective

There is an alternative perspective on the politics of advising which differs substantially from the orientation of our discussion above. Arnove's book, *Philanthropy and Cultural Imperialism*,[8] and Illich's scathing essay, 'To hell with good intentions,'[9] both reflect this alternative critical view of international advisers. Unlike other critics of advisers such as the Paddocks,[10] Seers,[11] Luce,[12] or Hazzard,[13] who emphasize a lack of effectiveness, Arnove and others would argue that advisers are in fact perhaps too successful. In fact, their very success may have adverse effects on the developing nations. These critics do not deny that there may be individual advisers with good intentions, and who may sincerely want to help. They argue, however, that the overall impact of such advisers is clearly detrimental. Illich's words are indeed harsh and totally blunt:

> Next to money and guns, the third largest North American export is the U.S. idealist, who turns up in every theater of the world: the teacher, the volunteer, the missionary, the community organizer, the economic developer, and the vacationing do-gooders. Ideally, these people define their role as service. Actually, they frequently wind up alleviating the damage done by money and weapons, or "seducing" the "underde-

veloped" to the benefits of the world of affluence and achievement. Perhaps this is the moment to instead bring home to the people of the U.S. the knowledge that the way of life they have chosen is simply not alive enough to be shared.[14]

A number of elements constitute this critical perspective on international advising. Gouldner, for example, argues that there is an international occupation or profession of experts and technicians.[15] These individuals as a group have important status and economic interests to protect and advance. Because of the many perquisites associated with international advising such as travel, special financial incentives and rewards, prestige, and tax privileges, advisers themselves benefit substantially and directly from their work.[16] If Gouldner's argument is correct, then the ideal of advisers working themselves out of jobs is likely to be mythical. Instead advisers will seek to promote the need for their services and try to foster continued dependence rather than self-reliance. A statistical correlational analysis confirms Gouldner's view (see Appendix I). Arnove and Roberts emphasize that advisers represent a subtle form of neocolonialism; they facilitate the continued domination of developing countries in the periphery by rich industrial countries at the center. Foundations and other international agencies attempt to place their advisers in influential positions. Given the high prestige and access to international development funds of such agencies, their employees gain considerable access to powerful individuals in developing countries. They may persuade such policy-makers to pursue development paths compatible with the major interests of the Western industrial powers.

Many writers and thinkers critical of international advisers are *dependistas*, those adhering to the dependency theory of development. They stress that international advisers foster cultural, intellectual, and economic dependence. The networking emphasized by major foundations such as Ford and Rockefeller incorporates intellectuals from developing nations into a transnational system of interdependent elites.

Advisers, in our experience, almost never think of themselves in these terms. They are, from the critical perspective being considered here, 'salesmen' for Western industrial products and services such as technological gadgetry, books, supplies, and higher education in Western countries. The Japanese have been most severely criticized from this perspective, since many Japanese technical assistance projects normally involve the exclusive purchase of extensive supplies and equipment from Japan. In Southeast Asia, IBM in the late 1970s donated a large amount of sophisticated computer hardware to the Asian Institute of Technology (AIT) for its new Regional Computer Centre. IBM also provided technical experts to train AIT staff members in the use of the donated equipment. AIT serves students from throughout the Asian region. When they return to their home countries they are likely to be oriented toward purchasing computer hardware and software from IBM since they were trained using their products and services. Many social science advisers from the US serving abroad promote the use of SAS and SPSSX computer software. Both of these packages are marketed by organizations in the United States. Many advisers overseas also promote study abroad back in their own countries. Such study abroad introduces nationals from developing nations to the modern consumer society. As the World Bank has carefully documented, study abroad by LDC nationals represents a large foreign exchange drain. Direct economic benefits, as well as indirect multiplier effects, accrue to the rich host countries providing these educational services.

Still another element in this critical perspective on international advisers relates to the role of international advisers in co-opting radicals and leftist intellectuals in the developing countries. In Latin America, for example, the Ford Foundation and its advisers have on occasions actively supported certain radical intellectuals. With such support to enable them to pursue their research and intellectual interests within the establishment, they are less likely to leave for the jungles or hills to become potential leaders of revolutionary movements which seek to overthrow established capitalist regimes. International advisers through their networking activities may integrate these radical intellectuals into a transnational research system. The end result is that the audience for the critical and radical thoughts of these intellectuals is a dispersed and elite international group which poses no threat to the local regime. Also their research work may appear in English rather than in a local language, and thus reaches few people in the local polity.

A final dimension in this radical critique of international advising relates to the type of research promoted by such advisers and the type of related institution-building promoted. Arnove and his associates argue that such advisers normally promote 'value-free' research designed to legitimize the status quo and to sustain privileges and inequalities reflecting the existing political–economic structure. Highly normative research with a critical dimension would be considered nonscientific and not fundable. With respect to the educational field, Farrell argues that much educational gadgetry untested in the US is exported to the developing nations, and he considers this a blatant manifestation of 'intellectual colonialism.[17] An example would be manpower planning, an approach strongly supported by many US advisers abroad, but never actually used or tested in the US itself. Advisers involved in research also gain access to extensive information about LDCs which they routinely transmit back to their own nations.

The building of institutions in the LDCs, often with training and research functions, has been a major element in the technical assistance programs of many donor agencies. In his review of the Rockefeller Foundation's China Medical Board and Peking Union Medical College (PUMC), Brown is highly critical of the Foundation's elitist approach to medicine in China.[18] Brown argues that the PUMB trained only a tiny cadre of physicians while ignoring traditional medicine in China relevant to the masses. There is also the argument that these new institutions promoted by outside advisers tend to serve primarily those of higher socioeconomic backgrounds. Since the curriculum of PUMC was in English, only those elite Chinese from missionary schools could gain admission. In Thailand the Rockefeller Foundation supported the building of an excellent graduate program in economics at Thammasat University. The most prestigious graduate curriculum in economics is the English one developed with Rockefeller support. Since excellent English is required for admission to the program, it favors those from elite and urban socioeconomic backgrounds.

Given this radical critique, what then is to be done? There are no doubts in the mind of Illich. For those who would like to serve in Latin America, his advice may not be pleasant to hear:

> I am here to entreat you to use your money, your status and your education to travel in Latin America. Come to look, come to climb our mountains, to enjoy our flowers. Come to study. But do not come to help.[19]

In a box at the top of Mt Kilimanjaro there is a copy of the Declaration of Arusha. This important document outlines new political and moral guidelines for leadership in Tanzania. It emphasizes self-reliance and a war on exploitation. The declaration also emphasizes the importance of sharing a basic code of conduct and respecting fundamental principles. Glyn Roberts, a former member of the Swedish Peace Corps in Ethiopia, who has written critically about both foreign experts and volunteers in developing countries, argues that the Declaration of Arusha should serve as the basic philosophy underlying volunteer and technical assistance efforts overseas.[20] Later in this study we present a professional code of ethics for international advisers which we hope is responsive to the concerns expressed in the Arusha Declaration. Unlike Illich, Roberts sees a role for volunteers and experts, but fundamental changes are necessary in organizations such as SIDA and various volunteer organizations and the behavior of their staffs. Without such changes, Roberts sees volunteers and experts as contributing to the preservation of an unequal and unjust status quo.

Others would argue that developing countries must actively seek to reduce dependency links. Their use of outside experts and consultants should be restricted and eventually eliminated. By relying on their own efforts they will develop their own capacities and abilities more effectively. Rather than aid, these countries should seek more equitable prices for their products and better and broader markets for their exports.

Ironically, in the radical literature on international advising there is rarely ever any mention of the Soviet Union, or of the advisers it sends to various developing countries, primarily in Africa, the Middle East, and Asia. It would seem logical that many of the same criticisms offered by Arnove and his associates of US advisers in developing nations would similarly apply to Soviet experts serving in areas such as Ethiopia, Cuba, Afghanistan, and Laos. In a book intended explicitly to parallel Burdick and Lederer's *The Ugly American*, Victor Lasky in his book *The Ugly Russian* is highly critical of Soviet advisers working in developing nations. The following quotation related to Guinea illustrates the tone of his work:

> Moussa Diakit, Governor of the National Bank of Guinea, has charged that much of the Soviet-bloc goods and equipment sent to his country were 'not appropriate for our requirements and it is impossible to use them.'[21]

Padmai Desai reports that Soviet technicians in Egypt were considered to be high-handed and condescending.[22]

Of various technical assistance advisers and experts, the Chinese, working in countries such as Tanzania, appear to be most responsive to both the criticisms of Arnove and Lasky. The German scholar Bartke is highly laudatory of overseas Chinese experts.[23] He praises them for their salary structure, which is in accord with the standards of the receiving country. He also describes Chinese overseas experts as working in ways which are extremely responsive to local needs. It appears that Israeli experts sent overseas have also established an excellent record for sensitivity and effectiveness, though there is controversy about their success in countries such as Guatemala and Costa Rica.[24]

The perspective described above is blunt and aggressively critical. There is, however, a much softer and more subtle variant of this critique. This view relates to those instances in which advisers are highly effective in promoting constructive change bringing about greater equity and/or efficiency in another society. Ladejinsky's work on land reform in Taiwan would be a case in point, or Grant's work in pre-revolutionary China to promote public health more broadly. There is no doubt that such efforts may help a capitalist regime to survive politically by improving its responsiveness and performance. Thus, such advisers may help a government to overcome a revolutionary threat to buy time in facing such a challenge. The role of the advisers actively involved in promoting the 'Green Revolution' in Latin American and Asia, in our view, certainly helped a number of governments to buy time with respect to the explosive nature of population growth and related potential political 'time bombs.' Even here, however, critics might well argue that important inequalities generated by the 'Green Revolution' may actually hasten prospects for political revolution.

We do not necessarily adhere to all elements in the radical perspectives outlined above. The critique, however, helps to illuminate important realities which cannot be ignored. We also hope that our empirical analysis of global data and trends related to the provision of international advisers will help us to evaluate the extent of validity in the radical critique as articulated by authors such as Arnove and Illich. We do believe that the radical critique lacks balance and does ignore important contributions made by some international advisers, as illustrated in our exemplary case studies.

The provision of effective international advice is indeed a complex process. No one single perspective or orientation can adequately explain this important phenomenon, which varies widely dependent upon the particular context, including the individuals, institutions, and nations involved.

It is our major concern that all relevant and related viewpoints be carefully considered and assessed, based on the best and most thorough empirical evidence available.

Notes

1. P. Freire, The people speak their word: learning to read and write in Saõ Tomé and Príncipe, *Harvard Educational Review,* **58**, 28 (1981).
2. G. Benveniste, *The Politics of Expertise,* Boyd & Fraser, San Francisco, California, 2nd edn, 1977, p.45.
3. See J. Habermas, *Legitimation Crisis,* Beacon, Boston, Massachusetts, 1975.
4. A. Curle, *Planning for Education in Pakistan: A Personal Case Study,* Harvard University Press, Cambridge, Massachusetts, 1966, p.9.
5. The phrase, 'speak truth to power' derives from A. Wildavsky, *Speaking Truth to Power: The Art and Craft of Policy Analysis,* Little, Brown & Co., Boston, Massachusetts, 1979.
6. H. Cleveland *et al., The Overseas Americans,* pp.142–9.
7. G. Benveniste, p.80.
8. R. Arnove (editor), *Philanthropy and Cultural Imperialism.*
9. I. Illich, To hell with good intentions.
10. W. and E. Paddock, *We Don't Know How.*
11. D. Seers, Why visiting economists fail, *Journal of Political Economy,* **70**, 325–38 (1962).
12. D. Luce and J. Sommer, The big adviser, in *Viet Nam—The Unheard Voices,* Cornell University Press, Ithaca, New York, 1979, pp.202–17.
13. S. Hazzard, *Defeat of an Ideal.*
14. I. Illich, p.3.
15. R. F. Arnove, Foundations and the transfer of knowledge, in R. F. Arnove (editor), *Philanthropy and Cultural Imperialism,* p.318.
16. See R. Coggins, The development set, *Adult Education and Development,* **14** (1976); L. Frank, The Development game, *Granta,* **20**, 229–43 (1986).
17. Cited in E. H. Berman, The foundation's role in American foreign policy: the case of Africa, post 1945, in R. Arnove, p.212.
18. E. R. Brown, Rockefeller medicine in China: professionalism and imperialism, in R. Arnove, pp.123–46.
19. I. Illich, p.7.
20. G. Roberts, Volunteers and neo-colonialism, pp.13–16.
21. V. Lasky, *The Ugly Russian,* p.33.
22. P. Desai, The Soviet Union and the Third World: a faltering partnership? in J. Bhagwat and J. Ruggie (editors), *Power, Passions, and Purpose: Prospects for North-South Negotiations,* MIT Press, Cambridge, Massachusetts, 1984, pp.268–9.
23. W. Bartke, *China's Economic Aid,* C. Hurst, London, 1975.
24. L. Laufer, *Israel and the Developing Countries: New Approaches to Cooperation,* Twentieth Century Fund, New York, 1967.

CHAPTER 5

The Economics of Advising
and Consulting

The services envisaged should aim at increased productivity of material
and human resources and a wide and equitable distribution of the
benefits of such productivity, so as to contribute to the realization of
higher standards of living (Resolution of the UN's Economic and
Social Council).[1]

The Economic Benefits of Advising and Consulting

There are two types of economic benefits which may accrue from the
services of foreign advisers. First, there may be direct economic benefits
deriving from the work and advice of consultants. Alexander, for example,
cites many concrete examples of how certain UN technical assistance experts
have contributed to dramatic cost reductions, employment-generating projects, or productivity increases.[2] Advisers have affected significantly the
allocation of economic resources.[3] Foreign technical assistance personnel
such as J. G. Harrar and Norman Borlaug, working at applied agricultural
research centers—for example, the CIMMYT (International Maize and
Wheat Improvement Center) in Mexico—have contributed to dramatic
yield increases in wheat production.[4] For such efforts Borlaug was awarded
a Nobel Prize. Deming's advice in Japan regarding quality control helped
that nation in its goal to become a leading world exporter. Arthur Young,
serving as an adviser in Taiwan in 1958, urged control of population growth
as a major policy.[5] Taiwan's subsequent family planning program is considered exemplary and has definitely been a factor underlying the country's
economic success.

The CIMMYT and Taiwan examples, however, raise some fundamental
methodological issues related to assessing the economic impact of foreign
advisers. Charles Madge, writing about the evaluation of technical assistance, raised the fundamental question of what difference the presence of an
expert has made to the development of a country. It is not adequate to cite
the progress made in the country during the time the expert was there, or the
period immediately following.[6] Basic here is the problem of causality,
complicated by the many factors affecting a country's development and
productivity in various economic sectors. The Paddocks, for example,

66

carefully analyzed increased wheat yields in Mexico. They found that applied research is only one of a number of important factors contributing to increased wheat yields. Indeed, Hick's research showed that two-thirds of Mexico's increased wheat production in the Northwest area was attributed to expanded acreage in irrigated land.[7] Similarly Hertford, an agricultural economist, argues that well over half the total change in Mexico crop yields has been due to the increased use of chemical fertilizers.[8] A strong price-support system by the Mexican government has also provided important incentives to Mexican wheat growers. Thus, to attribute all of Mexico's increased yields to the work of CIMMYT would be an exaggeration. Methodologically, it is virtually impossible to ascertain precisely how much of the economic benefits associated with Mexico's improved wheat productivity derive from the applied research and the involvement of foreign technical assistance in that research and related training.

Apart from direct contributions to economic progress, indirect economic benefits may result from the presence of foreign experts. These have been largely ignored in the literature. If their salaries are paid by international agencies or donor countries, then the presence of foreign advisers in another nation results in a direct inflow of foreign exchange. The effect is similar in nature to that of tourists. The size of the positive foreign exchange impact depends on four factors: (1) the size of their salaries, (2) their propensity to save/consume, (3) the extent to which they consume imported products, and (4) the aggregate number of advisers. Unfortunately we lack empirical information on the consumption patterns related to the second and third factors. We know of no survey of the consumption behavior of foreign experts. Based on our research and experience, however, we offer some tentative hypotheses concerning such consumption patterns.

Our first assumption is that advisers working overseas tend to have rather high propensities to save; thus only a portion of their salaries represents foreign exchange inflow. Also they tend to save in institutions outside of the host nation. With respect to imported goods, there are two basic types of economic behavior. The first we term the 'PX syndrome.' Individuals tend to buy familiar products from their own countries and, often living in 'golden ghettos,' remain isolated from local markets.[9] Overseas Japanese have been criticized severely for restricting their consumption to Japanese products and services.

The second type of behavior we call 'internationalist.' Such advisers have a genuine fondness for things foreign. They take an interest in local arts, crafts, literature, and services. We are aware of one foreign expert in Indonesia, for example, who developed an avid interest in impressive Indonesian cloth and batiks. He spent a rather sizeable portion of his salary on such items, thus contributing to the local economy. We know of advisers in Thailand who have strong interests in indigenous books and literature and spend heavily in those areas, thus contributing to the economics of the local

TABLE 5.1.   *Foreign Exchange Impact of International Advisers in Thailand*

Propensity-to-consume ratio	Estimated inflow of foreign exchange ($)
0.50	15,000,000
0.70	21,000,000
0.90	27,000,000

publishing industry. Such expenditures on local products and services will also have substantial multiplier effects.

Such foreign exchange inflows can be flexibly utilized by the host government. Once foreign advisers have exchanged their salaries into the local currency, the resulting increment of foreign exchange can be used for any of a wide variety of purposes. Our major finding is that the positive foreign exchange impact of foreign advisers has been largely ignored. If such advisers are internationalist, and consume many local products and services, then they can have a positive foreign exchange impact, apart from any direct economic contributions resulting from their advice itself.

It may be useful to estimate this foreign exchange impact for a specific country. Given the precise data available on number of advisers serving in Thailand reported in Appendix I, it is possible to estimate the foreign exchange impact of their presence in Thailand. Since we lack precise data on the local consumption function of these advisers, we present three alternative assumptions. Our analyses assumes propensity to consume ratios of 0.50, 0.70 and 0.90, respectively.

The annual expenditure for each adviser is based on empirical data from James Coleman's study of institution-building in Thailand and Zaire.[10] Thus, for 1981, the 529 person-years of international advisers in Thailand is the equivalent of approximately $30 million potential inflow of foreign exchange. If the propensity to consume locally is 0.50, then this would represent an inflow of approximately $15 million (see Table 5.1). Thus the impact, while significant, is rather small. It would be roughly equivalent to the foreign exchange impact of an additional 50,000 tourists in one year (assuming an average stay of three days and expenditures of $100 a day).[11] Another interesting comparison is with foreign remittances. This has been a rapidly increasing new source of foreign exchange for Thailand, primarily resulting from large numbers of overseas Thais working in the Middle East and Los Angeles. For 1983 such remittances were approximately $580 million, indicating a much larger foreign exchange impact than international advisers.

The Illusion of a Free Good

In many instances foreign expertise is provided 'without charge' by international or bilateral aid agencies. Thus, local governments may bear

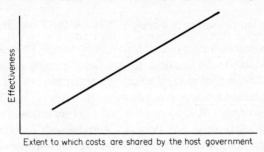

Fɪɢ. 5.1. Hypothesized Relationship Between Cost Sharing and Effectiveness

little of the financial burden of supporting foreign expertise. In some cases the only local cost is the provision of office space and/or local transportation. Also as pointed out above, there are likely to be positive foreign exchange benefits associated with the 'free' provision of foreign experts. In these cases local institutions will perceive of the foreign expert as a 'free good.' The contributions of such experts can be far below their genuine international costs. But since their costs to the local institution are close to zero, it is extremely easy for benefits to exceed 'costs.' Also local nationals working with advisers may receive related perquisites such as air-conditioning (which remains long after the adviser has departed).

In Fig. 5.1 we pose a direct relationship between effectiveness and optimal utilization and the extent to which a host country bears the burden of financing foreign expertise. The hypothesized relationship is based primarily on Japanese development experience.[12] The Japanese for the most part financed foreign expertise from their own resources, and thus could gear it specifically to their own requirements. Throughout their development experience after the Meiji Restoration the Japanese made creative, effective, and highly selective use of foreign expertise.

A second basic hypothesis is that the demand for foreign expertise will diminish significantly if host countries must bear more of the burden of financing. While presently there may be an overreliance on foreign expertise, total local financing would certainly put countries with limited foreign exchange at a severe disadvantage in attracting needed foreign expertise. Also with total reliance on local funding of foreign expertise, the potential of TCDC may not be realized. Our basic recommendation is that some combination of local and foreign funding may often be an attractive alternative. Since its inception the US Peace Corps has adopted this formula. The host government provides for housing of volunteers, while the Peace Corps provides funds for the monthly subsistence allowance and travel. This model appears to have worked well.

The Compensation of Foreign Advisers and Consultants

This has been continually a controversial issue. Currently, there is basically a two-tiered salary structure. One tier involving rather low salaries is that for individuals provided by volunteer organizations such as the Peace Corps and Japanese Overseas Cooperation Volunteers (JOCV). The other end of the tier is represented by salaries consistently much higher than local salaries in the host country. The People's Republic of China is an exception in that its experts are provided compensation at rates far lower than normal international standards. Bartke estimates that Chinese experts are provided at approximately one-fourth the cost of other nationals.[13]

With respect to the compensation of foreign advisers, a basic question is whether it is necessary to provide them 'bonus compensation' for serving overseas. It has been common for many international and bilateral aid agencies to provide such compensation as an incentive to attract highly qualified individuals to overseas posts. There are several reasons for such extra compensation. First, individuals serving abroad are removed temporarily from their own professional mainstream, and may miss important professional meetings and opportunities in their own country. Second, individuals serving in tropical environments face certain health hazards such as tropical diseases and higher accident rates. Third, individuals serving abroad may not have access to many of the amenities and entertainment opportunities they are accustomed to in their own countries. Fourth, individuals serving in large cities such as Lagos and Bangkok may lose excessive amounts of time in extraordinary traffic congestion. Despite these reasonable arguments for providing special compensation, in the literature there is much criticism of the high salaries of foreign experts and the related resentments created.[14] Thus, the compensation issue creates genuine dilemmas.

With respect to local resentment about high salaries, we feel that this primarily derives from the ostentatious consumption and many special perquisites associated with such levels of compensation. Regardless of actual salary levels, local resentment would be reduced if advisers and consultants lived more modestly. An example in this regard is the privilege of having a chauffeur. If an adviser has a chauffeur while the host country counterpart does not, this is likely to cause serious resentment. Local nationals in Malaysia have complained bitterly about the special privileges of foreign advisers. One means to try to force more modest living styles is to bank part of the consultants' salary in a special account, which becomes available after completion of the assigment.[15] The US Peace Corps has utilized this approach. Housing allowances could also be more modest. Another means to facilitate more modest living styles is to eliminate all special PX-type privileges abroad. These privileges particularly arouse host-country resentment and skepticism. They also greatly reduce the potentially positive foreign exchange effect of advising and consulting.

We would also like to propose a third tier salary structure, primarily based on China's experience in providing expertise at low costs to other nations, particularly in Africa. It is our assumption that many experts who were formerly volunteers and who have learned 'to live on the cheap,' would still be attracted to international advising, even at lower levels of compensation or without special bonuses. Such individuals often know how to purchase local commodities and services easily at costs far below those paid by most foreign nationals. Such individuals may stretch a $20,000 salary to become the equivalent of a $40,000 salary for another individual who does not know how, or is unwilling, to economize.[16] Even with significantly lower salary levels it should be possible to recruit quality individuals, and in this sense the Chinese have provided an inspiring example. Thus, the costs of providing foreign expertise can be reduced. Greater utilization of TCDC could also reduce the costs of providing technical expertise transnationally.

Use of Local Expertise as an Alternative to Expensive Foreign Expertise

Given that local expertise is much less expensive than foreign expertise, there are strong economic arguments for the greater utilization of local talent. With respect to the cost differentials, in Thailand foreign expertise is roughly four to eight times more expensive than the use of local expertise. In the Ivory Coast, where salaries of local officials are relatively much higher, the cost differential is estimated to be two to one.[17] Given these cost differentials, the cabinet of Thailand established the policy of using local experts in development projects whenever possible. Also local experts know the administrative and cultural setting far better than most experts and, of course, are fluent in the local language.

Though local consultants are less costly than those from other countries, there are nevertheless some important drawbacks related to reliance on local consultants. In countries where intellectuals and high-level manpower tend to be overemployed, such as in Thailand, local consultants may be able to devote only a limited amount of time to a project. Other commitments may interfere with their capability to concentrate on a particular development project. Some local experts may also suffer from what Goodwin and Nacht term professional and intellectual decay. It may have been a number of years since local experts completed their advanced training. Thus they may not be in touch with the latest developments in their fields. Professional obsolescence may also, however, characterize *second-rate* foreign consultants.

Another issue relates to the development of new perspectives and orientations. An outside consultant may possibly bring a fresh, unorthodox perspective to a problem. In projects where ability to draft communications in an international language is important, outside advisers may have a decided advantage.

Finally, we must not ignore the foreign exchange implications of outside advice. Though local experts may be much cheaper, their employment does not generate any foreign exchange inflows. In fact if they have strong Western consumption patterns, their employment may contribute to foreign exchange outflows.

Major Economic Alternatives: The Peter the Great Approach vs the King of Siam Option

The Peter the Great Approach emphasizes sending students abroad for training, while the King of Siam Option brings in the expert from abroad.[18] These two alternatives to technical assistance have decidely different economic implications which seem to have been ignored in the literature. As the costs of overseas study have accelerated, the foreign exchange drain of study abroad has become dramatic. A recent World Bank study estimates that the study of LDC students in foreign countries resulted in a loss of $2.9 billion of foreign exchange.[19] This constitutes 10 percent of the value of exports of 31 of the poorest LDCs of the world.[20] Also the positive economic multiplier effects of such spending accrues to the rich industrialized nations. There is another implicit hidden foreign exchange cost of study abroad. Individuals who study abroad are often incorporated into modern high-consumption cultures. Foreign students often return to their countries with consumer items such as cars, refrigerators, stereos, and computers. Settled back in their own country they need to fulfill an acquired taste for more expensive imported goods. Given such tastes, they may oppose local tax reforms and other political changes which might impair their opportunities to retain such lifestyles.

We are not against foreign study. In fact there are many potential positive benefits—motivational, cultural and intellectual—associated with study abroad.[21] Our main concern is that both the high direct and indirect economic costs of study abroad be fully recognized. Given increased awareness of the genuine economic costs of study abroad, LDCs may begin to be far more selective in sending students abroad.

The King of Siam Option has different economic implications. As discussed previously, this option normally leads to foreign exchange inflow and economic multiplier effects which benefit the local economy; also some advisers may develop new attitudes and understandings of problems in the LCDs. For example, E. F. Schumacher's service in Burma and India had a dramatic impact on his thinking about economics and development. Given Schumacher's influence as founder of the 'Small is Beautiful' movement, his service in Burma and India has had an impact transcending his actual accomplishments while advising in Asia. Barbara Ward's experience as an overseas adviser may have contributed to her keen insights on development problems. The number of those individuals, both volunteers and experts, who have served in LCDs has grown dramatically (see figures in Appendix I). These individuals constitute a potentially powerful group who may favor policies in their home countries more favorable to economic improvement in the LDCs.[22] Ironically, this reverse effect could in the long-run result in the most significant economic impact of international advising, consulting, and volunteer work.

Notes

1. Y. ALEXANDER, *International Technical Assistance Experts: A Case Study of the U.N. Experience*, Praeger, New York, 1966, p.7. For a detailed study of the economics of international consulting in Australia, see P. J. RIMMER, *Consultancy Services: Supply to Southeast Asia from Australia*, ASEAN–Australia Joint Research Project, Kuala Lumpur and Canberra, 1984.
2. Y. ALEXANDER, p.171.
3. See, for example, G. FRY and R. KAEWDAENG, Budgeting for greater equity: a normative regression analysis, *International Journal of Policy Analysis and Information Systems*, **6**, 115–31 (1982).
4. J. G. HARRAR, *Strategy toward the Conquest of Hunger*, Rockefeller Foundation, New York, 1967, pp.25–39.
5. A. N. YOUNG, Observations on the financial and economic situation. Report to the Prime Minister of the Republic of China at the request of President Chiang Kai Shek, p.6.
6. C. MADGE, *The Evaluation of Technical Assistance*, OECD, Paris, 1969, p.31.
7. W. and E. PADDOCK, *We Don't Know How*, p.212.
8. Ibid., p.213.
9. J. TENDLER, *Inside Foreign Aid*, Johns Hopkins University Press, Baltimore, 1975, p.33.
10. J. S. COLEMAN, Professorial training and institution building in the Third World: two Rockefeller Foundation experiences, in E. BARBER, P. ALTBACH, and R. MYERS (editors), *Bridges to Knowledge: Foreign Students in Comparative Perspective*, University of Chicago Press, Chicago, 1984, p.37 and 53.
11. See S. RATANAKOMUT, Tourism industry in Thailand, in *Proceedings of the International Conference on Thai Studies 3–6 July 1987*, Research School of Pacific Studies, ANU, Canberra, vol. 3, 1987.
12. P. T. BAUER and B. S. YAMEY, The Pearson Report: a review, in T. J. BYERS (editor), *Foreign Resources and Economic Development*, Frank Cass, London, 1972, p.53.
13. W. BARTKE, *China's Economic Aid*, p.12.
14. P. J. ELDRIDGE, *The Politics of Foreign Aid in India*, Weidenfeld & Nicolson, London, 1969, p.81.
15. J. TENDLER, p.33.
16. M. THOMSON, *Living Poor: A Peace Corps Chronicle*, University of Washington Press, Seattle, 1969.
17. Data from Unesco, Paris.
18. C. D. GOODWIN and M. NACHT, *The Impact of American Higher Education on Foreign Students with Special Reference to the Case of Brazil*, IIE, New York, IIE Research Report no. 5, 1984, p.16.
19. K. H. LEE and J. P. TAN, *The International Flow of Third Level LDC Students to DCs: Determinants and Implications*, Education Department, World Bank, Washington, DC, 1984, p.4.
20. G. PSACHAROPOULOUS, Memorandum on Study Abroad to Education Sector Staff, The World Bank, 2 April 1984.
21. G. W. FRY, The economic and political impact of study abroad, in *Bridges to Knowledge*, pp.55–72.
22. G. T. RICE, *The Bold Experiment: JFK's Peace Corps*, University of Notre Dame Press, Notre Dame, Indiana, 1985, pp.295–6.

CHAPTER 6

In-service Training at Home

Only by emphasizing the training aspect of foreign assistance is it possible to develop permanent roots and to achieve continuity and multiple benefits from an enlarging force of competent personnel able to serve national needs (J. George Harrar, Rockefeller Foundation).[1]

As the costs of study abroad have accelerated, particularly in countries such as the United Kingdom, Australia, and United States, in-country training is increasingly thought of as a cost-effective alternative to technical assistance. The International Institute for Educational Planning (IIEP) in Paris, for example, has arranged many training programs of this type in various locations around the world. Training of this kind varies in duration from approximately one to six weeks, with three weeks being a common norm. Local training programs raise a number of important issues. Prior to discussing such issues we would like to summarize the major advantages of the in-country training option.[2]

The first and most obvious advantage is cost savings. It is much cheaper to bring an expert from Paris for three weeks to an LDC than to send 20–30 trainees to Paris. Second, the economic opportunity costs of short-term in-country training are much less than for extended periods of training or study abroad. A third advantage relates to the learning environment. There is an inherent anomaly in discussing problems of the rural poor in such touristic venues as Honolulu, Paris, London, or Victoria, British Columbia. A training site in a remote part of Indonesia or Thailand would be a more relevant environment. Participants in such settings can take field trips to examine and evaluate concepts introduced during the training. Robert Chambers's excellent ideas concerning rapid rural appraisal could be much more appreciated in a rural LDC setting that at, say, Sussex or Stanford. Fourth, training seminars or conferences generate income for the surrounding community. If they are held in the poorer provinces of LDCs, positive economic multiplier effects accrue to local communities. Fifth, in local training, individuals of lower socioeconomic background have a greater opportunity to participate. To undertake overseas training, foreign language proficiency is normally a requisite competence. Opportunities for acquiring foreign language competence are normally greater among those of higher socioeconomic background.

Despite these important advantages, local training as a form of technical assistance raises a number of complex issues and potential problems. A first major issue is the choice of the training language. If a local language is not used, then interpreters must be provided. Simultaneous translation capability may only rarely be available. Having local interpreters or experts translating all comments by the outside trainers is an inefficient and tedious process. This issue is normally not significant in countries such as Costa Rica or Ivory Coast using international languages, where the training would naturally take place in Spanish and French, respectively. In countries such as Thailand, Indonesia, Nepal, or China, the language issue is far more complex. One alternative is to restrict participation only to those with excellent proficiency in the training language. This has the drawback of eliminating potentially capable trainees of lower socioeconomic background. Another alternative is to use foreign trainers fluent in a local language such as Swahili, Thai, and Indonesian. This alternative is often not feasible since individuals with both the needed language proficiency and relevant technical expertise cannot be identified or recruited. A final option is to rely only on local experts. This option is economical and eliminates the language problem. There are, however, certain problems related to exclusive reliance on local experts that was discussed in Chapter 5, above.

Another approach is to use a mixed team of local and foreign trainers. The foreign trainers in turn may represent different nationalities with varying development experiences. In a recent training program in Rayong, Thailand, the IIEP employed this approach. Trainees were exposed to local Thai expertise as well as perspectives from British, French, German, and Vietnamese trainers. This provided for a pluralistic learning environment with an exposure to many diverse ideas and approaches. In this training program local experts were extremely helpful in dealing with any language problems arising. Local experts also benefited from the contact with diverse foreign expertise. This mixed-training model has many attractive features.

A second major issue relates to the cross-cultural dimensions of such training. Foreign trainers must be sensitive to local cultural values which may affect pedagogy and learning styles. Individuals who are effective trainers in their own cultures may not necessarily be able to communicate their ideas well in other cultures. Prior to engaging international trainers, it is important to ascertain their level of competency in providing training in cross-cultural settings. Demonstrated prior effectiveness in such settings is perhaps the clearest criterion to apply. Such trainers should be highly skilled in communication, both cognitive and nonverbal, and aware of the many issues discussed earlier in Chapter 3, on the 'Tongue-tied Adviser.'

Another major problem relates to preparation. Good training programs require an intensive prior planning effort; also learning materials must be *adapted* to local conditions and contexts. Many individuals involved in international training are extremely busy professionals; thus, they may not have adequate time to prepare and plan for overseas training programs. In such cases the quality of local training suffers. Agencies sponsoring local training must ensure that trainers devote adequate time for preparation, and financial compensation should be provided for this important aspect of training.

Trainees participating in programs of this type often vary dramatically in terms of their background preparation. Thus, it is important for trainers to use pre-tests and/or background surveys at the beginning of training programs. Without such information, trainers may badly underestimate or overestimate the initial competency of trainees, or fail to appreciate the diversity of learner backgrounds. Trainers must then adapt their training to the level of ability of the participants. Where significant differences in background exist it may be necessary to break trainees up into smaller learning groups, where communication is easier.

Unfortunately many training programs are not rigorously evaluated. To provide a meaningful evaluation of local training programs three elements are essential. First, pre-tests and post-tests should be administered to assess degree of changes in knowledge, skills, and attitudes. Second, both individual and group evaluations should occur at the end of the training. The individual evaluations should not only include objective questions, but should also provide opportunities for extensive open-ended evaluative comments. A training program should also involve some type of follow-up activity in which participants have an opportunity to use active concepts, skills, or knowledge acquired. There should then be follow-up evaluation to ascertain if participants have been able to apply concepts learned in the local setting.

Still another potential problem is the learning environment itself. In some cases training is held in major tourist resorts such as Pattaya and Chiang Mai in Thailand, Bali in Indonesia, or Antigua in Guatemala. Such settings can provide a major distraction to effective training and learning; also in local settings traditional leisure habits such as card-playing and gambling may prevail. Such an environment can have adverse effects on the quality of training.

Despite the numerous problems related to in-country training, it still is a highly attractive technical assistance option.[3] Well-organized and carefully planned in-country training, utilizing a mix of local and international trainers, and involving local site visits, can be extremely cost-effective. This option also facilitates equity with respect to broader participation and representation of groups who may be of rural and/or lower socioeconomic backgrounds. In the years ahead we foresee a much greater proportion of technical assistance devoted to in-country training. International trainers who are sensitive to cross-cultural differences, and who can adapt their expertise to local conditions, can play an important role in this important type of human resource development and capacity-building. W. Edwards Deming's effective training in Japan related to quality control in the early 1950s reflects the remarkable potential impact of this approach to sharing technical expertise.[4]

Notes

1. J. G. HARRAR, *Strategy toward the Conquest of Hunger*, Rockefeller Foundation, New York, 1967, p.189.
2. J. KERRIGAN and J. LUKE, *Management Training Strategies for Developing Countries*, Lynne Rienner, Boulder, Colorado, 1987.
3. W. S. SAYRE and C. E. THURBER, *Training for Specialized Mission Personnel*, Public Administration Service, Chicago, Illinois, 1952.
4. See W. E. DEMING, A view of how quality began in Japan, in *Quality, Productivity, and Competitive Position*, Center for Advanced Engineering Study, MIT, Cambridge, Massachusetts, 1982, pp.99–110.

PART III

The Effective Cross-Cultural Adviser/Consultant

CHAPTER 7

Assessing the Effectiveness
of International Advisers
and Consultants:
An Ecological Perspective

But how does one evaluate the "success" of experts? To be sure, assessment of the substantive accomplishments of experts constitutes one of the most baffling problems of technical assistance (Yonah Alexander).[1]

Perhaps the best experts are those who recognize the many ways in which the rural people themselves are the best experts (Robert Chambers).[2]

In developing criteria for assessing the effectiveness of international advisers, we must recognize the complex interaction between the qualities of individuals and the contexts in which they are working. That context is defined by a wide range of historical, political, administrative, cultural, and economic factors. Table 7.1 lists a number of these factors which impinge on the potential effectiveness of advisers. The same individual might be highly effective in one setting, while failing in a rather different context.

The first factor, nature of colonial experience, is rather important. If the colonial experience of a nation was not particularly harsh, and if it experienced a smooth evolution to independence, this provides a positive climate

TABLE 7.1. *Contextual Factors Affecting
the Success of International Advisers
and Consultants*

Nature of the colonial experience of the host country
Level of economic development
Nature of bureaucracy in the host country
Quality of planning for, specification of, adviser's role(s)
Extent of local financing of advisory services
Nature of adviser's organizational affiliation
Host country's commitment to developmental goals
Participation of host country in selection of adviser
Pattern of communications in host country
Elements of chance and luck

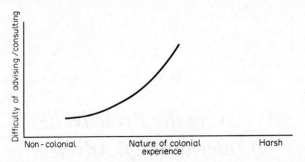

FIG. 7.1. Hypothesized Relationship Between Nature of Colonial Experience
and Difficulty of Advising/Consulting

for the outside adviser. Western Samoa would be an example. We
hypothesize that it is easiest for advisers to work in countries such as
Thailand, Nepal, or Tonga, which were never colonies. Our fundamental
proposition is that the harsher the colonial experience, the more difficult it
will be for advisers to be effective (see Fig. 7.1), primarily because of the
strong resentment against outsiders.

With respect to stage of development, Fig. 7.2 shows our basic hypothesis,
a U-curve. We feel that advising is more difficult at the earliest and then the
later stages of development. At the earliest stages of development, often
appropriate counterparts are not available, and advisers often end up in
operational, directive roles. Also in such settings, complementary resources
to implement needed programs may simply not be available. In countries at
later stages of development (e.g. Saudi Arabia, Brazil, Malaysia, and
Singapore), many foreign advisers may be resented, because they are
perceived as blocking capable local individuals from having opportunities to
assume greater and more challenging responsibilities.

Bureaucratic structures differ significantly from one LDC setting to
another.[4] In some settings major changes are extremely difficult to achieve,
while in others changes are possible. For example, advisers working in
countries with high levels of bureaucratic corruption will find their tasks far

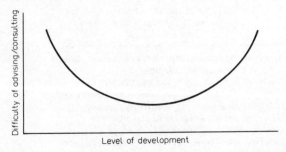

FIG. 7.2. Hypothesized Relationship Between Level of Development and
Difficulty of Advising/Consulting

more difficult than for their colleagues working in countries where such practices are rare or less common. In his research on US voluntary aid John Sommer finds that the extent of local political and bureaucratic impediments is a key factor related to success.[5]

Many failures in technical assistance relate to a lack of *a priori* planning. The timing of advisers' presence must be carefully worked out and roles and objectives clearly delineated.[6] Impressive individual qualities will mean little in an ambiguous undefined role.

As mentioned in our discussion of the economics of advising, the nature of financing an adviser can directly impinge on effectiveness. Excessive compensation, for example, can lead to resentment. Advisers and technical assistance workers of the People's Republic of China have not faced this problem, given the modest salaries received by PRC experts and overseas technical assistance workers. Also local financing of part of the adviser's compensation can encourage and facilitate maximum utilization of the adviser.

The nature of an adviser's organizational affiliation is also important. Advisers may benefit through a 'halo effect' from the professional reputation of the organization employing them. Similarly, those working for organizations with poor reputations may suffer adversely from such associations.

Another important external factor affecting an adviser's potential effectiveness is the host country's commitment to development. Developmental changes may be extremely difficult to introduce in nations where preservation of the status quo is the major economic and political concern. A major technical assistance project of the Ford Foundation in Thailand was largely successful because of the willingness of an open-minded director-general to take the risk of approving a new budget allocation system oriented toward greater equity.[7] In many other LDC settings the success of such a technical assistance project would have been much more problematic.

Increasingly, host governments are playing a role in the selection of consultants and advisers. Advisers having been reviewed and selected by the host governments will inherit a much more favorable working environment than those advisers selected and recruited wholly by outside agencies and organizations.

Another important contextual factor is the nature of communication patterns in the host country and how much these differ from the culture of the advisers. Our basic proposition is that, other things being equal, it is easier for advisers to be effective to the extent that communication patterns in the host country are similar to their own.

A final external contextual factor of considerable importance is the element of chance or luck. For example, much of Currie's success as an economic adviser in Colombia was based on relations with two successive heads of an agency who were influential with the nation's president. A Ford Foundation adviser's role in Thailand became more influential when his

Thai superior was named to the Thai cabinet. These types of events are largely based on chance, but can have significant impact on an adviser's successful performance.

Recognizing the importance of the many contextual factors described above, we now turn to the specification of criteria for assessing the effectiveness of international advisers and consultants.

Technical Expertise and its Creative Application

To be successful an international consultant or adviser must have first-rate technical expertise. In fact, in the literature, concern is expressed that the best potential experts are not normally available, because they are often too busy to accept assignments.[8] Projects then must use second-rate people. T. T. Krishnamchari, former Minister for Commerce and Industry in India, indicates that roughly only one in four experts were of good quality.[9] Indian doubts about the quality of foreign experts have been periodically expressed in the *Lok Sabha*.[10] Those advisers and consultants who have become most famous for their successful advising and consulting, such as J. G. Harrar, Norman Borlaug, William Edwards Deming, and Wolf Ladejinsky all possessed unquestionable excellence in their respective technical fields.

Highly specialized expertise in particular disciplines is now rather common. But in LDC contexts, expertise which transcends traditional disciplinary boundaries is often critically needed.[11] This type of interdisciplinary expertise is much more difficult to obtain.

Finally a major criterion of succes is whether international advisers can creatively adapt their technical expertise, and communicate this expertise to local nationals in a different cultural and political setting. Highly successful consultants such as Borlaug, Deming, Harrar, and Ladejinsky have demonstrated this impressive type of creativity.

Communicative Competence

This concept derives from the work of the important German social scientist, Jürgen Habermas.[12] This competency is crucial for international advisers and consultants. Exceptional technical expertise means little, if advisers are unable to communicate their ideas effectively in the local cultural setting. Success in this domain is indicated, for example, by advisers who are able to communicate effectively and genuinely with people of diverse social, ethnic, and linguistic backgrounds.

Ethnic Humility

Another important measure of success is the extent to which advisers can overcome ethnocentrism and cultural arrogance, to become genuinely multicultural protean individuals. Protean individuals are able to adjust and adapt themselves to varying cultural norms. Ethnic humility also means evaluating an individual's own culture with open eyes and recognizing its faults and weaknesses. Living in a 'golden ghetto' abroad does not reflect ethnic humility. Based on his research on Swedish technical assistance personnel serving in Africa, Lindholm was disappointed to find that few Swedes in Dar es Salaam associated with people outside the Swedish 'colony.'[13] In contrast, Israeli technical assistance personnel working in other countries never have a special housing compound or office mission.[14] In their extensive work in Tanzania on the Tan–Zam railway project, the Chinese have been praised for their ethnic humility, illustrated by their willingness to eat and live with the Africans.[15] Advisers with ethnic humility strive to be emic; that is, to understand local notions and concepts. They recognize the essential importance of local knowledge. They are sufficiently open intellectually to appreciate the richness of Asian or African thought. Rita Liljestrom, in her study of successful Peace Corps volunteers in Africa, emphasizes the importance of having a cordial compassion for their fellow-men.[16] Such compassion is directly related to ethnic humility.

Success in Building Local Capacity

One of the major signs of success of international advising is to create the local capacity (individual and/or institutional) which eliminates the need for further technical assistance in the particular area of concern. Green echoes this concept when he argues that all technical assistance work in Tanzania should be oriented toward building up Tanzanian capacity.[17] In a similar vein, Loxley argues that advisers have the primary responsibility of doing all that they can to effect their own replacement by a Tanzanian in the shortest possible time.[18] This basic ideal is elegantly expressed in Spanish by César Engaña:

> En este sentido, el trabajo fundamental del experto en alguna rama de la asistencia técnica, es el de compartir y repartir los beneficios del conocimiento especializado que posee, de manera tal, que cuando él termine su misión, dejará tras de sí, personas que son más capaces de lo que eran, para comprender sus problemas de manera tal, que puedan diseñar las mejores y más adecuadas soluciones a la situación local.[19]

During the late 1960s in Thailand, the Ford Foundation provided considerable technical assistance, including 14 experts (27 person-years), to help develop the National Institute of Development Administration, a graduate school oriented toward development studies and research.[20] Currently that institution has no foreign advisers, and has clearly established its own total self-reliance. With the exception of an occasional Fulbright or visiting scholar, its faculty is now entirely indigenous. Similarly with respect to Soviet technical assistance projects in India, there is an emphasis on eventual complete Indianization.[21] In the US Point 4 program there was considerable emphasis on 'working oneself out of a job,' but this perspective has been less common in more recent years.

Thus, the true success of advisers or consultants is reflected actually more in what happens after they leave, rather than in specific accomplishments during assignments. The extent to which project goals and activities are self-sustaining after the consultant's departure reflects the degree of success in building local capacity. Unfortunately, there are many cases of projects or programs which failed to meet this criterion, and which gradually dissolved after the consultant's exit from the scene. Other consultants, however, have reported unsuspected successes after the passage of time. They may have left Indonesia or Guatemala thinking of themselves as failures, or as only moderately successful. Upon return four or five years later they are surprised to see their project take root and develop a life of its own. The Dutch goverment, however, has expressed concern that most donor countries are not specifically concerned to aid developing countries in creating a national research and development capacity of their own, thus fostering continued intellectual and scientific dependence.[22]

Ability to Foster Local Participation

In the development field there is growing emphasis on citizen participation.[23] This is a major goal, for example, of Canada's International Development Research Centre (IDRC). Currie's success as an economic adviser in Colombia was largely based on his ability to convert a foreign report into a national program. He accomplished this using a participative device, modeled on the British Royal Commission, which enabled prominent Colombians to serve their country in an influential and prestigious capacity.[24]

Without adequate opportunites for local participation, important local knowledge and folk wisdom may be ignored. Advisers sometimes can charter and legitimate the creative ideas of ordinary citizens who normally would not have an opportunity to share their ideas more broadly.

To be successful, advisers should involve as many local nationals in their work as possible. Both John Grant in China and H. E. Maude in the South Pacific were notably successful in this regard (see case studies in Chapter 9). This type of participation facilitates the building of local capacity and self-sustaining projects. Advisers working alone, or primarily as individuals, may produce brilliant reports, but their failure to induce local participation adversely affects the long-term impact of their work. This type of failure is illustrated by our case study, The Loners.

Sense of Diplomacy and Politics

Just Faaland argues that the art of the development diplomat is much more difficult to master than other types of diplomacy.[25] Faaland's basic point is that diplomacy is the key to being persuasive. If advisers are not liked because of a lack of diplomatic skills, then their ideas or recommendation (regardless of how sound or brilliant) may never be given serious consideration. M. Kubr, in his work on the profession of management consulting, places similar stress on the importance of having excellent personal relations with clients and their staffs.[26] Thus, the effective consultant must also be a successful diplomat.

Harlan Cleveland, in his important work *The Overseas Americans,* emphasized as one of his five major criteria a sense of politics.[27] There are actually two dimensions to this domain. The first relates to developing an understanding of the local bureaucratic and political system, so as not to propose naive or unrealistic suggestions. The second concerns potential involvement in local partisan politics. Harari, in his research on technical assistance experts, found that a highly successful French expert with 13 years of overseas service stressed the importance of her having maintained political neutrality and discretion.[28] Thus, the successful consultant needs to understand local politics, but in a detached, discrete way. To the extent that the adviser may in certain contexts become involved with influential political figures as a means to achieve impact, such contacts should be broad and diverse.

Degree of Commitment and Willingness to Serve

Another measure of success is degree of commitment and willingness to serve. Successful consultants cannot simply work from nine to five each day. They may from time to time be expected to commit themselves on weekends or in the evenings. Jim Stirtin, known as 'the man who built Aramco in the Middle East,' is reputed to have 'thrown away the clock.'[29] They also must be willing to endure hardships by traveling to remote areas of a country, if that is relevant to their consulting work and requested by the local authorities. Upon arriving as US Ambassador in India, John Galbraith received the following instructions from President Kennedy:

> Modern diplomacy requires a close understanding not only of governments but of people. . . . Therefore, I hope that you will plan your work so that you may have time to travel extensively outside the nation's capital.[30]

Somewhat ironically Galbraith claims in his memoirs that 'getting out among the people' achieved little.[31]

The opposite pole of this syndrome is what might be termed the 'junket adviser,' who is often preoccupied with having adequate time to play golf or tennis, to swim, and to travel to tourist resorts. This pattern creates resentments and may leave inadequate time for performing consulting tasks with commitment and excellence.

Sense of History

In developmental work there is a tendency to ignore the historical context and lessons from prior related experience,[32] and an inadequate willingness to learn from failure.[33] The effective adviser demonstrates a sense of history and institutional memory by not proposing approaches which have already been attempted without success. Awareness of historical conditions may also alert the adviser to important political and administrative constraints that may impinge on the effectiveness of proposed projects or programs.

Degree of Selflessness

A degree of selflessness is an important element in successful advising. To what extent has the adviser been willing to share credit with local nationals? Has the adviser been willing to accept blame for mistakes or ineffectiveness without bitterness or rancour? It is also important that the adviser not compete with host country individuals or institutions involved in similar activities or programs.[34] It is also easier for selfless advisers to retain a low profile, since they do not seek undue publicity for their efforts or achievements. In many cultures boasting or praising one's own efforts is considered distasteful. For these many reasons a degree of selflessness achieved is an important factor in assessing successful advising. Much of Dr Tom Dooley's fame for his work in Laos derived from his committed selflessness. At the same time, advisers should not hide their successes. One of our colleagues gave a television series in Costa Rica on his speciality. The series was well received.

Ability to be a Team Player and to Work in Groups

Many development projects and consulting assignments involve working in groups. For example, 80 percent of Israeli foreign technical assistance personnel work in teams.[35] Many Chinese overseas projects involve teams of outside expertise. US AID projects often utilize teams of consultants or advisers. Individual advisers will also frequently work with host country teams. The ability to work smoothly in such groups is another important indicator of successful advising. The group-oriented adviser will also have more opportunites to share his expertise with local nationals.

Willingness to Listen and Learn

Successful advisers must be willing to listen and to learn from local nationals. Such an orientation is essential to enable advisers to adapt their expertise to local conditions. Advisers sincerely committed to listening to and learning from others show a respect for human dignity which transcends class and national boundaries. Advisers with this orientation can be potentially advocates for the 'little ones' and the disenfranchised, whose voices are rarely heard in influential circles. To use Wildavsky's apt term, advisers with this commitment to listen and learn can help to 'speak truth to power.'[36]

Summary

In discussing overseas advising, Hills stresses three dimensions: (1) the attitudes of the recipient nation, (2) the attitudes of the organization employing the adviser, and (3) the adviser's own attitudes, behavior, and competencies.[37] Viewed from an ecological perspective, success in international advising derives from the interaction among these three basic dimensions, represented by the triangle in Fig. 7.3.

With respect to the organizational factor, advisers' employers may set severe constraints which affect success.[38] Such constraints have adversely affected some Japanese experts working abroad. Individual advisers may have little or no influence over such organizational factors affecting their work.

To achieve effectiveness all three elements in the basic triangle need to be favorable. A favorable country and organizational climate does not guarantee success, since the adviser's individual talents may be lacking. On the

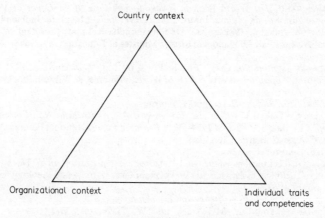

FIG. 7.3. A Three Tier Perspective for Assessing Success in International Advising and Consulting

other hand, dynamic individuals with impressive expertise and personal traits may achieve little in certain contexts where country and/or organizational contexts are not favorable. It is unfortunate that much of the literature on overseas advising and consulting is reductionist in that it ignores the important ecological contextual factors which condition potential for individual success or failure. Advisers or consultants do not operate in a vacuum, and their degree of professional talent interacts in a complex way with major contextual conditions.

Notes

1. Y. ALEXANDER, *International Technical Assistance Experts: A Case Study of the U.N. Experience*, Praeger, New York, 1966, p.68.
2. R. C. CHAMBERS, Cognitive problems of experts in rural Africa, in J. C. STONE (editor), *Experts in Africa*, p.101.
3. See MULTATALI, *Max Havelaar, or, the Coffee Auctions of the Dutch Trading Company* (translated by R. EDWARDS), University of Massachusetts Press, Amherst, Massachusetts, 1982.
4. R. GONZALEZ and A. NEGANDHI, *The United States Overseas Executive: His Orientation and Career Patterns*, Graduate School of Business Administration, Michigan State University, East Lansing, Michigan, 1967, p.7.
5. J. SOMMER, *Beyond Charity: US Voluntary Aid for a Changing Third World*, Overseas Development Council, Washington, DC, 1977, p.61.
6. Y. TANDON (editor), *Technical Assistance Administration in East Africa*, Almquist & Wiksell, Stockholm, 1973, p.15.
7. G. FRY and R. KAEWDAENG, Budgeting for greater equity: a normative regression analysis.
8. L. JOO-JACK and C. TAN (editors), *Southeast Asian Perceptions of Foreign Assistance*, Institute of Southeast Asian Studies, Singapore, and Institute of Asian Studies, Bangkok, 1977, p.97.
9. K. SNIDVONGS, Responsiveness of local environment to aid programs, in *Technical Assistance and Development*, Harry S. Truman Research Institute, The Hebrew University of Jerusalem, Jerusalem, 1970, p.126.
10. P. J. ELDRIDGE, *The Politics of Foreign Aid in India*, p.81.
11. R. LEMARCHAND, *The World Bank in Rwanda—The Case of the Office de Valorisation Agricole et Pastorale du Mutara*, International Development Institute, Indiana University, Bloomington, Indiana, 1982, p.236. Dr Sippanondha Ketudat, President of the Petrochemical Authority of Thailand and former Minister of Education, also made this point in an interview.
12. J. HABERMAS, *Legitimation Crisis*, Beacon Press, Boston, Massachusetts, 1973.
13. S. LINDHOLM, *Appointment with the Third World*, Almquist & Wiksell, Stockholm, 1974, p.71.
14. L. LAUFER, *Israel and the Developing Countries*.
15. J. LIM and C. TAN, p.179. See also *Communist Aid Activities in Non-Communist Less Developed Countries, 1979 and 1954–79: A Research Paper*, National Foreign Assessment Center, CIA, Washington, DC, 1980.
16. Cited in S. LINDHOLM, p.126.
17. R. H. GREEN, Technical assistance and Tanzanian administration, in Y. TANDON, p.40.
18. J. LOXLEY, Technical assistance, high-level manpower training and ideology in Tanzania, in Y. TANDON, p.67.
19. C. ENGAÑA, in *Technical Assistance and Development*, p.87.
20. C. KARNJANAPRAKORN, L. McKIBBEN, and W. THOMPSON, *NIDA: A Case Study in Institution Development*, International Development Research Center, Indiana University, Bloomington, Indiana, 1974, p.103.

21. E. N. KOMAROV, *Indo-Soviet Cooperation: Historical Background and Present-Day Development,* Allied Publishers, Bombay, 1976, p.88.
22. *Development Cooperation and the World Economy: Cooperation Between the Netherlands and Developing Countries,* Development Cooperation Information Centre, The Hague, 1980, p.187.
23. See G. GRAN, *Development by People: Citizen Construction of a Just World,* Praeger, New York, 1983.
24. L. CURRIE, *The Role of Economic Advisers in Developing Countries,* p.60.
25. J. FAALAND, *Aid and Influence: The Case of Bangladesh,* St Martin's, New York, p.182.
26. M. KUBR (editor), *Management Consulting, A Guide to the Profession,* ILO, Geneva, 1976, pp.24–5.
27. H. CLEVELAND *et al., The Overseas Americans.*
28. D. HARARI, *The Role of the Technical Assistance Expert.*
29. Jim Stirtin, 'Man who built Aramco,' retires after 38 years, *Sun and Flare,* 10 April 1958, pp.1,4.
30. J. K. GALBRAITH, *A Life in Our Times Memoirs,* p.392.
31. Ibid.
32. W. and E. PADDOCK, *We Don't Know How,* p.300.
33. D. KORTEN, Community organization and rural development—a learning process approach.
34. W. and E. PADDOCK, p.98.
35. L. LAUFER, p.31.
36. A. WILDAVSKY, *Speaking Truth to Power.*
37. R. C. HILLS, *Technical Assistance: Towards Improving the Underlying Framework,* Development Studies Centre, ANU, Occasional paper no. 14, 1979.
38. S. HASEGAWA, *Japanese Foreign Aid: Policy and Practice,* Praeger, New York, 1975, p.125.

PART IV

Case Studies

Introduction to Case Studies

Our methodology for this study has emphasized the use of *both* qualitative and quantitative approaches. An important aspect of our qualitative research is a set of case studies presented in Chapters 8 and 9. In our view there is a tendency for social scientists to overemphasize the identification of the 'representative' case. In contrast, the physical sciences often stress the study of anomalies. An understanding of the latter phenomena may lead to brilliant or creative insights. For the latter reason we have selected case studies that tend to reflect extremes. Several of the anonymous case studies show serious dimensions of failure, while the identified cases highlight examples of impressive success and impact. The careful examination of these anomalies will, we hope, lead to a deeper understanding of the essence of *effective* international advising and consulting.

CHAPTER 8

Anonymous Case Studies

The Loners

Every American should realize that he is here to assist and not to run. It is a common failing of the American technical personnel to attempt to control rather than advise. Everything must be done, on the contrary, to assure our counterparts that the responsibility for running the institution is theirs. Our hosts are so sensitive about this point (Director of a team of American advisers).

Our first case is based on the experiences of two foreign consultants serving in as many developing countries. One was European and the other from the US, both selected by the same international organization. Though serving in two quite different countries, their experiences as what we call 'loners' were remarkably similar.

The assignment of the European consultant was to advise host country nationals on a major policy study with significant implications for the allocation of the country's national budget. The adviser in question has an outstanding international reputation in his field of expertise. Given commitments to his own organization in Europe, however, the adviser was able to spend only a year on his assignment abroad.

Because of the high status of this adviser, as well as his lack of ability in the local language, he was able to work with only a small group of local researchers on the policy study. The rather extensive task of data collection itself was carried out entirely by local nationals. Probably no more than five to ten local researchers had any significant direct contact with the foreign consultant.

Interviews with local nationals concerning this consultant revealed considerable resentment. His aloof manner in dealing with local staff was the primary complaint. In recognition of the need to carry out a complex policy study involving a large survey within a year, we consider it understandable that the adviser guarded his time carefully. This, however, drastically reduced opportunities for casual informal contact with local colleagues. In addition, the consultant received an impressive salary in accord with his professional stature internationally. This produced an enormous financial distance between the expert and his colleagues.

Unfortunately it was necessary for the adviser to return to his home country prior to completion of the policy study. Responsibility for completing the analysis and writing much of the final report itself was left to another foreign consultant resident in the country at that time.

From this description it should be quite obvious that the consultant was decidedly task-oriented rather than process-oriented. The individual saw his assignment as producing an end product: a high-quality policy research report conforming to international standards. Actually the international organization hiring the consultant and the host government expected the consultant to build a considerable local research capacity while, at the same time contributing to the production of a major policy study. There was ambiguity, however, as to the relative importance of the task and process roles. Given a strong task-orientation, the consultant designed the entire study. Local nationals then carried out various analyses and all the data collection. The adviser was clearly in a dominant, superior position, and was the *sole* author of the final report.

To evaluate the effectiveness of this consultant, it is important to consider both the task (the quality of the research product and its impact) and the process involved. It is also necessary to consider both the perspectives of the host government and the international organization providing the consultant's services. The research product resulting from this consultant's services was an impressive policy study, which was several years later published by the consultant as *sole* author in a prestigious international journal. The study has been frequently cited in subsequent years by host country researchers in local publications. Government budget allocations in the country have shifted in directions suggested by the study, although it would be difficult to prove that the report 'caused' such policy changes. As suggested by our earlier discussions of the role of consultants, the report may have served primarily to legitimate shifts of this type already planned by the government. Despite the overall quality of the report, several key variables in the study were poorly operationalized. They failed to reflect local cultural phenomena. From a task perspective, however, the adviser was considered to be a success.

With respect to the process involved in building local research capacity, however, both the local government and the international organization providing his services were seriously disappointed. The consultant's expertise was not broadly shared with local colleagues. Some indirect influences, possibly deriving from the design of the study were evident. It appears that only one local national involved in the project seriously benefited professionally from the consultant's presence. Other local nationals were primarily involved in purely routine aspects of implementing the research study.

Apart from the failures related to process, two other problems emerged. The consultant returned to his/her country with the data but without making adequate efforts to ensure that such data would be readily available for future researchers in the host country. It is not completely clear who was most responsible for this 'oversight,' but it is quite unfortunate that future researchers have not had access to the rich data underlying this important policy study. A second problem was that the study was not translated into the local language. Thus, access to the study has been limited to Westerners and local nationals fluent in English.

To conclude, the major problem was this consultant's conception of his/her role as a 'loner,' a research scholar who would design and write the policy study essentially alone. The adviser failed to involve local nationals adequately in the creative design and development of the study. Given a lack of local language skill, and a manner of professional aloofness, the impressive expertise of this consultant was shared only in a sharply limited way.

The second loner experience, similar to that above, involved a US expert also asked to provide advice on a major policy study. Like the first individual, this consultant also had an outstanding reputation as a professional in his field of expertise. He, too, employed an exclusive task-oriented approach.

In this case language was not a serious problem, since the country was a nation where English was widely spoken among professionals. However, a major problem did arise since many young professionals had been sent abroad for further training. Thus, a number of the consultant's potential colleagues and counterparts were not physically present in the host country. Given this situation, it was even easier to become a 'loner' and highly task-oriented.

This consultant, like the earlier one, took on the major design of the study. The individual also spent hours alone at a local computer center, running various quantitative analyses. He saw local nationals primarily as technicians, available to help carry out research tasks.

Various interviews with local nationals suggested a similar resentment toward this consultant. 'Excessive' financial remuneration and professional aloofness were mentioned most frequently. The 'high lifestyle' of the expatriate expert was a particular irritant to local nationals in this setting.

As in the first example, however, an impressive study was produced, which has been frequently cited in subsequent years. It too has served to influence and legitimate major national policies. In this case, as with the first, a high-quality research product was produced, but little human capacity-building took place. Given the low priority assigned to process, the expert's impressive expertise was shared in only a limited circle.

Several 'lessons' emerge from these two highly similar cases. First, they suggest the need to have clearer role specifications prior to the initiation of consultancies developed in close cooperation between the host government and the organizations providing consultant services. Second, they illustrate how easy it is for advisers or consultants to confirm the stereotype of 'academic colonialist.' To minimize such problems it is imperative that research done by advisers or consultants be genuine joint ventures with cooperative writing and publishing with host country nationals. Finally, from a more optimistic perspective, the two cases do at least illustrate that foreign advisers can play an important role in policy research abroad.

The Expatriate Livestock 'Expert' in the Tropics

The expert of this case study served in an island nation in the tropics.[1] A serious balance of payments problem existed, and there was deep concern about the high cost of imported meat. The cabinet therefore decided in 1971 to initiate a livestock development program to achieve greater self-sufficiency in meat production. Ironically, the local Department of Agriculture became involved in the project only *after* the cabinet decision had been made. As might be expected, the Director of Agriculture was rather skeptical about the potential success of the project. Outside experts were sought even though the government had a general policy of hiring qualified local nationals if possible. Unfortunately local people adequately trained in livestock management were not available.

A donor nation responded positively to a specific request for both financial support and for the provision of expert services. The first step was a feasibility study to be performed by a foreign expert. Unfortunately, none of the existing staff members of the Department of Agriculture of the donor nation could be released for the proposed project. Thus it was necessary to hire a *retired* officer who was available and who had experience with many types of farming. The retired expert chosen by the donor nation had, however, no experience whatever in tropical agriculture or in hill-country cattle farming. Nor had he ever worked on any international projects, and he was totally unfamiliar with the bureaucracy and culture of the host nation.

Prior to the feasibility study by the foreign livestock expert, two local nationals (then graduate students returning home for field research) prepared a careful report on strategies of livestock development for the Director of Agriculture. In this report they also specified the desired qualities to be sought in an expatriate project director. They emphasized that the individual chosen should have livestock experience in the tropics. They also wanted an expert who would work collegially with local farmers and train local individuals to manage the project. The Director of Agriculture thought highly of this report.

Soon thereafter the Director of Agriculture departed on six months leave, attending an international conference and visiting agricultural projects in other countries. An expatriate veterinary officer was made Acting Director of Agriculture in his absence. This expatriate, who, like the 'loners,' was considered rather aloof, handled the initial visit of the foreign expert. Unaware of the directly relevant study made by the two local nationals, the

Acting Director did not mention this to the visiting expert. Totally ignorant of important local knowledge relevant to his task, the visiting expert relied almost entirely on the Acting Director, who himself had been in the country for only six months. After spending a 'lengthy' two weeks on the island, the visiting expert prepared an extensive feasibility report outlining 21 tasks to be completed over a three-year period.

This report was well received in the donor nation, and resulted in foreign funding for the project and approval by the cabinet of the tropical island nation. Our visiting expert was then selected as project manager to implement the livestock development scheme over a three-year period.

The proposed project was bureaucratically complex, involving at least one department in the host country and two departments in the donor nation. The need to implement 21 separate and specific tasks was indeed ambitious, especially because the visiting expert had *never* had responsibility for the overall management of a project, even in his own country.

The expert was found wanting in his ability to relate to and communicate with local nationals. He in turn expressed dissatisfaction with local nationals' lack of initiative and carelessness. As a result there was a serious deficiency in the coordination of project activities. There was also considerable inefficiency in the procurement of project resources from both nations involved. The various tasks comprising the project were not integrated, resulting in frequent delays. Even more shocking was the expert's failure to inform the small farmers (the intended 'beneficiaries' of the project) of project developments and their relevance to them. Without this type of communication it was difficult for the expert to *adapt* the livestock scheme to the complex and crucially important land tenure customs of the island.

Despite the delays and multiple cost overruns, various project tasks were completed and a foundation was provided for herd expansion and improvements at the department's experimental farm. Success related, however, only to the expansion of existing government farm facilities.

Upon termination of his contract the expert had developed no plan to transfer management of the project to host nationals. This was the result of the expert's failure to train local nationals to replace him. Thus, he recommended that a new expatriate be appointed to continue the project. The local government was extremely disappointed with this outcome.

Though this foreign livestock expert may have had good intentions, his experience exemplifies a common pattern of failure in technical assistance projects. The major elements in this series of failures can be summarized as follows:

1. The project itself was imposed by high-ranking politicians and technocrats without the involvement and participation of the department concerned. Thus, the foreign expert faced an adverse bureaucratic climate from the very beginning.

2. The expert failed to acquaint himself with prior *local knowledge* relevant to the project.
3. The expert could not adapt his technical expertise in farming to a tropical context in which land conditions and tenure arrangements were dramatically different from his own country.
4. The expert failed to communicate with local peasants directly affected by the project.
5. The expert lacked management skills necessary to implement a complex international project in a foreign setting.
6. No provisions existed to ensure continuation of the project by local nationals following departure of the expert.

'The Back Door Channel'

We use the term 'back door' in this instance to refer to an attempt to utilize friendship with a spouse of an influential politician or policy-maker as a means of gaining access for influencing an important decision.[2]

The subject of this case is a remarkable individual, whose entire career has been devoted to overseas consulting. Possessing an impressive and exceptional command of the local language, his understanding of the local culture and bureaucracy is deep and perceptive. Using our imagery of peasants and princes we would describe this consultant as desiring to serve those princes committed to improving the quality of life of peasants in rural areas.

This case grew out of the competing politics played by bureaucratic factions, a feature common to many organizations. The critical incident involved was the demotion of a higher-level civil servant, a remarkably committed and loyal individual, who during his career had made a major personal sacrifice to serve his government. The nature of his demotion was severe and uncharacteristic of the bureaucracy in question. He was demoted by the powerful leader of a competing faction in the bureaucracy.

The foreign consultant in this case knew the demoted civil servant and his committed public service. In fact they were close personal friends. This consultant felt because of his strong moral commitments, that he could not sit quietly by and remain neutral. He was outraged by the personnel decision which adversely affected his dedicated colleague. He thus took decisive action on behalf of his friend.

Our knowledge of the action taken in this case derives from accounts reported in the local press. They alleged that a foreign expert had utilized his friendship with the spouse of a high-ranking individual to attempt to influence bureaucratic decisions. The local newspapers were extremely critical of the foreigner because of his 'interventions' and 'interference' in local affairs. The accounts proved embarrassing to the high-ranking individual approached through the 'back door.' The consultant's deep involvement in bureaucratic politics became widely known as a result of the newspaper reports and ironically, even assuming their accuracy, the 'back door' ploy failed. The high-ranking politician in question felt that it was inapproprate to interfere with personnel issues at the civil service level, and that such action would constitute a bad precedent.

Within the year the consultant in question left his overseas post and returned home, disappointed that he had been unable to help his friend who had been so inappropriately punished. There were a number of personal and organizational factors which explained his decision to leave his overseas post. This incident was not the only factor involved.

Ironically, the consultant is now back in the host country serving in the same ministry. His friend, the wronged civil servant, has been restored to an even more important post in the bureaucracy and his faction is now clearly the dominant one. The civil servant has never forgotten the consultant's previous commitment and support, and their cordial relationship has brought many benefits.

In cultures of this type, memories are long and reciprocity is particularly important. The foreign aid folklore is, however, full of examples of situations like this which, in fact, didn't work out well at all.

It should be obvious that it is not easy to remain 'neutral' in highly politicized bureaucracies. Also, individual consultants may have moral and ethical commitments that transcend national boundaries or concerns about appropriate image and behavior.

The Ecotopian Adviser

Our ecotopian adviser[3] works as an expert for a major bilateral technical assistance agency. His lifestyle and approach to advising differ markedly from many overseas advisers or consultants. In fact some Westerners are critical of him because they consider that he has 'gone native'.

This adviser has two decades of experience in the country in which he is working. His knowledge of the language (a difficult Third World one) and culture is impressive. His ability to deliver articulate, clear and humorous formal speeches in the vernacular language is the envy not only of many Westerners but even of some local nationals. He has also mastered writing in the local language, a skill attained by extremely few Westerners, limited to a handful of highly experienced missionaries. His understanding of the ways of the complex bureaucracy in which he works is exceptional; he constantly seeks to build personal contacts in a wide range of governmental offices relevant to his work. It is in fact hard to find individuals in related bureaucracies unaware of this unusual expert and his work. These impressive skills have enabled this adviser to accomplish in only a few years tasks that normally would have taken other advisers much longer, if they were accomplished at all.

This adviser clearly sees himself as subordinate to host country nationals and he is noted for his loyalty to local superiors. He is always willing to help when needs rise. His reliability is unquestioned.

We term his personal style ecotopian because of his modest approach to living. He earns a handsome international salary, but his lifestyle is not ostentatious. He lives in a simple, but spacious local house with no air-conditioning and little furniture. Guests, both local and international, are welcome. They frequently sleep on the floor with covering mosquito nets, as is traditional in this tropical country. Our ecotopian adviser owns no private car and travels either by motorcycle or a ten-speed bicycle. He dresses simply but politely.

This adviser is particularly popular among most local nationals for a number of reasons. One of the most important is his sense of humor. He has an impressive dry and sarcastic wit, with which he is able to express himself easily in the local language. This had endeared him to many in a culture which emphasizes humor and prefers indirect, subtle forms of criticism. Though he is extremely popular, this consultant is frequently outspoken in his criticisms of both the local bureaucracy and of his international employer. His criticisms usually relate to the failure of such bureaucracies to encourage local participation in the formulation of development programs. His approach to criticism is sufficiently subtle so as not be overly offensive to his counterparts and host agencies. For example, in one of his most critical articles, published abroad, he was careful to use a pseudonym.

With respect to his job performance this adviser is noted for his deep concern that individuals affected by development projects have a serious voice in determining their structure and methods. He also strives to ensure that innovations introduced do not have adverse effects on the rich local culture in which he is working. Though our ecotopian adviser would be the first to admit that his success in these areas has been limited, he has courageously resisted tendencies among his international and local employers who too often ignore the needs and voices of those being directly affected by major innovations.

Individuals of this type, in our experience, are rarely employed by international aid agencies. A naive fear that such individuals have 'gone native,' or will give priority to the interests of the host country, seems to prevail. Lederer and Burdick, authors of *The Ugly American*, would be pleased to learn that international agencies may now begin to employ individuals such as our ecotopian adviser.

Lessons to be Drawn from Anonymous Case Studies

The anonymous case studies suggest several lessons, which can be briefly summarized:

1. Given the emphasis in the West on outcomes and products, it is easy to

neglect important *process* aspects of international consulting. Training and capacity-building may be even more significant than a specific consulting or policy report *per se*.

2. Excessive concern for 'perfectionism' may lead to too little delegation of important tasks to local nationals.

3. The adviser–counterpart(s) relationship remains a special part of the technical assistance process. Absence of appropriate counterparts can adversely affect the potential impact of international consultants.

4. An ostentatious style of living can create serious resentments. There are clearly feasible alternatives to such lifestyles in developmental contexts.

5. Involvement by outsiders in local personnel processes associated with bureaucratic factionalism can be hazardous to the 'health' of all involved.

6. Data collected as part of international consultancies should remain the intellectual property of the host country.

7. This set of case studies reflects the importance of having a set of professional and ethical standards to guide our profession (see Appendix II).

Notes

1. This case study is based on material from R. N. LOVE, Pacific island livestock development: South Pacific, in L. J. GOODMAN and R. N. LOVE (editors), *Management of Development Projects: An International Case Study*, Pergamon, New York, 1979.
2. This case is partially based on a Thai language newspaper account, *Daily Mirror*, 29 May 1980, p.6.
3. The term 'ecotopia' we borrow from the novelist, Ernest Callenbach. Relevant to this anonymous case study is the article by S. McNABB and J. SOMSAK, What has 3 heads and preys on rural populations? or bureaucratic politics and hill tribe education in Thailand, *Adult Education and Development*, 22, 135–42 (1984).

CHAPTER 9

Exemplary Case Studies

The collaborative approach maximizes the substantive contact
between the expatriate analysts and the host country officials resulting
in a better appreciation of each other's problems. It is far more likely
under such an approach that policy recommendations would be jointly
determined. Thus, the policy changes recommended would be appropriate and the understanding of the local setting would be built into the
recommendation (LeAnn Ross).[1]

Lauchlin Currie—The Economist–Farmer[2]

Lauchlin Currie came to prominence during World War II as an cconomist
on the White House staff. After the war he became a consultant to the World
Bank, and in due time became head of the Bank's mission to Colombia in
1949. During his stay in that country Currie decided to become a Colombian
national. In following up on the recommendations of the World Bank
mission he gained extensive experience serving as an economic adviser to the
Government of Colombia. Currie is modest about his accomplishments,
stating that he may hold the world's record for the number of policy
recommendations rejected. Since 1949 he has intermittently, and in many
different capacities, advised the Colomiban Government. Even more
unusual, Currie, after settling in Colombia, for 10 years had first-hand
experience as a dairy farmer in that country. In that sense Currie exemplifies
some of the qualities of the Samurai adviser mentioned earlier in this book.

The major evidence for Currie's success is that the Colombian Government, despite frequent political changes and shifts in political ideology,
seems to call regularly upon Currie's advice. He served as adviser to the head
of the Colombian Government Planning Agency for nearly 40 years. It may
be helpful to summarize the nature of Currie's major successes.

Currie's World Bank mission report had a direct impact on Colombian
economic policy even though many suggestions were not directly
implemented. Nevertheless, it is remarkable how Colombian economic
policy over the years mirrored the recommendations of the World Bank
report. In this case a foreign report was influential in the development of a
national program. It also seems clear that Currie did much to foster a close
and cordial relationship between the Bank and the Government of Colombia. (This is a definite contrast, for example, with the situation in Brazil.)

Evidence of this has been Colombia's success in drawing upon Bank resources. By the end of 1974 Colombia had received, in per capita terms, the largest volume of loans from the World Bank of any major developing country. Some critics, however, would hold that World Bank loans create excessive dependency; to them Currie's 'success' would definitely be questioned.

Currie also wrote a working paper, *Operation Colombia* (1961), which proposed a controversial and non-conventional approach to agricultural policy. Though formally rejected in 1961, the basic ideas were later revised and actually adopted in 1971. Thus, Currie's major success was in bringing 'truth to power,' to use Wildavsky's apt term.

There are a number of reasons for Currie's success in exerting influence on Colombian economic policy. Currie clearly had impressive credentials related to the formulation of government economic policy to share with Colombia. He had played an important role in developing the economic recovery program of the New Deal in the 1930s. He had served first as assistant to the chairman of the Board of Governors of the Federal Reserve System and later as a special assistant to President Roosevelt. From 1942 to 1944 he had been a *de facto* director of the Foreign Economic Administration and handled all lend-lease aid to China. His academic credentials were also an advantage: degrees from the London School of Economics and from Harvard University.

Moreover, Currie effectively borrowed the idea of a 'Royal Commission' from Great Britain to channel ideas to key policy-makers and to legitimate them in Colombia. He recommended that an eminent group of Colombians carefully review the various elements of the Mission Report prepared by Currie and his foreign colleagues. Thus the recommendations of the commission of prominent Colombians carried great weight both with the World Bank and the Government of Colombia.

Currie also recognized the importance of having the Mission Report published in both Spanish and English. Had the report been available only in English, its potential for influence would have greatly diminished. Throughout his work as an economic adviser in Colombia, Currie carefully maintained a low profile. While doing so, he developed an extensive network of relationships with important figures within the Colombian bureaucracy. The use of Currie's services by many different governments suggest that his bureaucratic contacts have been diverse and politically neutral.

Finally, Currie clearly recognized that, in making economic policy recommendations, the ideal must be tempered with the practical, and that many sweeping reforms will not be politically feasible. Looking back on his own advising experience, Currie felt that he perhaps pushed too hard and too rapidly, and that he might have had greater impact if he had not aroused heated opposition to his rather controversial ideas.

Currie's career clearly reflects the complex challenge that advisers face in attempting to promote significant change in national policies and institutions.

Adam Curle: Enlightened Self-Critic[3]

As part of the Harvard Group providing technical assistance to the Pakistan Planning Board (later, Commission) in the 1950s and 1960s Adam Curle had $8\frac{1}{2}$ years' association with Pakistan. He worked in Pakistan on numerous occasions both as a short-term and long-term adviser.

Professor Curle is rare among international advisers in that he has written frankly about his advising experiences abroad. These reflections are presented in *Planning for Education in Pakistan*, a book containing refreshing insights into the personal element in development assistance. The candor of Curle's reflections is a valuable contribution to the literature on international advising and consulting.

Curle reveals his own original naive assumption that he would be quickly ushered into the corridors of power. He had imagined that his suggestions and solutions related to Pakistan's educationaal problems would be readily acepted by Pakistan's prime minister and cabinet. Curle openly admits that this anticipatory vision was remote from the reality he experienced as an educational adviser in Pakistan.

Soon after arriving in Pakistan, Curle developed what he terms the *adviser syndrome*. Associated with this syndrome are feelings of uselessness, worry, depression, ineffectiveness, and guilt about wasting other people's and his own valuable time. This syndrome rapidly develops when individuals are not able to contribute as quickly and fully as they had *hoped*. The sense of ineffectiveness was particularly troubling to Curle since it cast doubt on the validity of his own basic intellectual foundations.

Curle outlines two possible responses to the *adviser syndrome*: the schizoid and the depressive. Those responding in the schizoid pattern tend to be dogmatic and impatiently adhere to a simple and often reductionist theory of development. Schizoid advisers will not admit or accept their own failure, but blame local nationals for being lazy, stupid, irresponsible, and corrupt.

The depressive response to *adviser syndrome* differs markedly from the above. Curle admits that he, himself, responded in the depressive pattern. He felt a miserable sense of uselessness and shame from his impotence. Despite the many visible problems around him, he did not know how to contribute. Though Curle was an expert in planning, the Pakistani context was alien to him. While he was willing to recognize his own inadequacies (a central element in the depressive response), he also realized that he had to endure a painful processs of *unlearning* much that he had previously known.

After several months Curle began to overcome the depressive psychology of the *adviser syndrome*.

Curle expressed a fundamental difficulty with the concept of 'adviser' which he thought implies a subtle continuation of colonial domination. He objects to the notion of the *éminence grise*, exercising marked influence on the mind of an important ruler. In Curle's view the emphasis should not be on advice *per se*, but on help, in doing whatever needs to be done at any point in time. He saw his task primarily as educational and cooperative. For example, during one of Curle's advising assignments he was not assigned a counterpart. Thus there was no personal involvement of the kind essential for training, cooperation and exchange of ideas. In his next assignment a year later, Curle was fortunate to have an exceptionally good counterpart. His colleague was an important, influential personage in Pakistan's planning process. Curle made it clear to his counterpart that he should make whatever use of him he wished; his energies were to be directed at his counterpart's priorities. Curle's service orientation was impressive.

Curle expresses his keen awareness that it is easier to construct than to implement a plan. Moreover, Curle views short-term advisers as having little impact on implementation, arguing that it takes time to learn how to contribute.

Curle's modesty about is own contributions is striking, giving great credit to his Pakistani counterpart, Namdarkan, for profound and important contributions to Pakistan's Third Five Year Plan.

Reflecting critically and openly about his own advising role in Pakistan, Curle emerges as an unusual development expert. Philip Coombs elegantly describes Curle in these terms:

> One wishes that the many hundreds of technical assistance experts around the world—specialists away from home—all possessed his sensitivity, perspective, and wisdom.[4]

John Grant, Radical Adviser in China[5]

A son of a missionary born to Canadian parents in China, John Grant differed substantially from many international advisers. As a child in China, Grant reacted negatively and at first-hand to the arrogant racism which prevailed in some missionary schools. Grant worked in China as an adult from 1921 to 1938, after joining the International Health Board (IHB) of the Rockefeller Foundation. For 14 years he was Professor of Public Health at the Peking Union Medical College (PUMC), and for three years he was Co-director of the Rockefeller Foundation's progressive rural China program.

Grant brought an impressive array of versatile skills to his job. His fluency in Chinese, and earlier China background, brought him to the attention of the Rockefeller Foundation. In addition to his cross-cultural and linguistic competencies, his technical skills were of a high order, including an M.D. degree from the University of Michigan, continued study at the Johns Hopkins School of Public Health under noted public health authorities, and practical experience on a Rockefeller-supported county health project in North Carolina. The latter experience significantly influenced Grant's ideas on social medicine, and increased his awareness of the need for integrating preventive and curative health services.

After arriving in China, Grant realized that one of his main tasks was to raise China's public health consciousness. To do so he did *not* maintain a low political profile. Instead he attempted to develop personal contacts with influential Chinese leaders such as the Minister of Education, the Minister of Foreign Affairs, and even progressive warlords. Grant knew all but two members of the first Nanking cabinet on a personal basis. He also held discussions with Chinese authorities in various provinces.

In his work, Grant emphasized the need to build local capacity by training qualified Chinese public health experts. With respect to his early proposals and initiatives, Grant tried to have local Chinese colleagues and organizations take the lead. As indicated in the following quotation, he became increasingly impatient with many Western advisers who wanted to do everything themselves:

> The foreigner in China is everlastingly thinking in terms of the foreigners as being the only worthwhile thing in China and the foreigner in China has done practically nothing in being able to get the Chinese to adopt his methods. It is far more important to support Chinese efforts that are 60% efficient than western ones that are 100%.[6]

Grant's impact on institution-building in China was made jointly with two important Chinese colleagues. These were Fang, the first director of the Health Station, and Liu, the Vice-Director of PUMC. They proposed to create a Ministry of Health. Their petition, an elegant document (the Chinese writing in it represented a work of art), was accepted in 1928, after only six week's consideration. China did then establish a Ministry of Health, and the country began a policy of direct government involvement in medical care.

While in China, Grant was far more than a representative of the Rockefeller Foundation. He played a major role in persuading the League of Nations to become involved in China's public health program. Grant felt that multilateral assistance from the League would be more politically acceptable to Chinese doctors trained in Europe or Japan than would bilateral American aid. Grant, for example, arranged for Borislav Borcic, a

Croatian, to serve as a two-year medical adviser in Nanking under auspices of the League.

Perhaps Grant's major problem in China was his relationship to Rockefeller Foundation headquarters in New York. Given his boldness and enthusiasm, he had a tendency to commit the Foundation to programs which had not yet been approved in New York. Staff members at headquarters were alarmed that Grant was moving ahead too rapidly without prior Foundation awareness or consideration.

In 1952, after the Chinese revolution, the views on Grant's 'accomplishments' changed dramatically. Wu, a former graduate of PUMC and then a professor at Peking University Medical College, reflected:

> The department of public health, headed by a big spy (J. B. Grant) offered the earliest opportunity to go abroad. Health Centers were headed by PUMC graduates and all the health services in colleges, middle schools and primary schools were dominated by PUMC graduates . . . to spread the poison. . . . Through the public health work, the poison was spread to workers and the public in general.[7]

This assessment of Grant's work, obviously motivated by revolutionary ideology, does seem to recognize that Grant was indeed influential and that his programs were disseminated broadly.

It may be useful to try to present an overall assessment of the effectiveness of Grant's work in China. Four criteria may be useful in making this assessment: (1) extent of relationships with Chinese counterparts, (2) technical knowledge and ability to adapt this expertise to Chinese conditions, (3) local human capacity-building through training, and (4) institution-building.

With respect to the first criterion, Grant appears to have been eminently successful. His fluency in Chinese and early childhood experiences in China were certainly a major asset which facilitated building personal relations with Chinese counterparts. Grant frequently visited Chinese restaurants and bars with Chinese colleagues, which helped build important informal relations. For example, Grant once enjoyed a raucous three-day New Year's celebration with his intimate Chinese friend, J. Heng Liu. Liu was to accept considerable advice from Grant regarding the organization of the National Health Administration. Grant had great success in developing friendships with high-level Chinese politicians and officials.

Grant's knowledge of medicine and public health appears to have been excellent, though he was not renowned as a researcher. What was most significant was Grant's ability to *adapt* his expertise to local conditions. He quickly realized that a system of private health care with a curative orientation was inappropriate for China. Instead he focused on preventative public health care. He noted that a community approach to health was necessary in an affiliative and group-oriented society like China.

Grant's most notable success perhaps was in training Chinese students and colleagues. Particularly noteworthy were Ch'en and Yang. The first adapted the metropolitan health model to meet the needs of rural China. The second established midwifery training programs all across China. The majority of PUMC graduates remained in China after the revolution and many achieved prominence in the medical field. For example, in 1955, seven of the nine representatives in the field of biomedical science in the prestigious Chinese Academy of Sciences were either former PUMC faculty or graduates.[8] Ironically, many of the programs advocated by Grant, such as improved health services in the rural areas, and paraprofessional training, became more feasible under the PRC regime.

Grant's successes with respect to institution-building are more moot. It is undeniable that the PUMC was an elite institution. Its student body was strictly limited in size. Because English was the language of instruction, it served exclusively students from private and mostly missionary universities.[9] Its students led a luxurious life compared to other students in China. Undeniably, the PUMC became increasingly a Chinese institution. At the time Grant went to China with the Rockefeller Foundation, approximately 30 percent of the faculty were Chinese.[10] in 1940, several years after Grant's departure, the Chinse constituted more than 90 percent of the staff. It is doubtful, however, that such a trend would have been so dramatic but for the Japanese invasion of China. Overall, Grant did not change PUMC's elitist orientation.

Although Grant strove to accomplish things through Chinese colleagues, his own dynamic and charismatic presence was often critically important. Victor Heise, who visited Grant's newly established health station in Peking, felt that 'if Dr Grant's push and energy were withdrawn, the project would soon collapse.'[11] Mary Brown Bullock offers a much more positive view of Grant's success in institution-building:

> Perhaps it is because Grant worked so diligently to overcome the institutional encumberances of Western medicine that one reflects favorably upon his career. But perhaps more revealing is the fact that he did not make himself indispensable to the progress which he started. Therein lies the measure of his success.[12]

Than Mo American

The woods are lovely, dark and deep
But I have promises to keep,
and miles to go before I sleep (Robert Frost)[13]

Tom Dooley is one of the best-known US citizens who have worked abroad in technical assistance. This is perhaps because he is the subject of a well-known Kingston Trio ballad and a feature film. The Frost poem quoted above, a favorite of President Kennedy, guided Dooley's life from 1954 onward. Dooley's first overseas duty was as a Navy medical officer working with thousands of Vietnamese refugees in the port city of Haiphong. He also worked as a French interpreter in Vietnam, having previously studied at the Sorbonne in Paris.

After completing his military service in Vietnam, Dr Tom Dooley organized a small private medical missionary team to return to Indo-China to work in the remote parts of Laos where health conditions were extremely poor. There he was known as *Than Mo American* (Lao for Mr American doctor). This mission was subsidized by profits from the sale of Dooley's book, *Deliver Us from Evil*, about his refugee work in North Vietnam. According to Dooley, his commitment to this kind of mission was inspired by his personal acquaintance with Albert Schweitzer.

Dooley's orientation to technical assistance was consistent with a philosophy popularized by Schumacher in *Small is Beautiful*. Whenever asked by a government, like that of Laos, Dooley and his colleagues would go to a remote rural area and establish a small 'hospital.' Their goal was to train the villagers to maintain the hospital on the simplest possible basis. After a period of two to four years the hospital was to be turned over to the local government.

Dooley was keenly aware of the critical criterion for success in overseas technical assistance. His basic philosophical orientation toward the work of his team in Laos is reflected in the following statement:

> I am not interested alone in the amount of antibiotics that circulate in the bodies of our patients. But I am most interested in the amount of education that circulates in the hearts and minds of the people of our high valley. After *our departure* this will last longer than will their blood level of penicillin.[14]

Dooley and his colleagues also insisted that the host nation promise to sustain and maintain after their departure what they had helped to establish.

Dooley was an individual skilled in networking *par excellence*. He strove to increase the medical resources being shared by rich countries like the US with poorer nations such as Laos. Dooley had his own 'personal law,' namely to write at least ten letters a night seeking such assistance.

Dooley was highly skilled in developing good personal relations with his Lao counterparts. He saw them not as employees of a Westerner, but as members of a team. He also tried not to be patronizing and to treat the Laos in the same manner as he treated his US colleagues. Though he continually stressed tenderness, Dooley frequently spoke roughly to his Lao students when they were careless, or neglected their duties. Though such roughness violated the Lao norm of politeness, it was essential if Dooley and his colleagues were to instill a medical ethic of carefulness, precision, and perfection.

Dooley always stressed patience as the companion of wisdom. He was proud of his colleague, Earl Rhine, because he treated all peasants as visiting royalty. Rhine had an extreme gentleness of manner which characterized his work with Lao villagers. Dooley and his colleagues took an active interest in the local culture and were aware of local legends and ancient Buddhist prayers. Though Dooley's two colleagues had to utilize an interpreter, Dooley himself appears to have learned considerable Lao. Based on material presented in *The Night They Burned the Mountain*, it also appears that Dooley and his colleagues had a sound appreciation of Lao humor. He and his colleagues were for the most part culturally sensitive. Some degree of ethnocentrism, however, was evident. For example, they saw their first task as explaining to their Lao students that they must not pick their noses, although a sense of personal hygiene may have prompted this concern. Such remarks led Daniel Ramsdell to criticize Dooley's book on Laos for being patronizing.

The knowledge of Dooley and his team's work spread well beyond Laos. Twenty-three nations were later to request teams from MEDICO such as that organized by Dooley in Laos. *The Washington Post* and *Times Herald* (16 July 1956) praised Dooley's work as 'the ultimate example of effective person-to-person contact with foreign people.'[15] Senator Mike Mansfield, former US Ambassador to Japan, entered the following statement into the *Congressional Record* (9 April 1956):

> If the United States had abroad more ambassadors like Dr. Thomas A. Dooley, I think it not only would be better off, but would be better understood in the countries which are underdeveloped and which need understanding at this time.[16]

It is interesting to speculate as to whether Dooley's example might have had an impact on either Senators Humphrey or Kennedy who proposed the Peace Corps concept when Dooley's work in Laos was attracting national and international attention.

Ironically, while still a young man, Dooley fell victim to malignant cancer, leading to his premature death in 1961. Dooley was impressively stoical and philosophical about his bout with cancer. He saw his disease as building a bond of fellowship between him and those who knew the mark of pain. Even while suffering from cancer, Dooley prepared to return to Laos and continued to strive to achieve the inspiring dream articulated by Anne Frank:

> Things will change, and men become good again, and these pitiless days will come to an end, and the world will know once again order, trust, and peace.[17]

Harry Maude: Proconsul in the Pacific[18]

Former colonial officials, especially those from Britain and France, often became international advisers and consultants. Harry Maude is one such individual; he had a remarkable career as a British colonial officer in the South Pacific, later becoming an adviser to a number of Pacific island nations and regional organizations. In the end he became a noted Pacific historian.

As a colonial officer Maude's work was primarily in the Gilbert Islands during a ten-year period, 1929–39. He served in a variety of posts such as Census Officer, Administrative Officer, Native Lands Commissioner; and adviser to Queen Sālote of the Kingdom of Tonga. Finally in the postwar period he was Executive Officer for Social Development of the South Pacific Commission.

Though noted for his personal low-key approach, attributed to his modesty and shyness, Maude was determined from the beginning of his service to get close to the 'natives.' He early on made a commitment to learn Gilbertese, and passed the higher standard language examination. This included competence in writing Gilbertese. His wife, Honor, more outgoing than Harry, also developed fluency in Gilbertese.

Throughout his career in the South Pacific, Maude demonstrated an impressive capacity for developing personal relations with ordinary islanders. He loved to participate in the islanders' games, contests, and community singing. He also recognized the importance of humor in South Pacific cultures. Later in his career, Maude was appointed Resident Commissioner of the Gilberts. He was not comfortable living in a European 'ghetto,' as he would have called it, and having to entertain fellow-Europeans. He preferred spending his leisure time with the islanders. Though Maude's shyness may have been a liability as Resident Commissioner, it may also have helped him in dealing with islanders by making him less directive and arrogant than some others. Though Maude had the ability to communicate with princes, his preference was clearly for contact with the ordinary peasants of the Pacific.

Maude, in spite of a modest personal manner, actively sought to bring about social change. When first working in the Gilberts, Maude encountered a ludicrous set of puritanical regulations, established by a previous British administration. Such regulations, for example, prohibited dancing except for a few limited hours, and resulted in jail sentences and fines for a number of islanders. Maude used important and influential contacts in London to obtain a review of these regulations. Maude was then asked by London to amend and redraft the entire code. Maude did not take on this task as an 'expert' working in isolation, but instead personally visited all 16 islands, and in a series of public meetings sought out the views of the islanders themselves with respect to a new code. More than 100 of the old regulations were abolished and the remainder were substantially modified.

Maude also achieved success in Pitcairn, the so-called 'Bounty Island.' Maude was sent there to frame a constitution, a code of laws, and to open a post office. Again Maude did not draft the constitution as a European 'expert,' but instead had meetings with the people of Pitcairn and based the constitution on the unanimous decision of the islanders themselves. Maude also initiated the now famous postal service of Pitcairn, which serves to this day as the island's major source of foreign exchange.

While working for the Western Pacific High Commission, Maude helped deal with the grievances of the Banabans who had been badly exploited by the British Phosphate Commission. Maude, highly sympathetic to the Banaban position, helped secure a new island for their resettlement.

As a special adviser to Queen Sālote of Tonga, Maude reviewed the structure of the Tongan Civil Service and provided ideas on possible ways to reorganize the service. Maude's frank recommendation, unusual for a European adviser, was that Tongans should be trained to take over the key posts from Europeans.

Perhaps Maude's most impressive accomplishment was his effort to establish a cooperative movement in the Gilbert Islands. All commerce had been controlled by foreigners, but when Maude left after 17 years of service, all major commerce was in the hands of native-run cooperative societies.

While working the South Pacific, Maude also fought vigorously to expand the land area of the Gilberts by acquiring additional island groups such as the Phoenix group and the Line Islands. Maude felt that the Gilbertese had an inadequate land area, relative to the size of their population. Maude's success in this domain has major economic implications today. The new nation of Kirabiti (formerly part of the Colony of Gilbert and Ellice Islands) now has an enormous exclusive economic zone, given the currently accepted principle of the 200-mile economic zones stipulated by the Law of the Sea.

Maude's remarkable successes and accomplishments in the South Pacific were largely the result of his ability to communicate with peasants, princes, and even scholars, and his perseverance to struggle effectively for needed change.

W. Edwards Deming: 'Quality Guru' [19]

Famous in Japan, Deming was not widely known in the United States until around 1980. Deming's impact on Japan in promoting the concept of quality control is one of the most striking examples of the catalytic influence an outside expert may provide.

Deming's involvement with Japan began in the late 1940s. He went to Japan in 1946 to advise the postwar Allied occupation government on the use of statistical sampling techniques for census, nutrition, and business reports. Later in 1949 the Union of Japanese Scientists and Engineers (JUSE) sponsored a quality control seminar. In connection with that seminar Japanese statisticians began reviewing relevant foreign literature and became familiar with Deming's work and his excellent reputation as a statistician and interpreter of statistics for the US federal government. JUSE learned that Deming would be coming to Japan for a second time to advise the occupation government on statistical matters. They asked Deming to speak on the topic of what statistics could do for Japan's industry. Ichiro Ishikawa, the dynamic president of JUSE and also president of the influential Keidanren, urged Japan's top industrial leaders to come to hear Deming speak at the Industry Club on 26 July 1950. In this key lecture Deming stressed the importance of company-wide statistical quality technology and the responsibility of management to emphasize service to customers.

Deming expressed great confidence in the ability of the Japanese to implement the ideas he was advocating, and predicted that Japanese quality could become the best in the world. Many who listened to Deming were intially skeptical about his methods and his optimism.

During that same summer Deming conducted a series of lectures focusing on new ways to build statistical knowledge into the education of engineers. Approximately 400 Japanese engineers attended this series of lectures during that same summer of 1950.

Deming returned to Japan six months later to check on the progress of his quality control suggestions. The president of Furukawa Electric Company, initially a skeptic, already was able to report reduced accidents and faulty production by utilizing the techniques proposed by Deming. Within a year and a half after the first courses in 1950, 13 Japanese companies reported significant strides in improving quality and productivity. In recognition of Deming's remarkable contribution to Japanese industry, the Japanese established The Deming Award, to be given annually to the Japanese company showing the most impressive gains in quality.

Following Deming's initial stimulus, JUSE itself continued the teaching of statistical quality control methods to engineers and managers. Between 1950 and 1970 JUSE provided such training to nearly 15,000 engineers and thousands of foremen. As late as 1984, courses in statistical quality technology for management were booked to capacity with a waiting period of seven months.

Deming has visited Japan more than 20 times, and has received the ornate Second Order Medal of the Sacred Treasure from Emperor Hirohito. Though Deming's recent fame derives from his advising in Japan, he has also consulted in many other countries, including Taiwan, Mexico, India, Turkey, Austria, Germany, and Hungary. A speech on quality control in Budapest, in 1980, was reported to have significantly influenced the First Secretary of Hungary, Janos Kadar.

How can we account for Deming's remarkable success as an international adviser? Perhaps most important is Deming's possession of specialized expertise strongly desired by the Japanese. In many respects Deming's expertise is rather unusual in that it is highly interdisciplinary. He initially taught engineering at the University of Wyoming and later physics at the Colorado School of Mines. Later he taught and received his doctorate from Yale in physics. At a later stage of his career he was a professor of statistics at the NYU Graduate School of Business. Deming had not only extensive academic knowledge, but considerable practical experience with US government organizations such as the Department of Agriculture, the Budget Bureau, the Bureau of the Census, and the Bureau of Standards. Thus, Deming was a classic 'inner and outer' shifting back and forth between academic and practical settings, and between domestic and international assignments. Thus, Deming was keenly aware of the many practical applications of theoretical statistics, and his current professional identity is as a theoretical statistician. Upon beginning his lectures in Japan in 1950, Deming was bringing with him a highly unusual blend of interdisciplinary and practical orientations, in addition to his excellent reputation as a quality control statistician.

Deming has recently published a major work outlining the basic principles underlying his statistical approach to management and quality control. A careful examination of this work, entitled *Quality, Productivity, and Competitive Position,* provides some important clues as to why Deming was so successful. Most striking is Deming's ability to convey complex ideas simply and clearly. A high-school graduate with a good background in mathematics and science (the norm in Japan, by the way), should be able to read Deming's work without difficulty. In many respects Deming emerges as strikingly populist in ideology. He is always concerned about the worker on the assembly line and the ordinary consumer. Deming's work also suggests a strong interest in human potential. Instead of criticizing the Japanese for their poor quality, he stressed the positive and their remarkable potential for growth and improvement.

Deming is also a man of unusual drive and energy. He is, at the time of writing, 88 years of age, but continues to work an active 12-hour day as a consultant and writer. As a circular reverse adviser he is now helping many US companies to improve their quality and productivity. Like a number of our exemplary US advisers, his own roots are in a small Midwestern town, this one in Iowa.

Deming's case illustrates the crucially important contextual element that conditions potential success of advisers. The Japanese displayed impressive initiative in ensuring that Deming's expertise would be utilized and disseminated. In this regard credit belongs to Ichiro Ishikawa for providing a forum for Deming to present his ideas to Japan's most influential businessmen and industrialists. Ishikawa, JUSE, and Keidanren must also be praised for their extensive efforts in establishing training courses to promote statistical quality techniques after Deming's initial stimulus. The establishment of the Deming Prize was also a clever and culturally appropriate mechanism to promote and continue emphasis on Deming's ideas and orientations. The Deming case, in sum, is an extraordinary example of the right man being in the right place at the right time, and the impressive Japanese capability to learn from foreign expertise.

The Protean Agrarian Reformer, Wolf Ladejinsky[20]

We must recognize the need to bring only our most skilled consultants to work as colleagues with you, and then only within the framework of your own national government or voluntary program (John C. Cool).[21]

Now we know from Greek mythology that Proteus was able to change his shape with relative ease from wild boar to lion to dragon to fire to flood. What he found difficult . . . was to commit himself to a single form, a form most of his own. . . . The Protean style of self-process, then is characterized by an interminable series of experiments and explorations (Robert J. Lifton).[22]

In his book *Boundaries,* Robert Lifton (1969) portrays the ideal of protean man, the individual who can readily assume different roles and who thrives on diversity. Similarly, in *Cooperation in Change,* Ward Goodenough echoes the theme of the multicultural individual who can shift smoothly from one operating culture to another.[23] Wolf Ladejinsky, born in Ekaterinopol, a small hamlet in the Russian Ukraine, epitomizes the protean ideal in a professional career devoted to foreign advising and consulting in many Asian nations over a period of four decades.

In this case study we look first at Ladejinsky's accomplishments as an adviser, and then attempt to examine the numerous factors underlying his remarkable success and achievement of professional excellence in overseas service. Ladejinksy's diverse professional career itself is an interesting example of diversity, both with respect to countries and organizations served. His career began initially with an 11-year stint in Washington as a staff member of the Office of Foreign Agricultural Relations of the US Department of Agriculture. Ladejinsky's first major overseas work was in postwar Japan. In fact, many have credited him with having been the chief architect of Japan's successful land reform program. In 1949 Ladejinsky was asked to help the Joint Commission on Rural Reconstruction (JCRR) with respect to its work on agrarian reform in China and Taiwan. From 1950 to 1954 he was again in Japan as agricultural attache. Chester Bowles, US Ambassador to India in the 1950s, urgently requested Ladejinsky's services to review tenurial conditions in key areas such as the Punjab. Later Ladejinsky left the government and subsequently worked for foreign governments, the Ford Foundation, and finally the World Bank in countries such as Nepal, Vietnam, India, the Philippines, Indonesia, and Sri Lanka.

In considering the success of Ladejinsky's many and difficult assignments, it is perhaps best to cite directly those whom he served abroad. Kozen Hirokawa, former Minister of Agriculture in Japan, reflecting on Ladejinsky's contribution there, states:

> Our country owes you [a] heavy debt for your share in the successful accomplishment of the Land Reform Program. The world knows that this is the most significant reform which Japan accomplished under the Occupation, and I know that the reform was carried out with the closest cooperation and in the most friendly atmosphere between yourself and the personnel of our Ministry and I are convinced that the effect of the Land Reform will remain forever and so will your name in Japanese agriculture.[24]

He was held in similarly high regard in Taiwan, as illustrated by this cable from Premier Chen Cheng:

> I was glad to learn . . . of your willingness to come to Taiwan again. We are grateful for your invaluable assistance rendered to our country when you were last here (in 1949). Now we are planning to carry out a limitation of land holdings program in which your advice is greatly needed. We have requested General MacArthur to approve lending your services to our government and he has been good enough to give his approval.[25]

Indians, in general, have frequently been critical of foreign advisers and consultants.[26] Ashok Mitra, for example, writes of the legion of experts who 'come, write their report, go, and soon forget the country for which they had written it, their mental horizon . . . colored a cynical gray.'[27] But when commenting on Ladejinsky, Mitra offers a touching tribute:

> He wandered restlessly across the Indian countryside to comprehend the essence of agrarian truth. It was a bizarre, yet emotionally a moving experience, to see this near-octogenerian, who had lost the sight of practically both his eyes, who was . . . still determined to catch the plane, land on the airstrip in a distant town, and get into the jeep or station wagon, or take the ferry across the river, so as to reach some remote village where the *bataidar* would be able to tell him a little more about the mystique of the local land system, or of the local wage rates. This was no run-of-the-mill technical expert, this was a zealot. And the zeal came from a deep love for people whatever their civilization or the pigmentation of their skin.[28]

The high regard in which Ladejinsky was held by top officials of foreign governments and international development agencies was based on his many notable accomplishments, which can be briefly summarized as follows:

1. He is considered to have been a major architect of Japan's successful land reform program following World War II.
2. He made a major contribution to agrarian reform in Taiwan.
3. He had close and cordial relations with the Planning Commission in India and his work strongly influenced its policies. His major impact in India was, to inform the public debate about agrarian reform and to offer an inspirational example which raised public consciousness concerning India's rural problems. The ferment resulting from such a debate led to a number of programs in the early 1970s designed to enhance social justice.
4. He was influential in persuading the World Bank to recognize the central importance of agrarian reform in the development process.
5. Ladejinsky's prolific writing on agrarian issues in the Third World represents an impressive contribution to the development literature. Unlike many social science works on development which is overly mystified and reified, Ladejinsky's writing is practical, critical and understandable.

Given Ladejinsky's remarkable success as a foreign consultant and adviser, it is important to examine the personal and professional qualities which contributed to his excellence to overseas service. Harlan Cleveland, in his work on the overseas Americans, included technical skill as the first criterion for successful overseas service. Ladejinsky certainly excelled with respect to this criterion. According to the historian, Lawrence Hewes, he knew more about land reform in its various dimensions than did anyone else.[29]

But as Cleveland and Sanders point out, technical skill *per se* is a necessary, but not a sufficient condition for success overseas.[30] It was, in fact, Ladejinsky's protean qualities which explain much of his success. He had a remarkable communicative competence in being able to relate both to peasants in remote villages and also to those in the highest political offices. In contrast, too many foreign advisers become 'knights in air-conditioned offices,' relating predominantly with other consultants and foreigners, and not communicating with either peasants or princes.

Not only did Ladejinsky make an effort to meet peasants, but he also was highly emic in dealing with them.* He was able to *listen* and understand their perspectives. According to Walinsky there has been perhaps no other 'agricultural economist, development practitioner, or, indeed, government official who had made so close and direct an acquaintance with the peasant cultivators of Asia or had come to know so well the peasant condition.'[31]

* 'Emic' is an anthropological term derived from a basic linguistic concept, and refers to an orientation that stresses understanding how people different from ourselves categorize and see the world from their own perspective.

Ladejinsky had other important skills for dealing with princes, i.e. heads of governments and high-level policy-makers. He had a canny ability to relate the truth as he and his peasant colleagues perceived it, and to criticize governments without offending. His many papers presented to various governments are important examples of what Cleveland calls a 'sense for politics.'

Though having no formal training in anthropology, Ladejinsky emphasized direct field observation and was brilliantly perceptive in analyzing local situations. Robert Chambers, in an insightful article on rural poverty unperceived, lauds Ladejinsky for his insights on the Green Revolution after brief visits to the Punjab and Kosi area in Bihar.[32] Long before most development specialists were to understand the full implications of the Green Revolution, Ladejinsky was arguing that 'the new agricultural policy which has generated growth and prosperity is also the indirect cause of the widening of the gap between the rich and the poor.'

Louis Walinsky describes in detail the special personal qualities which enabled Ladejinsky to be so successful in his technical assistance work.[33] These impressive qualities can be briefly summarized as follows:

1. judicious evenhandedness reflected in his work in the Netherlands Indies and in British Malaya;
2. sense of fairness in dealing with the land tenure situation in Taiwan;
3. his ability to focus on the essential;
4. his impressive persuasiveness (Nepal);
5. his perseverance and persistence despite discouragement or obstacles encountered; and
6. the humility he showed with regard to his own work and accomplishments.

Walinsky also lauds his 'capacity for friendship, his passion for good craftsmanship, his sense of humor, the stoic fortitude with which he endured ill health and disappointment, and his love of beauty in music, literature, and art.'[34] But perhaps most important were his zeal, faith, and love.

Ladejinsky's combination of exceptional technical skills and impressive personal qualities was certainly crucial in explaining his success. But Ladejinsky also for the most part worked in highly favorable contexts. In Japan Ladejinsky was associated with a progressive occupation regime which had dominant power and influence. In Taiwan he was working with a government that was aware of tragic mistakes made on the mainland and the need for essential and immediate reforms. In India he worked in a liberal political context where he could roam freely and interact with individuals from all walks of life. Finally, Ladejinsky had the privilege of working with prestigious and influential international organizations such as the World Bank and the Ford Foundation.

To present a balanced view of Ladejinsky, it is important to recognize that there are several dissenting views about the nature of his impact, particularly in Japan and Taiwan. The Japanese scholar, Takekazu Ogura, for example, does not understand why Ladejinsky was deemed to be a main figure in Japan's land reform. Takekazu does admit, however, that Ladejinsky may have participated in preparing the Memorandum on Rural Land Reform of 9 December 1945. In fact that Memorandum was prepared for General MacArthur by Mr Robert Fearey. Fearey has openly stated that this memorandum derived from intensive consultations with Wolf Ladejinsky in Washington, DC. Takekazu found that Ladejinsky was a reliable and amiable person, but states that he was not involved in important talks with Hardy and others concerning Japanese land reform. In describing Ladejinsky's actual role, Takekazu presents an elegant cultural caricature of the meaning of low profile:

> He might have been like a 'kabuki' (Japanese classic drama) stagehand dressed in black to be inconspicuous, who assists the actors in various ways during the performance.[35]

With respect to Ladejinsky's work in Taiwan, a Chinese division chief of the Joint Commission on Rural Reconstruction (JCRR), was highly critical of Ladejinsky for not staying in Taiwan long enough to make his advice meaningful and useful:

> In spite of the extension of his time it was still too short for [Ladejinsky] to make a thorough study . . . , neither was it possible to enable him to see the results of the implementation of some of his recommendations as in the case of land purchase program, so that he may offer some new suggestions to correct the situation if something goes wrong during the . . . implementation. . . . Any length of time shorter than one year will not be long enough for any foreign expert to do the best piece of work, . . . [otherwise] there will be no time . . . for his careful thinking, deep study and thorough discussion of the problem that he is trying to tackle.[36]

Robert Moody, a former US diplomat who helped negotiate the agreement which established the JCRR, and who is familiar with Ladejinsky's role in Taiwan, felt that the criticism of this Chinese division chief derived from the highly critical and frank criticisms by Ladejinsky of Taiwanese tax and fiscal policies which he hoped to see become more consistent with the ideals of land reform. Moody argues that the criticism of the mechanism of providing expert services was masking the antagonism generated by Ladejinsky's critical policy recommendations. Nevertheless, the issue of advisers' length of stay raised by the Chinese critic is a serious one, which deserves considerable thought and consideration among those agencies and organizations providing advisory services.

Ladejinsky's excellence in overseas service provides an inspiration to those upholding the ideal of the multicultural individual. This man, an immigrant to the United States, for whom English was his third language, could shift from one cultural setting to another with ease. He also serves as an inspiration to those who believe that able and sensitive individuals can contribute significantly as advisers and consultants to enhance development, particularly in the areas of encouraging agrarian reform and fostering greater social justice.

Norman Borlaug: Samurai Agricultural Scientist

Norman Borlaug is the only overseas technical assistant to have received the Nobel Peace Prize. Borlaug was honored with this award in October 1970 for his leadership in promoting the 'Green Revolution.'

Since 1944, Borlaug has worked primarily in Mexico as an agricultural scientist under the auspices of the Rockefeller Foundation's international technical assistance program. For many years he headed the wheat research and production project of the Centro International de Majoramiento de Maize y Trigo (CIMMYT). His work in developing high-yielding and highly adaptable varieties of Mexican wheat has helped Mexico and other developing nations such as India and Pakistan to increase their food supplies dramatically. Pakistan became a net exporter of both rice and wheat, and Mexico is now a wheat exporter.[37] The dwarf wheats developed by Borlaug and his colleagues became the new cereal prototype for new rice varieties developed at the International Rice Research Institute (IRRI) in the Philippines during the mid-1960s. Though his major work has been in Mexico, Borlaug has also provided technical advice to Pakistan, India, Turkey, Afghanistan, Tunisia, and Morocco. Where his advice has been implemented, cereal production has increased by as much as 50 percent within two years.[38] Borlaug's research in Mexico has contributed significantly to a quadrupling of wheat production in Mexico since 1950, and a doubling of wheat output in both India and Pakistan between 1968 and 1972.[39]

In addition to his applied research, Borlaug has devoted extensive time to training young scientists from many nations by working with them in the fields of Mexico. Borlaug persuaded the FAO and the Rockefeller Foundation to support an international training program in Mexico.

A major concern of Borlaug and the Rockefeller Foundation was to build local institutions which would have the capacity to do applied agricultural research. The fusion of the CIMMYT cooperative program into the National Institute of Agricultural Research exemplified success in developing local institutions capable of implementing applied research projects of the type promoted initially by Rockefeller.

The 'Green Revolution' deriving from Borlaug's work in Mexico, is, of course, controversial. Borlaug himself is the first to admit that the new seeds themselves, without other changes, will have little impact. It is currently fashionable to criticize this revolution for a number of second-generation problems. For example, the revolution's benefits are differential, depending on access to key production factors such as water, credit, and fertilizer, and this has contributed to growing rural inequality. There are also concerns about the threat of disease to new varieties, though Lester Brown argues that this danger, while real, is often overrated.[40] Borlaug himself argues that 'more genetic variability is being put into grains now than ever before in the history of the world.'[41] Viewed from a broad global perspective, Brown sees the new seeds developed by Borlaug and his colleagues as a godsend:

> The new wheats and the high-yielding rices developed at the International Rice Research Institute and modeled after them, may possibly affect the well-being of more people in a shorter period of time than any technological advances in history.[42]

This technological advance may buy 10–15 years in which to stabilize population growth. Given Critchfield's highly optimistic assessment of demographic changes in village settings, Borlaug's important contribution may not be in vain.

Having documented the nature of Borlaug's significant technical achievements, we would like to turn now to consider his personal style of technical assistance work. Borlaug is clearly a Samurai-type technical assistant. Borlaug prefers to wear work clothes and spend time in doing dusty and sweaty chores in real fields. Borlaug stressed to his trainees that 'they should listen closely to what the plants themselves say.'[43] Borlaug totally ignored the local cultural norm that an educated man does not work with his hands. Borlaug's background as a farm boy in Iowa may explain his penchant for doing genuine fieldwork.

Borlaug was also fortunate to be able to devote almost his entire working life to his project in Mexico. Few technical assistance personnel are able to spend several decades in a particular setting. With his extensive knowledge of the Mexican cultural, bureaucratic, and agricultural context, Borlaug's potential for achieving optimal effectiveness was certainly enhanced.

With respect to personal qualities, Borlaug is considered to be a friendly and unassuming man, reflecting his rural Mid-west and Scandinavian background.[44] Science writer Alan Anderson aptly describes Borlaug's protean qualities:

> The man is at once a *jefe* and a *campesino*, an agricultural superstar and a down-home sodbuster.[45]

He warmly greets in Spanish Mexican colleagues at all status levels. He can communicate with both Mexican peasants and Egyptian policy-makers. Determinedly apolitical, he has dealt simultaneously with Pakistanis and Indians, with Israelis and Egyptians.[46] An admiring Mexican colleague praises Borlaug's ability to transcend narrow nationalism:

> He is some guy, that Borlaug. He isn't part of the U.S., and he isn't part of Mexico—he is part of the whole world.[47]

Borlaug is said to have infinite patience in training young scientists, but in contrast has a deep-rooted impatience with bureaucratic red tape which may inhibit project development or success. Borlaug's case illustrates the complex interaction between the particular context and personal traits needed. By being patient in training but impatient in dealing with bureaucracy, Borlaug reflects an important versatility. Borlaug is also impatient with external obstacles. He refused to accept the view that double-cropping was not feasible.

Like several other highly successful advisers, Borlaug has been an 'in-and-outer.' He had formal academic training in plant pathology at a major land grant institution, the University of Minnesota, where he is also taught and did research. He had practical experience with the US Forest Service and in the private sector with the Du Pont chemical company prior to his service in Mexico. These diverse experiences may have contributed toward Borlaug's practical orientation toward research.

Borlaug's perspective on communications is consistent with a major thrust of this book. Borlaug contends that it is difficult for the 'Green Revolution' to reach small farmers unless there are national programs to communicate with such individuals. As agricultural scientists must 'listen to the wheat;' governments must listen to their farmers and respond to their needs for water, credit, fertilizer, seed, and land reform. Otherwise, the genuine potential of the 'Green Revolution' cannot be realized.

The essence of Borlaug's success has been the ability to adapt technology to new settings, to train local nationals from Mexico and other nations in applied agricultural research, and to help create indigenous institutions with a capacity to carry on their own agricultural research. Borlaug's role in fostering a new agricultural revolution, affecting millions of villagers around the world, is an inspiring testimony to the role that the committed individual human being can have in confronting a major global issue such as hunger.

A Jewel from Down Under: Australia's Mr International

By the time of Sir John's last formal visit to New Delhi as the Bank's consultant in 1981, the Indian agricultural economy was as robust as the grain outturn was over 130 million tonnes. It would grow to 150 million tonnes in the next four years. While many people contributed to this result—and not least the tens of millions of Indian farmers whose toil has given the acomplishment its real measure—it is to Sir John that an immense debt must be acknowledged. It was he who generated the vision from the evidence around him; it was he who galvanised the donor community and the servants of the Government to the action needed to launch and sustain the conquest of India's hunger; it was he who quietly but with an iron gentleness guided both government servant and banker to making manifest the reality of what he foresaw.[48]

Fortunately with the recent publication of *Policy & Practice: Essays in Honor of Sir John Crawford*,[49] the contributions of Australians such as Sir John Crawford to international development through consulting can be more broadly shared. Sir John (or Jack as he preferred to be called) was Australia's international adviser and consultant *par excellence*. He made highly significant contributions to Australia's growing links with the Third World and its Asia–Pacific neighbors.

Sir John's most seminal role as an international consultant was as a member of the World Bank's Bell Mission to India in October 1964. The Mission, led by Bernard Bell, a well-known US economist and adminis-trator, undertook a full review of India's economy and was to suggest new courses of action to accelerate economic growth. Though not yet known internationally in the circles of agricultural development, Sir John was asked to lead the agricultural team of the Mission. With an insatiable appetite for information on India, and an impressive ability to probe and listen, he expeditiously began his task. Unlike other experts and advisers, he started his questions by asking about research.[50] After a week of becoming familiar with India and its agricultural situation, primarily through documents provided by the Ford Foundation and discussions with his associates on the agricultural team (Wolf Ladejinsky, Louis Goreux, L. Garnier, and W. David Hopper), Sir John then began discussions with India's top and senior officials with influence on agricultural policy, primarily individuals in the Ministries of Agriculture, Planning, and Finance.[51] He sought out a wide range of perspectives and policy options.

Sir John then moved into the field to become close to the realities of rural India. He visited various areas of India with W. David Hopper and later South India with Wolf Ladejinsky, a world-renowned authority on land reform (see case study above). Sir John was not convinced that institutional changes alone were sufficient conditions to foster agricultural growth. Instead he stressed an integrated approach to agriculture (use of credit, price incentives, new seeds, extension) based on the development of new varieties through applied research. He was particularly impressed with the potential of new Mexican dwarf wheat for adaptation in India.

Though the Government of India showed distaste for the macro-economic policy suggestions of the Bell Mission such as devaluation, its Minister of Agriculture put into place the main elements of the Crawford strategy. The World Bank agreed to provide fertilizer for the project. By 1968, India had produced its largest wheat crop in history, 18 million tons.[52] Though Sir John visited India rarely from 1967 to 1973, he visited there annually from 1973 until 1980 on behalf of the World Bank. These years 'saw the full flowering of Sir John's work in India.'[53] Successive national governments of India put into place the integrated service and support systems central to the Crawford strategy, reflecting an impressive commitment to national agricultural development detected back in 1964 during his initial consultancy in India. By 1981 India's grain output was 130 million tons, a remarkable exponential increase since the Bell Mission in 1964.[54] Crawford had clearly worked himself out of a job, and India no longer needed his counsel.[55] Though India's success in raising its grain output resulted from many factors, Sir John's role as part of the Bell Mission was certainly influential in significant ways.

A comprehensive guide to Crawford's multitude of accomplishments is provided in the volume edited by L. T. Evans and J. D. B. Miller. We will mention here only briefly those successes most directly relevant to international development. In 1971 Sir John was named the first Chairman of the Technical Advisory Committee (TAC) for the Consultative Group on International Agricultural Research (CGIAR).[56] These international and interdisciplinary groups resulted from the Bellagio meetings encouraged by the Ford and Rockefeller Foundations, and were designed to coordinate more carefully and expand support for international agricultural development. Under Sir John's brilliant chairmanship, TAC established several new agricultural research centers inspired by the International Rice Research Institute (IRRI) in the Philippines and the International Maize and Wheat Improvement Centre (CIMMYT) in Mexico. Among new applied research centers fostered by Sir John and his committee were the International Centre for Agricultural Research in Dry Areas (ICARDA), now in Aleppo, Syria; the International Crop Research Institute for the Semi-Arid Tropics (ICRISAT) in Hyderabad, India; and the International Potato Centre (CIP) in Lima, Peru. It was in his role as chairman of TAC that Sir John so clearly demonstrated his skill as an institution-builder. Also his ability to chair successfully a transnational and multi-cultural committee with equal representation from the LDCs was similarly an impressive accomplishment.

Sir John's record of accomplishment derives from a unique combination of intellectual skills, personality traits, and rich practical experience. Though primarily a practitioner, he had an impressive list of research publications relevant to his reputation as an expert. He possessed a special ability to absorb and synthesize vast amounts of information quickly.

With respect to personal style, Sir John was genuinely Australian with an excellent sense of humor.[57] He possessed a fascinating mixture of self-deprecation and personal pride.[58] Physically, he was small in stature and quiet-spoken. He could communicate effectively with both princes and peasants. He was a natural politician with a keen *sense of politics,*[59] the trait stressed so strongly by Harlan Cleveland and his colleagues as a key to success over-seas.[60] Among other personal traits exemplified by Sir John were the following:

1. highly pragmatic and utilitarian habit of mind,
2. not pushy,
3. able to work well with other experts,
4. able to ascertain the felt needs of other cultural groups such as Indians and Indonesians,
5. difficult to say 'no,'
6. extremely loyal to colleagues and institutions,
7. trusted by ministers of all colors,
8. able to get things done,
9. ability to listen to and accept perspectives other than his own.

In an era of individualism it is also interesting to note that Sir John did not allow his own personal life to stand in the way of his duty and broader responsibilities. This was certainly an important element in his success.

Like many of our other exemplary consultants, Sir John was an 'inner-and-outer.' He had experiences in a wide range of organizational settings, public, academic, and international. Prior to World War II he had highly formative experiences working many months with the old Bureau of Agricultural Economics in the US Department of Agriculture. He claims that his experience gave him a genuine appreciation of the role of applied agricultural research in improving the productivity of ordinary farmers.

Two statements summarize elegantly Sir John's style and character. The first is by J. D. B. Miller, who knew him intimately at the ANU:

> his combination of steadfastness, clarity of mind, understanding of the other side's interests and ability to find a reasonable consensus.[61]

Second, Lloyd Evans argues that there were four major elements in Sir John's life:

> namely, his Malthusian concerns, his taste for institution building, his outstanding skills as a chairman of committees to determine policy, and his experience and persuasiveness in ensuring the translation of policy into practice.[62]

Clearly, Sir John Crawford was a master of the art of 'speaking truth to power.'[63]

Reverse Impact: Ernst Friedrich Schumacher, A Circular Adviser[64]

Though best known for his popular books such as *Small is Beautiful*[65] and *A Guide for the Perplexed*,[66] Schumacher also had extensive experience as an international adviser, primarily in England, India, and Burma.

Born in Germany, Schumacher migrated to England and studied there as well as in the United States. Most of his early career was spent as an economist advising the United Kingdom. His advice in England had a major impact on the course of events. His plan for a new international monetary payments clearing system was adopted by Lord Keynes as UK government policy.

Given his prominent success as an adviser in the UK, Schumacher was invited to serve as a consultant in both India and Burma. These experiences were to have a dramatic effect on Schumacher and his thinking about economics and economic policy. His interest in Eastern throught stemmed from the years spent advising the Governments of Burma and India. In Burma he became aware of the richness and relevance of classical Buddhism to contemporary economic problems. These insights are reflected in his famous essay, 'Buddhist Economics.' While advising in India he developed a strong admiration for Gandhi's call for culturally sensitive decentralized 'production by the masses.'

After arriving in India in the early 1960s, Schumacher traveled the whole country using every conceivable conveyance as a means to understand local conditions and to listen to the perspectives of Indian peasants. As a former farm laborer in England, Schumacher had obvious advantages in being able to relate to ordinary peasants in India. Upon completion of his visits to the countryside he prepared a *small* memorandum to the Indian government. Their planners were then assembled for a two-day meeting to discuss Schumacher's thoughts and suggestions. It was at this meeting that he introduced his notion of intermediate technology. Initially his idea received a cool reception from Indian planners. Fifteen months later, however, an all-India conference was held specifically focusing on the issue of inter-mediate technology. It was at this meeting that the Indians expressed their preference for the terminology, appropriate technology. Thus, Schumacher's formidable challenge to existing economic paradigms derives directly from his experience as a consultant to Burma and India.

Schumacher also had advising experience in Africa. He was once asked by the President of Zambia to help assess problems related to the implementation of a Five Year Plan. After extensive discussions with many Zambian farmers, Schumacher found that they lacked packaging material to send eggs to the local market. To Schumacher's disdain he found that a major European multinational corporation had a virtual monopoly on the production of egg trays. Their egg trays were also not suited to conditions in

Zambia. Schumacher thus helped the Zambians come up with their own design of egg tray, and assisted them in the development of a local plant to manufacture such trays as a means to eliminate reliance on the European multinational corporation.

Hazel Henderson of the Princeton Center for Alternative Futures, and a leading proponent of soft energy paths, elegantly describes the impact of Shumacher's work and thought:

> Most of all it is the clarity of Fritz Schumacher's vision that electrified millions and galvanized them into action for a saner future. He broke the spell laid on citizens by the empty expertise and mystifications of intellectual mercenaries. . . . Fritz Schumacher helped us all to reconceptualize our situation in the now-declining industrial era. . . . But, in addition, he pointed to the new path we must travel. This is the dynamism of his work. Intermediate and appropriate technology are now the rallying cries of broad political movements in the United States, Canada, West Europe, and Japan, as well as of rapidly developing industries in conservation, recycling, solar and wind power, and bio-conversion. In Australia and New Zealand Schumacher's ideas underlie two new political parties, one of which captured five percent of the vote at the last election.[67]

We have stressed in this book project continuity and the institutionalization of innovations as major criteria for assessing the success of international advisers and consultants. Though Schumacher died in Switzerland in 1977, his projects and ideas persist. The London-based Intermediate Technology Development Group continues to receive thousands of requests for assistance from around the world.

The irony of the Schumacher case study is that of what we term reverse impact or circular advising. While Schumacher may have directly contributed while serving as a consultant in India and Burma, certainly his major impact was advising the industrial world based on the insights he acquired from Burma and India. Thus, the Schumacher case vividly exemplifies the concept of circular advising. Advising is not a one-way linear process. The adviser may be influenced even more than he influences. Thus international advisers are a potential conduit for the multidirectional and circular transfer of creative ideas transnationally and cross-culturally.

Central to Schumacher's success as an international adviser and consultant is his respect for the dignity and wisdom of ordinary citizens, particularly peasants. Schumacher was consistently critical of those who ignore traditional values and the traditional wisdom of mankind. The essence of the Schumacher approach is perhaps best summed up in his own words:

> no, if I want to help I must be genuine about it and become a poor man myself to understand it, and then I quickly realize what fits.[68]

Lessons To Be Drawn From Exemplary Case Studies

These case studies suggest a number of lessons which can be briefly summarized as follows:

1. Many of our exemplary consultants are what have been commonly called 'Inners and outers.' They move easily between academia and the world of *praxis*. They have a remarkable flexibility which enables them to work effectively in diverse organizational settings. As the distinctions between the public and private sectors become more blurred, this type of talent becomes increasingly important.

2. *Protean* adaptability is another distinctive trait of our exemplary consultants. Many have several operating cultures, and they have a genuine awareness of the critical need to *adapt* both their professional behavior and their expertise to new situations in other cultures. Failures in the field of international consulting most frequently result from a mindless mechanical adoption of Western approaches in non-Western settings. The consultants' appreciation and valuing of cultural diversity makes them open and willing to listen and learn from others, whatever their culture or status. This trait, perhaps more than any other, facilitates communicating with both peasants and princes.

3. Another common pattern among our exemplary consultants is an ability to transcend conventional disciplinary boundaries. For example, W. Edwards Deming in his work integrated expertise from physics, statistics, industrial engineering, and business administration. Wolf Ladejinsky combined a knowledge of practical 'development anthropology' and agricultural economics. No single disciplinary label could do justice in describing his impressive body of practical writing related to the crucially important policy question of land reform.

4. Our most successful consultants have the 'Samurai' trait of being able to penetrate other cultures by becoming close to those being served or affected by policies under debate. Whatever the risks or physical discomforts involved, they seek to understand genuine conditions *in the field*.

5. Finally, and of special significance, is the ability to inspire others to 'dream the impossible dream' or to explore new horizons. Deming's urging the Japanese to become quality-conscious was precisely that type of inspiration. Similarly, Norman Borlaug and Sir John Crawford inspired others to achieve highly significant agricultural innovation.

Notes

1. L. A. Ross, Collaborative research for more effective foreign assistance, *World Development*, **16**, 233–4 (1988).
2. This case is based on the book by L. Currie, *The Role of Economic Advisers in Developing Countries*, Greenwood, Westport, Connecticut, 1981.

3. This case is based primarily on two sources: A. CURLE, *Planning for Education in Pakistan: A Personal Case Study,* Harvard University Press, 1966; A. CURLE, *Educational Planning: The Adviser's Role,* IIEP, Paris, Fundamentals of Educational Planning Series, no. 8, 1968.

4. Archive of Philip Coombs at the Hanna Collection, the Hoover Institution, Stanford University.

5. This case study is based on M. B. BULLOCK's excellent historical study of the Rockefeller Foundation's medical technical assistance to China in the prewar period, M. B. BULLOCK, *An American Transplant: The Rockefeller Foundation and Peking Union Medical College,* University of California Press, Berkeley, California, 1980, particularly pp.134–61. Also relevant is the study by E. R. BROWN, Rockefeller medicine in China: professionalism and imperialism, in R. ARNOVE (editor), *Philanthropy and Cultural Imperialism;* and P. J. DONALDSON, Foreign intervention in medical education: a case study of the Rockefeller Foundation's involvement in a Thai medical school, *International Journal of Health Services,* **6,** 251–70 (1976).

6. M. B. BULLOCK, pp.140–1.

7. Ibid., p.212.

8. Ibid., p.216.

9. Ibid., p.219.

10. Ibid., p.83.

11. Ibid., p.146. See also V. HEISER, *An American Doctor's Odyssey: Adventures in Forty-five Countries,* W. W. Norton, New York, 1936, p.275.

12. M. B. BULLOCK, p.161.

13. Cited in T. DOOLEY, *Dr. Tom Dooley's Three Great Books,* Farrar, Straus and Cudahy, New York, 1980, p.277.

14. Ibid., p.288.

15. *Current Biography 1957,* pp.148–50.

16. Ibid.

17. Cited in T. DOOLEY, p.383.

18. This case study is based on R. LANGDON, Harry Maude: shy proconsul dedicated Pacific historian, in N. GUNSON (editor), *The Changing Pacific: Essays in Honor of H. E. Maude* Oxford University Press, Melbourne, 1978.

19. This case is based on the following materials: personal documents generously shared by Professor Deming; W. E. DEMING, A view of how quality began in Japan, in *Quality, Productivity, and Competitive Position,* Center for Advanced Engineering Study, MIT, Cambridge, Massachusetts, pp.99–110 (1982); W. M. RINGLE, The American who remade 'made in Japan,' *Nation's Business,* **69,** 67–70 (1981); S. PARKER, Dr. Deming: quality guru, *Friendly Exchange,* **4,** 44–45 (1984).

20. This case study is based primarily on L. J. WALINSKY (editor), *The Selected Papers of Wolf Ladejinsky: Agrarian Reform as Unfinished Business,* Oxford University Press, New York, 1977, particularly pp.3–22. The volume includes a helpful chronological bibliography of Ladejinsky's work, pp.580–5. Other writers have also commented on Ladejinsky's work. We found the following particularly helpful in preparing this case: R. CHAMBERS, Rural poverty unperceived: problems and remedies, *World Development,* **9,** 1–19; R. MOODY, Land reform in Taiwan, in H. TEAF and P. FRANCK (editors), *Hands Across Frontiers: Case Studies in Technical Cooperation,* Cornell University Press, Ithaca, New York, 1955; T. OGURA, *Can Japanese Agriculture Survive?* Agricultural Policy Research Center, Tokyo, 1982.

21. Cited in M. MINKLER, Consultants or colleagues—role of United States population advisors in India, p.417.

22. R. J. LIFTON, *Boundaries,* p.44.

23. W. GOODENOUGH, *Cooperation in Change.*

24. L. J. WALINSKY, p.20.

25. Ibid.

26. See M. MINKLER.

27. L. J. WALINSKY, p.18.

28. Ibid.

29. L. J. WALINSKY, p.6.

30. H. CLEVELAND *et al., The Overseas Americans;* I. T. SANDERS, *Interprofessional Training*

Goals for Technical Assistance Personnel Abroad; Report, Council on Social Work Education, New York, 1959.
31. L. J. WALINSKY, p.16.
32. R. CHAMBERS, p.11.
33. L. J. WALINSKY, p.18.
34. Ibid.
35. T. OGURA, p.221.
36. R. MOODY, p.177.
37. L. R. BROWN, Nobel Peace Prize: developer of high-yield wheat receives award, *Science,* **170**, 519 (1970).
38. *Current Biography 1971,* p.52.
39. A. ANDERSON, The green revolution lives, *The New York Times Magazine,* 27 April 1975, p.15.
40. L. R. BROWN, p.519.
41. A. ANDERSON, p.83.
42. L. R. BROWN, p.519.
43. *Current Biography 1971,* p.52.
44. S. and K. SEEGERS, p.135.
45. A. ANDERSON, p.80.
46. Ibid.
47. Ibid.
48. W. D. HOPPER, An interlude with Indian development, in L. T. EVANS and J. D. B. MILLER (editors), *Essays in Honor of Sir John Crawford,* ANU Press, Sydney, 1987, p.171.
49. This case study is based on an excellent anthology of commentary on the life and work of Sir John Crawford, L. T. EVANS and J. D. B. MILLER, *Essays in Honor of Sir John Crawford.*
50. W. D. HOPPER, p.162.
51. Ibid., pp.163–4.
52. Ibid., p.168.
53. Ibid., p.170.
54. Ibid., p.171.
55. Ibid.
56. Sir John's role in coordinating and fostering applied international agricultural research is described by L. T. EVANS, A Malthusian optimist at work on the world food problem, in L. T. EVANS and J. D. B. MILLER (editors), pp.173–89.
57. An intimate view of Sir John's personal style is provided by J. D. B. MILLER, The man, in L. T. EVANS and J. D. B. MILLER (editors), pp.191–203.
58. Ibid., p.192.
59. Ibid., p.193.
60. H. CLEVELAND *et al., The Overseas Americans.*
61. J. D. B. MILLER, p.196.
62. L. EVANS, p.173.
63. A. WILDAVSKY, *Speaking Truth to Power.*
64. Major sources for this case study are as follows: G. McCROBIE, Preface, in E. F. SCHUMACHER, *Good Work,* Harper & Row, New York, 1979; H. HENDERSON, The legacy of E. F. Schumacher, *Environment,* **20**, 30–6 (1978).
65. E. F. SHUMACHER, *Small is Beautiful: Economics as if People Mattered,* Harper & Row, New York, 1975.
66. E. F. SCHUMACHER, *A Guide for the Perplexed,* Abacus, London, 1978.
67. H. HENDERSON, p.35.
68. E. F. SHUMACHER, *Good Work,* p.133.

PART V

Cross-Cultural Advising and Consulting as a Profession

CHAPTER 10

The Emerging Professions of
International Consulting
and Development Assistance

In case after case of the Americans we rated on over-all job performance, technical skill loomed as a critical factor. . . . His expertness
must include not only a sound grounding in his own speciality, but the
imagination and adaptability of the general practitioner in a much
wider field of *professional* [italics ours] activity. He must constantly
adapt his skill to new and challenging situations—not just situations
that he has never encountered before, but situations that may never
have risen before (Harlan Cleveland).[1]

A serious interest in overseas careers and professions began to emerge about
1960, and was marked by the publication of two books: *The Ugly American*
and *The Overseas Americans*.[2] The first was a best-seller and had an impact
on the national consciousness, as reflected by the subsequent film and the
incorporation of the title in the popular culture. Unfortunately, the message
of the book was muted by its popularization, since the term 'ugly American'
was dominated by its downside meanings: rich Americans living in segre-
gated 'golden ghettos,' and knowing neither the native language nor the
indigenous culture. This vulgarization ignored the paradox that the actual
'ugly American' in the book was an agricultural engineer from Iowa who
practiced his art in rural areas, taught appropriate technology, and was a
model of cultural adaptability.

When John F. Kennedy introduced his concept of the Peace Corps, his
strategy for the Volunteer's lifestyle was a rejection of the Ugly American
syndrome. PCVs would, in his famous phrase, 'speak the same language, eat
the same food, and live in the same houses' as the indigenous peoples with
whom they worked.

The *Overseas Americans* was an academic treatise that sprang from the
discovery, based on 1960 census figures, that 1 percent of all US citizens were
not only living, but earning their livings, abroad. A more or less permanent
set of a substantial number of US citizens residing overseas as expatriates
was a noteworthy new development in our historical experience. The book
was based on interviews with 244 individuals living in Europe, Asia, Africa,

135

Latin America, and the Middle East. These interviews included businessmen, missionaries, diplomats and other civil servants, and teachers and university personnel. The authors were interested to discover the elements of successful performance overseas. They found that successful performance depended on a large number of traits which, for purposes of convenience, they divided into five groups: technical skill, belief in mission, sense for politics (the art of the possible), organizational skill (later to become known as institution-building), and cultural empathy.[3] *The Overseas Americans* immediately gained a reputation for touting a formula, the five-finger exercise, as the key to success. However controversial it became, nonetheless its deeper purpose was to explore the educational roots of such performance, and it examined in detail a number of international and foreign area-culture programs in US universities, seeking the educational high road to success. To some extent the book was an extension of themes explored nearly a decade earlier in *Training for Specialized Mission Personnel*.[4] As such, it soon joined in a familiar controversy which we might label 'the recruitment solution versus the education argument.' The issue was addressed in an article by Egbert Wengert in *The Public Administration Review*, entitled, 'Can we train for overseasmanship?[5] 'Yes and no' was the reply, but mostly no, since some of the basic attitudes and skills, such as those marking belief in mission and cultural empathy, likely arise from deep within personality structures, and are thus largely inborn. This was a widely held, but intuitive, view which, in a simplified reading, tended to transfer the problem into one of recruitment and selection (that is, the people with the right combination of experiences and skills are out there; all that is needed is to attract them into the program). Another and even more salient critique of *The Overseas Americans* was that the five-finger exercise did not isolate successful performance overseas, but identified traits marking the successful performer everywhere, even in entirely domestic settings.

Only a few years later such criticisms grew with the completion of 'The problem of training Americans for service abroad,' and a series of four related research projects at as many universities based on techniques of retrospective interview process.[6] Although these studies tended to confirm an educational and training gap of major proportions, they did not succeed in disproving the null hypothesis: there is no significant difference between professional service at home and abroad. Nonetheless, those who were looking for the establishment of a new profession of overseas service thought they may have found an important beginning in the United States Peace Corps. Moreover, in an extensive series of recent interviews in Canada, to jump forward to the 1980s, Clarence Thurber elicited a near-unanimous opinion that 'international development' has, after 35 years, already achieved the status of an important career or profession.

A parallel question that has to be explored is whether international consulting and advising (the development assistance professions) constitutes a collection of related professions or subprofessions, or whether, in any context, they can be considered a multiplex profession. The former view is the predominant and most widely held one. That is, an engineer is an engineer first, and an international consultant second. This perspective provides the fewest conceptual problems, and it is strongly held in the United States and other industrial countries, particularly by the recruiters at headquarters. Thus, to the extent that individuals may be identified as experts in the field of health, agriculture, administration, or education, their expertise in international consulting or in development assistance may not be considered as expertise at all, but merely as a series of 'pluses' or 'extras.' This suggests that expertise is almost always defined by domestic criteria.

On the other hand, we have also observed that the foreign experiences of consultants tend to draw them together. Professionals who have served, for example, in India, or Nigeria, or Brazil commonly express a feeling that they have more in common than with members of their separate professions who are domestically oriented.

Thus, the international consulting or development assistance professions are emerging as a group of closely related ones, somewhat akin to 'the health professions' (doctors, dentists, nurses, and technical specialists) and the 'helping professions' (psychologists, social workers, psychiatrists, and supporting personnel.) We may assume that this emerging integration is caused by the impact of cross-cultural service on professional practice, arising out of the common experience of working in developing countries.

Some fundamental relationships between profession and society are raised in this discussion. For example, profession as such may be distinguished from other vocations because it contains an ethical element—service to society, rather than an activity carried on primarily for profit. But other elements are also central to professions: (1) a recognized body of knowledge which is applied through a practice; (2) a means for the advancement of this body of knowledge, through research and experimentation; (3) a means for sharing research results, as through a professional journal; (4) a means for exchanging information among practitioners, as in a professional society and its meetings; and (5) a means for educating and socializing young and aspiring professionals, as in professional schools.

In fields where a client's health, or even life, may be at stake, or where confidential relations must exist, the state asserts the right to examine and to license members of the profession. Such professions generally take the position that they must be self-governing (only a professional can make the necessary judgments). For this purpose codes of ethical conduct are elaborated, and committees are appointed to deal with charges of unethical practice, and to invoke sanctions. In Appendix II we present an explicit code of ethics for international advisers and consultants.

Indeed the crux of the meaning of profession is carried in its basic definition; for example, 'a vocation or occupation requiring advanced

IEDC—K

training in some liberal art or science, usually involving intellectual rather than manual labor . . . especially medicine, law, theology (formerly called the learned professions).'[7] While 'professional' is defined as 'of, engaged in, or worthy of the high standards of, a profession.' The eminent sociologist Talcott Parsons wrote that profession requires 'an institutional means of assuring that such competence will be put to socially responsible use,' and asserts that profession is centered in universities and research institutes and that 'the professional complex . . . has already become the most important single component in the structure of modern societies.'[8]

Three or four basic professions have set the pattern—theology (clergy) medicine (doctors), and the law (lawyers). We may inquire, then, to what extent are the emerging professions of international consulting and advising (or development assistance), similar to these basic professions? And is this emerging profession one or many?

Evidence comes out on both sides of the question. We continue to find that individuals are selected primarily for their expertise in the standard disciplines or professions. But we also find an increasing emphasis on cultural empathy and understanding ('knows the language,' for example, and 'has worked in Country X on numerous occasions.')

There is scattered evidence elsewhere of the impact of overseas service on professional concerns. In professional meetings, such as the American Society for Public Administration, for example, there is a continuing Section on International and Comparative Adminstration, which sponsors panel discussions at annual meetings. The American Educational Research Association also has a special International Studies Section. Other professional societies may have only an occasional panel devoted to the international concerns of the society and its members. There may be an occasional article in the leading professional journal of the profession or, even more occasionally, a special issue devoted to a series of related concerns. In the leading professional schools we typically encounter one scholar who teaches the 'international course' of the curriculum, although in most cases several faculty members may have had foreign assignments. Such is the case at Boalt Hall, the Law School of the University of California, and many other similar institutions. But many professional schools have none, and there appears to have been a considerable regression in this area over the past decade.

In sum, the international and foreign experiences of professors and consultants have made some impact, at least, on the total professional infrastructure. But this has been a minimal impact. Since by far the majority of all US college students are enrolled in professional schools, this fact has great implications for the knowledge and attitudes of educated Americans about the world around them. The vast majority of professionals are educated on the assumption that they will practice at home, or, as in the licensed professions, in the same state. There is also the ethnocentric view that their 'body of knowledge' is universally applicable.

This is one of the reasons that a multidisciplinary, or a multiprofessional approach, may be somewhat more promising. By creating the necessary critical mass (in the educational and training audience) we can focus attention on the special problems of the development assistance and the international consulting professions. And we can see that, by trial and error, a good many attempts have been made along those interdisciplinary lines.

The Society for International Development (SID) is one of the leading examples. Founded in the mid-1950s, largely by veterans of the Marshall Plan, The Truman Point 4 Program, The World Bank, and the United Nations Technical Assistance Program, the SID has grown over the years to become a truly international society. Its headquarters is located in Rome, and its annual meetings have been held in New Delhi, Cairo, and Paris, as well as in New York City and Washington. The SID's journal *Development: Seeds of Change* (formerly *International Development Review*) is devoted to publishing articles written by practitioners who represent a number of professions and disciplines, articles that are often case studies of particular projects, of what worked or didn't work, in various cross-cultural settings. The largest number of SID members probably belong to what may be called the corps group of the development assistance professions, namely agency and program administrators, located in such organizations as the US Agency for International Development; the Foreign Agricultural Service of the US Department of Agriculture; the Canadian International Development Agency; the World Bank Group; the United Nations Development Programme; various specialized agencies such as the FAO, WHO, Unesco, UNICEF, ILO, ICAO, and others; as well as development administrators and technical specialists in various countries such as India, Tanzania, and Brazil.

The SID constitutes evidence of the existence of a group of development-oriented professions (including agriculturalists, educators, administrators, national and regional planners, health-science educators, social workers, and others). These people, who have become international consultants and advisers, currently total about 370,000 world-wide, including those from the West, the Soviet Union and Eastern Europe, and members of the TCDC group. If we include members of host country organizations that work as counterparts to them, the total number of individuals involved might multiply by a factor of ten. In either case this phenomenon, viewed from the perspective of several decades, has certainly involved as many as several million individuals.

In addition, considerable research has been done on the problems of development and of development assistance. This has been sponsored by official agencies, universities, and research institutes. The number of journals with the word 'development' in their titles has increased markedly in recent years, and related articles appear with somewhat more frequency in the standard journals (e.g. *The American Economic Review*) as well as in the area-and-culture journals (e.g. *The Journal of Asian Studies, The Latin American Research Review*). Special research projects have been carried out by a number of land grant universities, such as Michigan State University, the University of Wisconsin (especially through its well-known Land Tenure Center) and Oregon State University (weed research in South America) but also in other universities such as the Center for International Studies at MIT, Harvard's Institute for International Developent (HIID), along with its International Advisory Service (both apparently an outgrowth of Harvard's participation in the Pakistan Planning Board Project in the 1950s and 1960s). The Harvard activities have helped to create the professions of Development Economist and Development Administrator.

Certain professional schools have given special impetus to the training of young professionals for overseas work. They have done this alongside the preparation of foreign students for work in their homelands. The Maxwell School of Syracuse and the School of Public Administration at the University of Southern California pioneered technical assistance in their field, mainly under contracts with the US foreign aid program. Others also participated, such as Michigan State University and the University of Oregon. As a result of the work of the Comparative Administration Group of ASPA during the 1960s and 1970s, Development Administration was recognized as a new speciality, reinforced by George Gant's book of the same name published in the late 1970s.[9]

At one time the School of Public Health at Harvard provided leadership in the international aspects of its field, largely because of the active interest of its then dean and several faculty members. In the field of agriculture, Cornell's International Agricultural Program and the University of Wisconsin have both established high standards of performance. Though highly selective, these examples show clearly the significant role of universities in these training activites. They are all efforts undertaken by particular schools, but typically involved several disciplines and professions. A leading anthropologist, Benjamin Paul, was central to Harvard's effort in public health, while political scientists and economists were part of the team at Syracuse. Thus these programs were characterized by important interdisciplinary cooperation.

A major example of this interdisciplinary trend was a study, mounted in the late 1960s and early 1970s, of the international role of the professional school. A number of preliminary reports were prepared in which pairs of professional schools were examined and compared, such as public and business administration; medicine and public health; agriculture and law; and others. These were widely circulated and commented upon. Ultimately, they led to a series of regional conferences, and to the publication of an influential volume edited by Irwin Sanders, *The Professional School and World Affairs.*[10] This study revealed that professional curricula do not adequately reflect the reality that many graduates will practice in many parts of the world.

A number of international internship programs have been instituted to provide something of a bridge between domestic and international service. For example, the Maxwell School for a number of years ran a program in which young administrators served in South Asia and in Africa as assistant district officers. (The project was financed by the Ford Foundation.) Robert Edwards, later president of Carlton College, was the director of the program. In addition a number of universities, particularly those having contracts abroad, found room for internships, including Syracuse in Nigeria, Michigan State in the same country, Indiana University in Thailand, Princeton in Asia, and the Volunteers in Asia program of Stanford. Sometimes a sympathetic AID Director such as Robert Culbertson in Peru, or James Watson, head of the Public Administration Program there, or a Ford representative, such as Douglas Ensminger in India or George Gant in Pakistan, made room on their staff for interns. While Clarence Thurber was a professor at Penn State in the mid-1960s some of his graduate students benefited from such internships, and later wrote Ph.D. dissertations based on their experiences and documents collected.

The largest and potentially most significant intern-like arrangement, for careers in the development assistance professions, is undoubtedly the US Peace Corps. Alongside the somewhat similar programs sponsored by European governments, Japan, and by the UN in its Volunteer Corps, one of the effects of these programs is to provide pre-professional experiences for a large number of young men and women. For example, their experience represents one of the most thorough language training programs in US history.[11] A similar statement could be written about training in problems of cross-cultural adjustment, and in understanding the inner workings of other cultures 'as though from the inside.' Because of the high degree of idealism and commitment found in this group, it is often the case that many former PCVs aspire to become full professionals working cross-culturally and internationally. Former volunteers have been active in development-oriented organizations such as the Transcentury Corporation and Volunteers for International Technical Assistance (VITA).

Such a concept, for example, inspired the development of Study Fellowships for International Development (SFID), a consortium of ten US universities (Harvard, Columbia, Cornell, Penn State, North Carolina, Chicago, Wisconsin, Oregon, Stanford, and UCLA). The program, financed by the Ford Foundation,[12] was open to returning PCVs who wished to attend one of the leading professional schools in the country, take related work in development theory and technical assistance practice, and become available for work in the developing countries. About 350 Fellows benefited from scholarships during SFID's existence, 1963–70. A somewhat similar program was administered at the University of Hawaii during this time, called International Development Fellows.

Many of the efforts that began to establish a professional dimension to development assistance efforts were, as we have seen, carried out in the

1960s and 1970s. There were, however, both conceptual and practical difficulties. Among the first category there was no readily available model against which a career service, or a professional practice, could be based. Could we use the US Foreign Service as a model, or the British colonial office, or the experiences of missionaries abroad, or of business abroad?[13] All of these provided some clues, but none was more than analogous to the requirements. Thus it was necessary to proceed on a trial-and-error basis. In terms of the practical difficulties, whether reforming curricula of professional schools, or financing internships or fellowship programs, foundations did play their traditional pump-priming role, but were unwilling to do so indefinitely. Significant support from the private sector for such enterprises has failed to materialize on any large scale.

Moreover, the majority of such efforts had come to an end by the mid-1970s, suggesting the following: (1) attitudes changed as a result of the Vietnam War and its aftermath; (2) priorities of governmental grant programs shifted, responding to the needs of the civil rights movement and for inner-city renewal; and (3) scholarly and professional interests changed, at least temporarily, in response to these changes in national priorities.

Nevertheless, the beginnings of a professional infrastructure had been set in place, and many of these features persist. The period since 1974, following the end of the Vietnam War, may be seen as a period of consolidation. Now the question has to be faced: are we analyzing this experience in preparation for future developments? Or will this experience remain in the relatively unexamined and untested realm which has characterized it to date?

As we ponder this question and its implications we may, as a preliminary measure, take note of some of the changes that appear to have overtaken the profession in the past 20 years. More than 20 years ago, in 1965, the profession was growing rapidly, and it was possible for James Grant (then with AID, now Director of UNICEF) at a Princeton Conference to predict that within the near future, that it would encompass 75,000–80,000 individuals in the West.* At that time it seemed that the growth of US, UK, and UNDP programs would continue, at least on a modest scale, for the next several decades. There was a close association between AID and the US university which became subject to critical scrutiny—this scrutiny turning on the role of academic freedom under government contracts. A hope existed that the plenitude of government contracts, and opportunities for campus-based consultants, would have a major feedback effect on university curricula.[14] Although aid contracts tended to be located at US land grant universities they were by no means exclusively so. Moreover, The Ford Foundation had funded a number of such contracts, at least one with the explicit purpose of eliciting the feedback effect. An example was the contract between the University of California and the National University of Indonesia in the field of economic development.

---

* Grant was remarkably prescient; cf. Table 1.1, which indicates that the number of advisers from OECD countries in 1985 was roughly 83,000.

In sum, many of us in development-oriented fields believed we were laying the foundations for a long-term, career-oriented, professional approach.

Currently we see many changes which have overtaken the field. Though the profession is certainly growing in countries such as Japan, Australia, Canada, and the Netherlands, in many ways it is now smaller (in the US) and more compact than would have been foreseen. In some ways this may reflect the ideological strife—over Vietnam, over relations in the aid business with our European associates, and over direct versus indirect competition with the Soviet Union (in other words, the relationship of economic and social development to military development). These conditions have contributed to a certain hard-nosed, less hopeful quality of mind and spirit, than previously existed. This too may partially account for the declines in development advisory personnel from the US, UK, and France since the mid- and late 1960s (see Fig. A.1).

As mentioned earlier, a predominant role in the profession has been taken by administrators and program directors. Technical specialists as consultants were king of the walk in an earlier day, but division chairpersons, program officers, and mission directors have since come into their own. A newer development, however, is the growth to prominence of development scientists, such as Norman Borlaug, and aid statesmen, such as Ralph Cummings, Sr, and the able group who sit on the Technical Advisory Committee. The latter advises the World Bank Group of the financing of 13 research centers in agricultural development—the IRRIs and CIMMYTs of the world.

There is a new emphasis on short-term consultantships, the two-week, one-month, three-month variety that in the 1950s and 1960s would almost certainly have involved a one- or two-year contract. Much of this results from the pressure of budgets, but also results from the increase in experience and analytical capacity of a more fully professionalized corps of consultants. Concomitantly there has been a significant diminution in university participation, both in corporate contracts and in the use of individual professors. This has severely impacted the small corps of development specialists in the professional schools. At the same time there has been a great increase in consulting firms specializing in overseas work, such as the Transcentury Corporation.

Some of these developments were foreseen at the aforementioned Princeton Conference. In fact some of them were more or less directly predicted by James Grant, Robert Oshins, and others, of US AID. However, the diminished role of the universities and professional schools (although relations with many land grant institutions remain and have been strengthened) were not so clearly foreseen.

In addition, PVOs seem to be playing a much larger role in overseas programs. In some ways they are more attractive to idealistic young professionals, for example, those coming out of the Peace Corps. They are sometimes seen to be less a part of the foreign policy establishment.

In some ways, development professionals feel lucky to have survived at all; this may account for the somewhat less hopeful, less optimistic context in which professionals now operate. But alternatively the context may be more realistic, more tested, more proven over the long run. The earlier period may be characterized as one of the gifted amateur; the current one of the hardened professional.

In the next chapter we specify an explicit knowledge base underlying the emerging professions of international advising and development assistance.

Notes

1. H. CLEVELAND *et al.*, *The Overseas Americans*, pp.128–9.
2. W. LEDERER and E. BURDICK, *The Ugly American*; H. CLEVELAND *et al.*, *The Overseas Americans*.
3. H. CLEVELAND *et al.*, p.124.
4. W. S. SAYRE and C. E. THURBER, *Training for Specialized Mission Personnel*, Public Administration Service, Chicago, Illinois, 1952.
5. E. S. WENGERT, Can we train for overseasmanship? *Public Administration Review*, **18**, 136–9 (1958).
6. See, for example, C. E. THURBER, The problem of training Americans for service abroad in U.S. government technical cooperation programs. Unpublished doctoral dissertation, Stanford University, *Disseration Abstracts*, **22**, 1704 (1961); G. M. GUTHRIE and R. E. SPENCER, *American Professions and Overseas Technical Assistance*, Pennsylvania State University, University Park, 1965; F. BYRNES, *Americans in Technical Assistance*.
7. *Webster's New World Dictionary of the American Language*, World Publishing, New York, 2nd edn, 1970, p.1134.
8. T. PARSONS, Professions, in D. STILLS (editor), *International Encyclopedia of the Social Sciences*, Macmillan, New York, 1968, pp.536–47.
9. G. F. GANT, *Development Administration: Concepts, Goals, Methods*, University of Wisconsin Press, Madison, Wisconsin, 1979.
10. EDUCATION AND WORLD AFFAIRS, *The Professional School and World Affairs*, University of New Mexico Press, Albuquerque, New Mexico, 1968. With respect to training individuals for overseas technical assistance work, see C. E. THURBER, pp.171–350; T. F. TRAIL, *Education of Development Technicians: A Guide to Training Programs*, Praeger, New York, 1968. Of direct relevance to the important issue of evaluating training efforts is the report, Conference on Evaluation of Personal Effectiveness in Overseas Technical Assistance Programs, held in New York City, 28–29 January 1965, sponsored by the Carnegie Endowment of International Peace. See also the report, Conference on the role of the younger professional person in overseas development programs, held at the Princeton Inn, 24–26 September 1965, sponsored by the Ford Foundation.
11. G. RICE, *The Bold Experiment: JFK's Peace Corps.*
12. For an intensive discussion of the Ford Foundation's role in promoting international studies through its International Training and Research Program, see R. A. McCAUGHEY, *International Studies and Academic Enterprise: A Chapter in the Enclosure of American Learning*, Columbia University Press, New York, 1984. See also F. J. SUTTON, Philanthropy, politics, patronage, *Daedalus: Journal of the American Academy of Arts and Sciences*, **116**, 41–91 (1987).
13. See G. CUNNINGHAM, *The Management of Aid Agencies*, Croom Helm in association with the Overseas Development Institute, London, 1974, p.177.
14. See D. BOCK, Technical assistance abroad, in *Beyond the Ivory Tower: Social Responsibilities of the Modern University*, Harvard University Press, Cambridge, Massachusetts and London, 1982, pp.195–213; P. STREETEN, Reflections on the role of the university and the developing countries, *World Development*, **16**, 639–40 (1988).

CHAPTER 11

Knowledge Foundations for the Profession of International Consulting and Advising

Instead of overvaluing and overrewarding purely abstract theorizing and modeling, judged not by their usefulness, realism or relevance but by the standards of excellence evolved within the professional in-group, we shall encompass in our valuations and rewards the ability to apply our minds to problems of the real world, and to communicate our insights to a wider public and those responsible for action. . . . We shall value the ability to listen, to be open to different methods and approaches. Arrogance will give way to humility. Without becoming soft, we shall become less rigid, more flexible. Rigor will replace rigidity, and flexibility mushiness (Paul Streeten).[1]

One of the major elements characterizing a profession is the existence of a specific underlying body of knowledge. There is an important body of knowledge and skills essential for individuals engaged in international consulting and advising in developing countries. Our specification of these skill domains derives primarily from the empirical work and literature review underlying this book. Mastery of the proposed domains certainly implies a continual commitment to life-long learning.

Professional Specialty

Each international development consultant should have a professional specialty such as biotechnology, water resource management, public health, tropical medicine, computer science, or management information systems. It is such a specialty that provides the basis for the sharing of expertise. Knowledge and understanding of other cultures will mean little, if individuals lack excellence in a professional specialty. Thus the profession of international consultant has dual dimensions. There is a specific professional speciality complemented by the knowledge and competency relevant to adapting and transmitting expertise cross-culturally and internationally.

145

Knowledge and Understanding of the Development Literature

There is now available an extensive and diverse literature on development. Guy Gran has compiled a comprehensive bibliography of such materials.[2] Individuals should be familiar with the major alternative approaches to development, including, for example, modernization theories, dependency theories, Marxism, and newly emerging paradigms transcending both capitalist and Marxist ideologies. In one of the most thoughtful documents to come out of the UN, Sir Robert Jackson of Australia, in reviewing the UN's development efforts, comments that there are too few, within or outside the system, who genuinely comprehend development.[3]

Knowledge of the Literature on Technical Progress and Cultural Change

The experiences of recent decades have provided noteworthy examples of success and failure in introducing technical innovations in traditional cultures. Major writers such as Robert Textor, Ward Goodenough, George Foster, Glynn Cochrane, Ronald Nairn, Clifford Geertz, A. H. Niehoff, E. H. Spicer, Irwin Sanders, and others have described key issues related to technical change in the developing countries.[4] It is important for those engaged in development work overseas to be aware of this literature. Otherwise the same mistakes may be repeated, and we do not learn from failure. Mastery of this literature also provides an important institutional memory.

Competency in Cross-cultural Communication

Technical skills, no matter how outstanding, are meaningless if they cannot be communicated cross-culturally. The important German social scientist, Jürgen Habermas, has introduced the concept of communicative competence.[5] He emphasizes genuine dialogue freed from domination. Apart from cognitive verbal skills, individuals must be sensitive to the nuances of nonverbal communication and related cross-cultural variations in communications patterns, as stressed in Chapter 4. There is an extensive literature which focuses on this type of competency. Some of the most important work in this area has been done by individuals such as Edward Hall, Richard Brislin, and Duane Archer.[6]

Foreign Language Proficiency

As a minimal professional qualification we feel that all members of the international consulting profession should be fluent in at least one foreign language. Many outstanding overseas advisers and consultants have been fluent in several foreign languages. Individuals in this field should also be aware of various techniques for acquiring foreign language proficiency such as the use of language informants. Without foreign language proficiency it is difficult to appreciate other cultures and other ways of thinking. Einstein and other scientists have argued that alternating the languages in which we think helps to avoid intellectual myopia.[7]

Understanding of Comparative Bureaucracy

Bureaucratic patterns in developing countries may diverge significantly from those in the US, Canada, Japan or Europe. Most overseas advising and consulting requires direct involvement in foreign bureaucracies. Advisers and consultants must have an in-depth understanding of how such bureaucracies function and how to get things done in such contexts. Though it is possible to study such patterns cognitively, practical experience in various developmental settings is also essential to enhance this particular form of understanding.

Diplomatic Competency and Negotiating Skills

Unfortunately there is a common view that diplomacy is practiced only by diplomats.[8] As suggested many years ago by the title of Jonathan Bingham's book on Point 4, *Shirtsleeve Diplomacy*, diplomacy is a crucial and critical skill required by overseas consultants and advisers.[9] In fact, in some respects this skill may be the most important. If individuals do not have adequate diplomatic skills, it is unlikely that people will respond positively to their expertise, suggestions, ideas, or training.[10] In fact, host country nationals may actively try to seek fault in the work of individuals who are rude and lacking in diplomatic tact. Reflecting on his experiences in Nepal, Ladejinsky notes the critical importance of diplomacy in providing advice:

> This sort of advice, badly expressed to a ruler, would almost necessarily close the door thence forth to the adviser, whether or not the advice was accepted.[11]

Related to diplomatic competence is another skill of special importance to international consultants and adviser, that is, the ability to be a successful negotiator. Negotiation in cross-cultural and international contexts can be quite complex. Lucian Pye, for example, has prepared a special book on negotiating with the Chinese, who have the reputation of being polite but tough negotiators.[12] The complexity of international negotiating results from the existence of multiple needs and interests which may be conflicting. Host countries often seek development assistance on the most concessional terms possible. International agencies, on the other hand, may frequently have an interest in the long-term recycling of limited development funds. There may also be disagreements about the nature of development projects supported, which must be negotiated.

Some of the most complex and difficult negotiations relate to economic policy advice from institutions such as the IMF. Advisers from the IMF may support strict austerity programs to reduce trade and budget deficits in LDCs. The implementation of such policies may have high political risks for the policy-makers and political leaders of a nation. Such policies may also have short-term adverse effects on poor people. To arrive at policies mutually satisfactory to both the international agency, the IMF in this case, and the host government is usually difficult.

Key personal traits related to successful negotiation include toughness, persistence, creativity, listening ability, and ability to make viable compromises. The genuine art of negotiation involves the combination of these traits with diplomacy and politeness appropriately adjusted to cross-cultural settings.

Culture-Area Knowledge

It is important that individuals have cultural awareness of the geographic area in which they are working. They should be familiar with a country's history and culture. Though they may not state it directly, the Japanese find it highly offensive when foreigners working in Japan show ignorance of their rich culture. Fortunately, there is extensive written material available on most cultures, such as the Human Relations Area Files, at first developed by Yale University, and the area handbooks developed by AUFS. Also, most countries now have a rich locally published literature on their culture, with which outside consultants should become familiar. The area studies programs of various universities provide this type of knowledge and understanding.

Knowledge of Literature on Consulting and Advising

Given the experiences of recent decades, a significant literature on the practice of overseas consulting and advising exists. The bibliography at the end of this book indicates how extensive this literature is. We consider it particularly important that the relevant works of such authors as Harlan Cleveland, Warren Ilchman, Angus Maddison, Guy Benveniste, M. Kubr, Francis Byrnes, H. Peter Guttmann, Reginald Bidgood, and Stig Lindholm[13] become the common knowledge shared by those professionally engaged in technical assistance. With the increased emphasis on TCDC, consultants and advisers from the developing countries can build on the extensive experience of others. Such historical awareness may help prevent the repetition of mistakes and blunders which can have adverse effects on humans and their communities.

Health Practices in the Tropics

Health conditions in the tropics may differ markedly from those found in Western industrial societies.[14] It is important for consultants and advisers to be aware of these differences. Simple health precautions, for example, can minimize the possibility of contracting diseases such as hepatitis, which can result in suffering and much loss of productive work time. Based on our experience, we consider that the US Peace Corps provides perhaps the best training in this important area. The physical aspects of Peace Corps training are noted for their rigor. Exercise opportunities in the tropics may diverge from common expectations. Individuals may need to try new sports played in largely developing countries. Badminton, for example, is commonly played in many parts of Southeast Asia, and squash is popular in countries such as Pakistan and Singapore. Participation in such sports may add to the variety and richness of overseas experience.

Awareness of Third World Literature

A rich Third World literature exists, but apparently few Westerners are aware of it. In fact, many writers from the developing nations have received Nobel Prizes in literature. Novels, short stories, and poems of Third World writers frequently deal with universal development problems such as human rights, inequality, corruption, and cross-cultural collisions. A knowledge and understanding of this literature helps to develop insight into development problems and create empathy for the diversity and depth of Third World cultures. A liberal education normally includes the reading of Shakespeare, Dickens, and Tolstoy, for example. Similarly a professionally educated international development specialist will be aware of the great writers of the Third World such as Neruda (Chile), Asturias (Guatemala), Lubis (Indonesia), and Rizal (Philippines).

The Interdisciplinary Foundations of the International Consulting Profession

Thus, as we consider the multiple demands for knowledge, attitudes, and skills required by the international consultant, and relate them to levels of experience and responsibility, we are once more brought to the realization that there is no magic answer, no formula that fits every situation or every individual. The Renaissance man no longer exists and cannot be re-created. Nevertheless, we have often been impressed by the breadth and depth of knowledge of some of our contemporaries, as reflected in our case studies

(Chapter 9). We are also aware that there is an important difference between academic knowledge, which often depends on precision, completeness, and comprehensiveness; and the knowledge required by practitioners, which often depends in addition on intuition, perspective, and insight. There is a difference between a detailed knowledge of history, that enables one to write a book, and a sense for history, that enables one to locate a technical assistance project in its historical perspective.

With these caveats in mind we divide our list of interdisciplinary foundations of knowledge into three overlapping but still distinct categories: basic, intermediate, and advanced, as indicated in Table 11.1. For each skill area listed, it is best to think in terms of a continuum of skill levels. True professionals in this field should strive to improve their proficiency in each major knowledge and competence area through a process of life-long learning.

Table 11.1 indicates the various academic disciplines most directly related to each major knowledge–competence area. The development of competence in each of these areas requires a broad interdisciplinary background as a complement to the individual's specialty and area of genuine expertise.

TABLE 11.1.   *The Interdisciplinary Foundations of the Knowledge Base for Development Assistant Professionals*

Knowledge areas	Relevant academic disciplines
Basic	
Technical or professional specialty	Education (Curriculum, Administration, Planning, Research); Biotechnology; Public Health; Agricultural Economics; Water Resource Management; Public Adminstration; etc.
Foreign language	Humanities, Linguistics, Literature
Cross-cultural communication	Anthropology, Psychology, Linguistics, Speech and Telecommunications
Development studies and technical change	Economics, Sociology, Political Science, Anthropology
Health practices in the tropics	Public Health, Tropical Medicine
Intermediate	
Cultural area knowledge and Third World literature	History, Anthropology, Humanities
Art of consulting and advising	Political Science, Diplomacy, Management Science, Rural Sociology
Program building and project development	Development Administration
Advanced	
Relationship of technical assistance to development	Economics, History, Public Administration, Political Science
Diplomatic competence and high level negotiating skills	International Relations, International Business

There is also the important issue of how individuals acquire these competencies and knowledge. Clearly a mix of formal training, on-the-job learning, adult education seminars and workshops, and a commitment to self-study, are essential for professional growth and success in the field of international consulting.[15]

We do not advocate the establishment of a professional body to certify individuals for this field based on examinations, degrees, or diplomas. Such an approach to professionalization often restricts access to individuals of lower socioeconomic background, or those who have developed their competencies through experience and self-study. We share Illich's view that excessive professionalization of this type can have adverse effects.

We would like to conclude by stressing that there are different mixes of knowledge, attitudes, and skills depending upon the particular organization, its style and mode of operation, and the variety of skills found in the organization itself. There is also the key issue of whether service in headquarters or overseas is involved. The complex fit of individual talents with clearly defined agency and country needs represents a major challenge to organizations involved in providing technical assistance for development.

Notes

1. P. STREETEN, p.640.
2. G. GRAN, A bibliographical guide to development studies, in G. GRAN (editor), *Development by People*, pp.357–470.
3. Sir R. JACKSON, *A Study of the Capacity of the United Nations Development System*, United Nations, Geneva, 1969.
4. R. B. TEXTOR (editor), *Cultural Frontiers of the Peace Corps*, MIT Press, Cambridge, Massachusetts, 1966; W. H. GOODENOUGH, *Cooperation in Change; an Anthropological Approach to Community Development*, Sage, New York, 1963; G. FOSTER, *Traditional Societies and Technological Change*, Harper & Row, New York, 1973; G. COCHRANE, *Development Anthropology*, Oxford University Press, New York, 1971; R. NAIRN, *International Aid to Thailand: The New Colonialism?* Yale University Press, New Haven, Connecticut, 1966; E. H. SPICER, *Human Problems in Technological Change*, Russell Sage Foundation, New York, 1952; and P. HILL, *Development Economics on Trial: the Anthropological Case for a Prosecution*, Cambridge University Press, Cambridge, 1986.
5. J. HABERMAS, Towards a theory of communicative competence, *Inquiry*, **13**, 205–18, 360–75 (1970).
6. See, for example, E. HALL, *The Silent Language*, Anchor Press, Garden City, New York, 1973; R. W. BRISLIN, *Cross-cultural Encounters: Face-to-Face Interaction*, Pergamon, New York, 1981; D. ARCHER, *How to Improve Your Social I.Q.*, M. Stevens, New York, 1980; C. DRAINE and B. HALL, *Culture Shock! Indonesia*, Times Books International, Singapore, 1986.
7. R. PASCALE and T. ATHOS, *The Art of Japanese Management*, Warner, New York, 1982, p.142.
8. G. COCHRANE, p.73.
9. J. B. BINGHAM, *Shirt-Sleeve Diplomacy*.
10. G. COCHRANE, p.72.
11. L. WALINSKY, *The Selected Papers of Wolf Ladejinsky*, p.332.
12. L.PYE, *Chinese Commercial Negotiating Style*, Oelgeschlager, Athenaum, Konigstein; Cambridge, Massachusetts, 1982.
13. H. CLEVELAND et al., *The Overseas Americans*; G. BENVENISTE and W. ILCHMAN, *Agents of Change: Professionals in Developing Countries*; A. MADDISON, *Foreign Skills and Technical*

Assistance in Economic Development; M. KUBR (editor), *Management Consulting: A Guide to the Profession;* F. BYRNES, *Americans in Technical Assistance;* S. LINDHOLM, *Appointment with the Third World;* H. P. GUTTMANN, *The International Consultant,* McGraw-Hill, New York, 1976; and R. BIDGOOD, *Consulting Overseas: A Guide for Professionals in Construction,* Northwood, London, 1976.

14. J. P. CARTER and E. A. WEST, *Keeping your Family Healthy Overseas,* Delacorte Press, New York, 1971.

15. See W. S. Sayre and C. E. THURBER, *Training for Specialized Mission Personnel,* Public Administration Service, Chicago, 1952; H. CLEVELAND *et al., The Overseas Americans;* J. M. MITCHELL, *A Ten Point Training Program: Report on the Task Force on Training and Orientation for AID,* International Cooperation Administration, Washington, DC, 1961; C. E. THURBER, The problem of training Americans for service abroad in U.S. government technical programs, *Dissertation Abstracts,* **22,** 1704 (1961).

PART VI

Future Trends

CHAPTER 12

Future Trends in International Consulting and Advising

Participatory development implies open-ended egalitarian learning, not hierarchical authoritarian learning. How technical specialists can maintain both traditional self-esteem and the requisite humility and flexibility in development learning situations is a question that needs to be talked through before a specialist is contracted (Guy Gran).[1]

Giovanni Galeazzo Visconti used to say that the noblest form of commerce was to win to one's service men of excellent quality and that he did not spare any cost to draw into his employment men of every nation (Herbert Goldhammer).[2]

As thinking about the development process has changed rather dramatically in recent years, the nature of international advising and consulting is also in flux. We recognize that it is difficult to see in the dark. Nevertheless, it is essential to try to anticipate advising and consulting patterns in the 1990s and even the twenty-first century. It is also important to try to assess the impact of emergent technologies such as *informatique* and *télématique* on the international advising process. As we approach the next century it seems clear that the international transfer of technology and information is markedly accelerating.

Major Mechanisms for Technology and Information Transfer

There are five principal mechansims by which ideas, information, and new technologies are transmitted internationally:

1. books, journals, and other publications;
2. patents and licenses;
3. media such as newspapers, radio, and television programs and video cassettes;
4. computer software, expert systems, and KIPS (Knowledge Information Processing Systems);[3]
5. the human agent as professional colleague, adviser, teacher, trainer, executive, and student.

Despite the growing impact of information transfer via computers and mass media technologies, we maintain that the human agent will continue to play a critical role in the transfer of information, ideas, and expertise across national boundaries. L. Bouras, of the Centre d'Etudes et Recherches en Informatique, Oved-Smar, Alger, Algeria, stresses that quality training is essential if developing countries are to realize their potential in data processing.[4] He calls for increased aid to LDCs in training related to *informatique* since these emergent technologies will be so important for international relations in the years ahead. Consistent with Bouras' orientation the French government is currently assisting Senegal in developing its capability in using computers. The Institute of Systems Science at the National University of Singapore is drawing on expatriate expertise to develop its applied computer capabilities. Similarly, the Asian Institute of Technology, located in Thailand, has a genuinely international and interdisciplinary staff. It is training thousands of Asians in how to adapt emergent technologies to the specific needs of various developing countries in Asia.

Bruno Ribes and his colleagues, in their important study of technology transfer, stress that the process of personal contacts between individuals is the oldest and most rudimentary form of transfer of knowledge.[5] Similarly Emile McAnany, a specialist in evaluating emergent communication technologies, sees international consultants as the 'main vehicle for transferring technology, standards, values as well as agendas.'[6] We need the careful evaluation and adaptation of these new technologies; we believe that the role of culturally sensitive outside agents with high standards of professional ethics will be of growing, not diminishing importance.

The Internationalization of the Advising and Consulting Process

Much of the literature on advising and consulting utilizes a national or bilateral perspective, with much of the focus on US, British or French advisers overseas. Actually, US advisers constitute only a small portion of the total number of international advisers and consultants. In the mid-1980s only approximately 10 percent of international consultants were United States citizens. The same can be said of any single nation's advisers, while in recent years advisers from Austria, Australia, Denmark, Japan, Netherlands, Canada, and Switzerland have rapidly increased. Between 1970 and 1985 the number of publicly financed technical cooperation personnel from Japan working abroad increased 447 percent. Of Colombo Plan experts working in Asia, 50 percent are from Japan and only 29 percent from the United States. Currently experts from developing nations carry out 60 percent of the long-term assignments funded by the Commonwealth Secretariat in London.

As the internationalization of the advising and consulting process continues, China, Brazil, and India are likely to play increasingly important roles. China, for example, recently assisted Tanzania in developing plans for its new city of Zanzibar. The recently retired chief executive of Air India was brought to Jamaica and succeeded in providing advice which helped Air Jamaica to achieve a turn-around. The airline is now expected to show a profit.[10] In 1979 a major meeting was held in Delhi involving the Government of India and various Latin American goverments. The Latin Americans reacted enthusiastically to what they saw in India:

> During this discussion, the Latin American participants expressed particular interest in India's success in evolving patterns of development based on internal cultural values by combining a comprehensive import substitution approach with small-scale production techniques.[11]

Despite these encouraging trends, the majority of technical assistance is still tied bilaterally to a particular donor nation. If the funding is from West Germany, then the technical experts must be from that country, even though more relevant or capable professionals in particular fields, may be available in Denmark or India. At a major meeting on higher education and development held in Bellagio, Italy, sponsored by the Rockefeller and Ford foundations, a consensus expressed the opinion that universities in the developing nations should play a determining role in the selection of outside expertise.[12] Though US-based, foundations such as Rockefeller and Ford have been exemplary in their international approach to the provision of technical expertise. For example, they have funded experts from institutions such as Sussex, Toronto, and McGill as well as from developing nations such as India and the Philippines. Seventy percent of US bilateral aid, however, in recent years has been spent in the US, while Canada requires 80 percent of its bilateral aid to be spent there. These requirements, of course, do not apply to US and Canadian contributions to the World Bank or other multilateral agencies. Because of such tied aid, the potential for internationalizing recruitment for overseas technical positions is constrained in bilateral aid programs.

In the chapter on case studies we introduced the concepts of 'circular advisers' and 'reverse impact.' Ribes and his colleagues emphasize the sharing of knowledge as a two-way process.[13] Many individuals returning from assignments in developing countries have mentioned that they learned more than they taught. Kenneth Thompson stresses that 'the fate of American education is dependent on responsible and well-qualified people engaged in tasks for which there is recognized need.'[14] Returned technical assistance personnel can provide an important political influence in industrial nations. The economic policies of these nations have an important impact on the future of developing countries. Paul Tsongas, the former

Senator from Massachusetts, for example, was a returned Peace Corps volunteer. While in the United States Senate he supported liberal policies toward the developing nations. On 24 June 1984 in the US, a nation-wide coalition of returned Peace Corps volunteers was formed to serve as a political group to try to change the way the US views the rest of the world.

Our case study of E. F. Schumacher, circular adviser *par excellence*, perhaps illustrates best the two-way process of knowledge transfer. Knowledge which Schumacher acquired in Burma and India has affected both industrial and other developing countries. Similarly Barbara Ward was deeply influenced by her consulting experiences in India and Pakistan. The same process is occurring in the private sector. Occidental Petroleum in California has acquired new agricultural technologies from the People's Republic of China. Global survival itself may be dependent upon the industrial nations' ability to develop lifestyles influenced by traditional village concepts of simplicity and cooperation.

Richard Critchfield, a frequent sojourner in diverse village settings, reveals an impressive appreciation of what village culture may contribute to modern industrial society:

> we have a false picture of Afro-Asian villages as dreary collections of huts, flies, dust and grim fatalistic inhabitants. Whereas reality in the green and often idyllic pastoral world of the villages is completely different, with a truth and simplicity of its own. Once this world starts coming equipped with sanitation, pure water and adequate health care—and the day is not far off—our own overcomplex 20th-century existence may suffer from comparison. Then we will start learning from them how to find our way back to the simple society.[15]

While the advising and consulting process is becoming internationalized, this does not eliminate the potential for failure or adverse outcomes. An Egyptian working in Sri Lanka can potentially make the same cultural mistakes as a Russian, Japanese, or American. Edward Boorstein, former economic adviser to Che Guevara and Allende, carefully documents the failure of Czech advisers in Cuba to adapt their planning expertise to Cuban conditions.[16] Advisers and consultants of whatever nationality need to pursue the emic ideal. Emic advisers seek to understand the basic values and meaning of the host country's culture. They attempt to understand local ways of thinking and to discover local knowledge relevant to their work.[17] Emic advisers are concerned with service not power. They genuinely try to work themselves out of a job by helping their colleagues to become more self-reliant and less dependent on outside expertise. Thus, in the final section of this chapter, we focus on the crucial need to redefine the meaning of professionalism in international advising and consulting.

Redefining Professionalism in International
Advising and Consulting

We have seen some notable successes in international advising and consulting, but failures are still too common.[18] The following negative assessment of some Canadian experts appeared in a research report sponsored by a Canadian institution:

> Canadian experts can also be responsible for introducing inappropriate technologies and projects; their know-how, developed in economic and social conditions quite different from those of underdeveloped countries, often creates more problems than it solves.[19]

In the early stages of a major development project in Thailand, the rumors that circulated about the foreign advisers were horrendous.[20] Academic overspecialization and narrow disciplinary orientations have often resulted in misleading policy prescriptions which led to unanticipated adverse consequences.[21] Other critics view many social scientists as lacking in genuine policy interests and unable to communicate across disciplines and with other participants in the development process.[22]

The ideal model is represented by the rare individual of whatever nationality who can transcend conventional disciplinary or professional boundaries to understand the holism of the development process. As the French scholar Basile emphasizes, 'the most diverse disciplines are converging, meeting, mutually influencing and improving each other.[23] To facilitate the understanding of other cultures, broad interdisciplinary training with a genuine appreciation of the humanities is important. Jacques Maisonrouge of IBM World Trade, in discussing the training of international executives, emphasizes the need for individuals 'conversant with the special aspirations of the developing countries.'[24] Interestingly the head of IBM World Trade majored in foreign languages. While professional skill in a conventional discipline is necessary, it is not sufficient for effective cross-cultural work. An ability to transmit and adapt knowledge is a key competence, central to the profession of international advising and consulting. The true professional in this field is willing to accept a reversal of roles. This at times leaves the outsider as pupil, listening and learning.[25] Without such humility and an emic orientation, consultants are likely to ignore indigenous technical knowledge (ITK) that is, in fact, highly relevant to their work.

Inadequate orientation to their tasks and assignments has been endemic in our field. Investment in orientation and training would undoubtedly result in substantial benefits, but as consulting assignments have become shorter and shorter, organizations have been reluctant to make such a commitment. Thus, it is essential to be even more selective in recruiting individuals with the appropriate professional skills and sensitivities related to international advising. Alternatively, more patience could be shown in being willing to wait until skilled individuals become available. Meanwhile, it is important to provide individuals with carefully prepared orientation materials. In this regard, Aramco's handbook for overseas employees, the film 'Going International,' and the insightful piece on rural poverty unperceived, by Robert Chambers, are exemplary.[26]

As mentioned in our earlier discussion of the training of international advisers and consultants, intensive orientations of only several days can be highly cost-effective, even for individuals on short- or medium-term assignments. For example, we have a colleague in Thailand who conducts two-day intensive workshops on orienting expatriates culturally for work in Thailand. Staff members from a wide range of international agencies and transnational corporations have attended these workshops. Participants uniformly commend the workshop for helping them to work more effectively in Thailand, and to have a greater in-depth understanding of the behavior and values of their Thai colleagues. Also notable is the Institute for International Studies and Training (IIST) in Japan, which carefully prepares Japanese for overseas assignments. It offers training programs ranging from one month to one year. Perhaps the United Nations University, also in Japan, could arrange intensive orientation courses in various locales for UN and other international experts assigned to an unfamiliar cultural setting.

In the past there has been too much emphasis on merely 'putting warm bodies' in the field. If budgets and financial contracts are available, there is the tendency to try to fill funded posts even if genuinely qualified people are not available. This is unprofessional and has contributed to considerable resentment. Ngo Dinh Nhu in Vietnam complained bitterly about US advisers who were rigid and not sufficiently adaptable to the Vietnamese culture.[17] Vietnamese newspapers similarly lamented the aloofness of advisers who didn't try to understand the psychology and aspirations of the local people. In contrast, Sweden appears to have been reluctant to fund overseas technical personnel without appropriate qualifications. They would not, for example, send an expert to Mozambique who is not fluent in Portuguese.

In the future we anticipate a trend toward fewer but more professionally skilled and sensitive advisers and consultants. Developing countries, on the whole, are less and less tolerant of the provision of second-rate individuals with inadequate professional skills for working cross-culturally.

Greater Sensitivity toward Issues of Equity, Equality, and Participation

According to C. G. Weeramantry, the burning issue in developing countries is equity.[28] Frank Moore, a senior official in US AID, openly admits the perverse paradox that US efforts to upgrade technical competence often contributes to widening the gap between 'change agents' and clients.[29] As pointed out in our case study of John Grant, the efforts of the Rockefeller Foundation in China contributed to the development of a medical elite recruited from narrow socioeconomic backgrounds. Moore argues that we must make 'massive efforts to narrow the social and economic gaps that we have unwittingly helped to widen.'[30] In the past most international advising and consulting has focused on questions of raising productivity and efficiency. Creative and cooperative efforts are also important for developing policies and programs to enhance equity and participation as central elements in the development process. In the future we anticipate better balance between efficiency and equity in the work of international advisers and consultants. As an example of the latter, a Ford Foundation adviser in Thailand devoted four years working collegially with Thais on policy questions related to educational equity and equality. Paulo Freire's work in Africa and Latin American has focused on greater participation of the poor. Also impressive in this regard was an AID project in Ecuador focusing on rural nonformal education, which involved genuine and extensive participation by the *campesinos* for whom the project was being created.[31] To foster such participation in development projects it may be necessary to develop systems which will make advisers and consultants more accountable to relevant client groups.

Greater Concerns for the Links Between Technology and Culture

Donald Kennedy, President of Stanford University, expressed in inspiring language the excitement of better relating the sciences and the humanities:

> We cannot be human and whole without reference to both. Uprooting the humanities from science robs us of a critical understanding: that they are joint products of a coevolutionary process, just as surely as the brain and culture are. That unity is the brightest academic vision we could possibly have.[32]

In discussing what makes for effectiveness in technical assistance, Frank Moore, a senior AID official, argues that we must increasingly think in terms of the relationship between technology and culture. Technologies as such are neutral. Their use depends on the values and ethics of human agents. New technologies can be used to foster cultural diversity, or they can be used for dehumanizing political repression. As indicated by the tragic Union Carbide incident in India, the introduction of new technologies can have devastating human implications. This technological failure has had a significant and adverse impact on US–Indian cultural and political relations.

Those involved as experts in the international transfer of technology must be conscious of the cultural implications of their work. They must be open to adapt technologies to meet diverse cultural needs. Jasper Ingersoll has developed, for AID, helpful guidelines for doing social and cultural impact studies of proposed development projects.[33] Such caution is essential to avoid adverse unanticipated cultural effects.

Despite the possible adverse effects of technological change, there is also potential for positive cultural outcomes. As Frank Sutton points out:

> seeking the benefit of foreign example and expertise, as they (governments) most inevitably do, they have a chance to produce cultural hybrids of sorts that may persist and flourish, and be something new in the world.[34]

To achieve such creative outcomes suggested by Sutton requires a synergistic process. In such a process international partners work as *colleagues* joining their efforts and resources to develop original solutions directly relevant to the local problem of focus.[35] In this process, both partners learn from each other. As an example of this type of creative synergistic process is the development of an artificial intelligence system (HI-Q) in Western Australia. This project has involved the collaboration of experts from Malaysia, Singapore, the Middle East, Britain, and Vietnam.[36] Another impressive example related to the global problem of malnutrition is the Spirula project involving cooperation between French microbiologists at the Laboratoire de La Roquette and villagers in Africa and Asia.[37] Spirula is a high-protein nutritional supplement deriving from recycled village wastes. The successful spread of this appropriate technology depends on current Japanese technological research related to the production of low-cost photovoltaics and the cultural sensitivity of those involved to find a way to integrate this nutritious alga into traditional diets.

Becoming More Humble and Protean

At a South Pacific Conference there was a delegation from American Samoa which included a young American anthropologist as adviser to Tuiasosopo, an elderly Samoan orator. During the conference a question was put to the orator and his wry response reflects the new critical awareness concerning the role of the outside advisers:

> he put his fingertips to his forehead, affecting a western mannerism, and with a twinkle in his eyes replied, 'Do you mind if I consult my anthropologist? He is supposed to know how I think.'[38]

There is no longer tolerance for the arrogant narrow-minded advisers and experts popularized in the literature of the 1950s and 1960s. M. Coulibaly of the Ivory Coast elegantly expresses some of the essential qualities needed by international advisers and consultants of the future:

> . . . facilité d'adaptation, de contacts: l'expert apprendra d'abord le pays, sa société, ses hommes, pour pouvoir y adapter son savior et ses méthodes.
>
> . . . humilité intellectuelle, dont il saura faire preuve pour aborder les problèmes.
>
> . . . fermeté de caractère: il saura parler loyalement du possible. Un conseiller doit être l'opposé d'un courtisan.
>
> . . . de ne pas faire référence immodérément aux mécanismes économiques des pays développés.
>
> . . . de prendre conscience des différences fondamentales qui séparent certain pays.
>
> . . . de savior qu'améliorer les techniques, c'est d'abord améliorer les hommes.[39]

In addition to humility, advisers of the future must have the protean qualities emphasized by Robert Lifton. Akio Morita, director of the Sony Corporation, is noted for having such qualities.[40] Able to change his views, manners, and considerations within those cultures where Sony is active, he is considered to be a true internationalist. Jacques Maisonrouge of IBM similarly stresses the need for more internationalists who are 'mobile, adaptable, and at ease in cultures other than their own.' He argues that such individuals must have a world view that inhibits the growth of chauvinism.

Strengthening Incentive Structures

Henry Wriston suggests that first-class problems naturally attract first-class minds.[41] We, however, are skeptical that existing incentive structures adequately reward advisers who show the dedication and commitment called for by scholars such as Robert Chambers at Sussex. He suggests that many advisers schedule their visits to developing countries based on weather conditions rather that the genuine needs of the developing nations.[42] How much recognition is there for those advisers and consultants who do spend time in remote areas during the worst weather? In fact, the incentive structures of a number of technical assistance agencies tend to reward those who remain in the capital close to their superiors and other important individuals with high status who may promote their future careers. Tendler argues that AID has paid less to its adventurous and adaptive technicians than to its security-seeking and foreign-avoiding ones.[43]

While some individuals like Mother Teresa and Norman Borlaug have received international recognition for their dedicated developmental efforts, for the most part there have been inadequate prestige and awards for those advisers and consultants who have achieved excellence. Perhaps an international foundation could create a series of prizes to recognize exemplary and culturally sensitive international advisers in various fields such as agriculture, health, information science, telecommunications, education, community development, public administration, and science.[44] Such recipients of prizes could share more broadly, at the international level some of their insights and approaches. These prizes should be open to individuals of all nationalities. If monetary rewards were associated with such prizes, they could be donated to facilitate the broader dissemination of successful projects or innovations. Such a system should also facilitate the growth of TCDC by making industrial nations more aware of the technical assistance talent present in the developing nations themselves.

Becoming More Conscious of the Impermanence of Contexts

A major theme of our study has been the recognition of the complex interaction between the context and the adviser. Contexts vary dramatically from place to place and from time to time. Too often development experts fail to realize that a successful formula in one culture may fail disastrously in another setting or at another time.[45] Hugh Snyder, who has studied the performance of advisers in Peru and Thailand, contrasts the markedly differing perspectives on advisers in these two nations:

> Thai officials also had a different attitude toward advisors from the U.S. Traditionally, Thais had used advisers from powerful, far-away nations as counterweights to internal opponents or external enemies. This stands in contrast to the Peruvian distrust of the motives of its powerful (and close) Northern neighbor, the United States.[46]

Kenneth Thompson has carefully outlined four distinct phases for international advising and consulting.[47] In each phase the role of the adviser shifts rather dramatically. An appropriate role in one country at one phase may be totally inappropriate in another nation at another phase. His four basic phases are indicated in Table 12.1. Many developing nations, particularly in the Asia–Pacific region are already moving into phases III and IV which stress mutual problem-solving and technical cooperation among developing countries.

Thus, it is critically important that international agencies and advisers carefully consider the ever-changing contexts for their technical assistance efforts. Without an in-depth awareness of temporal and milieu-specific conditions, technical assistance personnel will likely fail to meet expectations and to realize potential for achieving constructive change.

TABLE 12.1 *Four Phases of Advising/Consulting in Development Contexts*

Phase I	Need for a critical mass of outside institution-builders. Consulting stays of significant duration, frequently longer than 3 years.
Phase II	Adviser role more prominent than institution-builder. Need to work through others while remaining in the background. Need for a smaller number of low-profile advisers. Consultant stays of 1–3 years.
Phase III	Application of trained intelligence to problem-solving. Genuinely mutual collaboration on development problems. Short-term consulting stays.
Phase IV	Time for giving back by those who have received. Stress on technical cooperation among developing countries.

Source: Kenneth W. Thompson *et al.*, 1972, pp.245–6.

A 'Common Market' of Advisers and Consultants

As there are those who argue for the free flow of commodities among nations, we stress the importance of fostering the transnational exchange of ideas and individuals. Philip Coombs echoes such an ideal by calling for a global 'Common Market' in the cultural and intellectual realm:

> What we are seeking, essentially, is the development of a world-wide 'Common Market' not of physical goods but of ideas, knowledge, talents, and cultural products. This 'Common Market' will tie the world together, modify some of the adverse aspects of nationalism, and allow people to come closer together than ever before.[48]

Currently, much creative talent in the world is directed toward narrow nationalistic and materialistic ends, including the production of goods and services which may adversely affect the human condition. Inadequate talent is being directed toward the applied problems of the developing nations, such as basic health, basic education, water resource development and management, soil conservation, and forest preservation. It is urgent that the best available talent, regardless of nationality, be brought to bear on these major development problems related to global welfare.

The causes and solutions to these fundamental development problems transcend both national and disciplinary boundaries. Thus we anticipate a growing need for both international and interdisciplinary collaboration. The well-known cross-cultural scientist, H. C. Triandis, argues that the 'major social psychological problem of the next century, then, is to learn how people with different subjective cultures can respect one another, cooperate together, and live in harmony.'[49] In some small way we hope that this study may help international advisers and consultants to achieve creativity, respect, cooperation, and harmony in their important cross-cultural endeavors.

Notes

1. G. GRAN, *Development by People*, p.238.
2. H. GOLDHAMER, *The Adviser*, p.81.
3. See E. FEIGENBAUM and P. McCORDUCK, *The Fifth Generation: Artifical Intelligence and Japan's Computer Challenge to the World*, Pan, London, 1984, p.20.
4. L. BOURAS, Training, an essential condition for the data processing development in developing countries. The role of cooperation, in *Computers in Education*, North Holland, Amsterdam, 1981, pp.583–7.
5. B. RIBES *et al.*, Domination or sharing, in *Endogenous Development and the Transfer of Knowledge*, Unesco Press, Paris, 1981, p.21.
6. E. G. McANANY *et al.*, Distance education: evaluating new approaches in education for developing countries, *Evaluation in Education: An International Review Series*, **6**, 357 (1982).
7. *Development Co-operation 1986 Report*, OECD, Paris, 1987, p.243.
8. *The Colombo Plan Annual Report 1986*, Colombo Plan Bureau, Colombo, Sri Lanka, 1986, p.21.
9. *Report of the Commonwealth Secretary-General*, Commonwealth Secretariat, London, 1983, p.71.
10. Ibid., p.73.
11. *Identification of Opportunities for Interregional TCDC and ECDC*, ESCAP, Bangkok and Comision Economica Para America Latina, Santiago [Report of Consultations between the Government of India and Latin American Governments, 5–7 June 1979 in New Delhi], 1979, p.12.
12. K. THOMPSON *et al.*, Higher education and national development: one model for technical assistance, in *Education and Development Reconsidered*, vol. 2 [Document prepared for a conference at the Villa Serbelloni, Bellagio, Italy 3–5 May, 1972, sponsored by the Rockefeller and Ford Foundations], p.244.
13. B. RIBES *et al.*, p.61. See also B. HAYDEN, The ethics of development: AID—a two way process?
14. K. THOMPSON, p.244.
15. R. CRITCHFIELD, Revolution of the village, *Human Behavior*, **1**, 26 (1979).
16. E. BOORSTEIN, *The Economic Transformation of Cuba*, Monthly Review Press, New York, 1968, p.154.
17. 'Emic' is an anthropological concept derived from linguistics. An emic approach stresses discovering the indigenous concepts and categories of those being served or studied. See G. FRY, S. CHANTAVANICH, and A. CHANTAVANICH, Merging quantitative and qualitative research techniques: a new research paradigm, *Anthropology and Education Quarterly*, **12**, 147–50 (1981).
18. H. C. TRIANDIS, *The Analysis of Subjective Culture*, Wiley, New York, 1972, p.344.
19. R. SWIFT and R. CLARKE (editors), *Ties that Bind: Canada and the Third World*, Between the Lines, Toronto, 1982, p.183.
20. C. KARNJANAPRAKORN, L. McKIBBEN, and W. THOMPSON, *NIDA: A Case Study in Institution Development*, International Development Research Center, Indiana University, Bloomington, Indiana, 1974, p.109.
21. R. CHAMBERS, Rural poverty unperceived, p.8.
22. G. GRAN, p.239.
23. J. BASILE, *The Cultural Development of Managers, Executives, and Professionals*, Helicon, Baltimore, Maryland, 1968.
24. J. MAISONROUGE, The education of a modern international manager, *Journal of International Business Studies*, **14**, 144.
25. R. CHAMBERS, p.12.
26. R. LEBKICHER *et al.*, *The Aramco Enterprise: A Handbook for American Employees of Arabian American Oil Company*, Aramco, Dhahran, Kingdom of Saudi Arabia, 1957; L. COPELAND and R. CUMMINGS, *Going International: Leader's Guide*, Copeland Griggs, San Francisco, California, 1983, a guide to an excellent four-part film series on cross-cultural aspects of working abroad; L. COPELAND and L. GRIGGS, *Going International: How to Make*

Friends and Deal Effectively in the Global Marketplace, Random House, New York, 1985; N. CHESANOW, *The World-Class Executive,* Rawson, New York, 1985.
27. Interview with Ngo Dinh Nhu, cited in *Journal de l'Extreme Orient,* 3 June 1958.
28. C. G. WEERAMANTRY, *Equality and Freedom,* Hansa, Colombo, Sri Lanka, 1976, p.10.
29. Memorandum to Owen Cylke, Deputy Director, AID, 15 January 1981, p.5.
30. Ibid., p.6.
31. J. HOXENG, *Let Jorge Do It: An Approach to Rural Nonformal Education,* Center for International Education, School of Education, University of Massachusetts, 1973.
32. D. KENNEDY, Science and 'culture', Convocation Address, University of Oregon, 4 October 1982.
33. J. INGERSOLL, *Social Analysis of Development Projects, a Suggested Approach for Social Soundness Analysis,* AID Development Studies Program, Washington, DC, May 1977.
34. *Technical Assistance and Development,* p.213.
35. P. CASSE, Technical assistance for the Third World: the role of U.S. universities, *The Bridge,* 5, 26 (1980).
36. *Business News from Australia,* 5, 4–5 (1984).
37. R. D. FOX, Spirulina: the alga that can end malnutrition, *The Futurist,* 19, 30–5 (1985).
38. C. G. R. McKAY, *Samoana: a Personal Story of the Samoan Islands,* A. H. and A. W. Reed, Wellington, 1968, p.151.
39. Son Excellence M. COULIBALY, Role des expertes dans les programmes de developpement, in *Technical Assistance and Development,* p.100.
40. N. LYONS, *The Sony Vision,* Crown, New York, 1976.
41. J. MAISONROUGE, p.143.
42. R. CHAMBERS, p.8.
43. J. TENDLER, *Inside Foreign Aid,* p.35.
44. R. CHAMBERS, p.16.
45. H. C. TRIANDIS, p.345.
46. H. SNYDER, *The Michigan State University-Aid Project with the National Economic Development Board, 1964–68,* Center for Studies in Education and Development, Harvard Graduate School of Education, Cambridge, Massachusetts, 1979, p.102.
47. K. THOMPSON, p.246.
48. P. COOMBS, U.S. Foreign relations: a new dimension, *AAUW Journal,* 55, 165 (1962).
49. H. C. TRIANDIS, p.344.

A Statistical Profile of International Advisers and Consultants: Where They Come From, Where They Go, and What They Do

Objectives

In this appendix we present a basic statistical profile indicating where advisers come from, where they go, and what they do. We also show how such profiles have changed over time. Also presented are some key indicators for various countries such as number of advisers utilized, relative to number of foreign scholarships received during a specified time period. Finally we conclude this appendix with several analytical models to explain both the demand for, and supply of, United Nations experts working as international consultants.

Also included in this appendix is a precise quantitative profile of technical assistance personnel provided to one developing nation, Thailand, as an example. These data reflect the extremely important role of nongovernmental agencies in providing technical assistance personnel.

Profile of OECD Experts and Volunteers

OECD data on public financed technical co-operation personnel include both experts and volunteers. OECD nations vary markedly in the extent to which they provide experts and volunteers for technical assistance work in the LDCs. Also there have been some rather dramatic shifts over time. In 1970, France alone accounted for 38 percent of all OECD experts and volunteers; as can be seen in Fig. A.1, however, France's provision of technical assistance has declined steadily since 1970, establishing a trend followed both by the US and the UK. Figures A.1–A.4 indicate the shift in the provision of experts and volunteers for each of the OECD nations during the period 1970–85.

Given that Japan's rapid transformation from a feudal state to a techno-logical society is unparalleled in the history of technology, it should not be

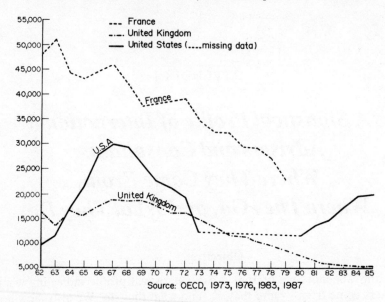

Source: OECD, 1973, 1976, 1983, 1987

FIG. A.1. Trend Over Time in Total Number of Experts and Volunteers Publicly
Financed by Specific OECD Nations

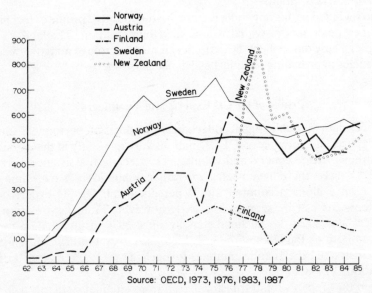

Source: OECD, 1973, 1976, 1983, 1987

FIG. A.2. Trend Over Time in Total Number of Experts and Volunteers Publicly
Financed by Specific OECD Nations

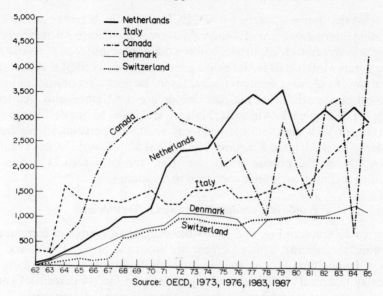

FIG. A.3. Trend Over Time in Total Number of Experts and Volunteers Publicly Financed by Specific OECD Nations

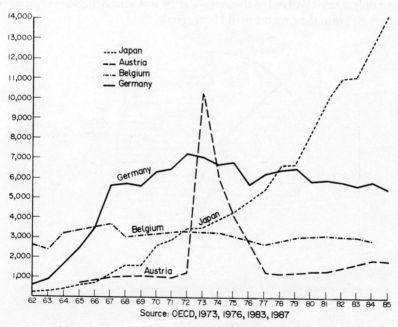

FIG. A.4. Trend Over Time in Total Number of Experts and Volunteers Publicly Financed by Specific OECD Nations

surprising that Japan leads the list of OECD nations in its rate of increase in providing international experts and volunteers. Japan, once a beneficiary of highly selective outside expertise, is now a major new source of expertise for other nations interested in developing their own technological capacities. Other nations showing dramatic increases in the provision of international technical personnel during the past decade are the Netherlands, Austria, Switzerland, Denmark, Australia, Finland, and Italy. Major declines in the provision of such international technical assistance personnel have been registered by the United Kingdom, the United States, and France. Figures A.1–A.4 show the precise trend over time for each OECD nation in providing technical assistance cooperation personnel.

Profile of Communist Economic Technicians

The circle graph in Fig. A.5 shows the geographic source of communist economic technicians. Thirty percent are from the Soviet Union and 11 percent from China. For example, currently there are large numbers of Yugoslav technical personnel working in Iraq. In fact 44 percent of communist technicians overseas are from Eastern Europe. Remittances from these personnel represent an important source of hard currency for Eastern European nations.[2] The largest proportion of communist economic technicians are working in Africa (63 percent) and the Middle East (27 percent), with only a few involved in the Asia–Pacific or Latin American regions (see Fig. A.6) (with the exception of Nicaragua).

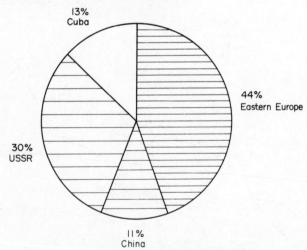

Source: *Communist Aid Activities in Non-Communist Less Developed Countries, 1979 and 1954–79: A Research Paper,* National Foreign Assessment Center, CIA, Washington, D.C., 1980, p. 21.

FIG. A.5. Geographic Origins of Communist Economic Technicians Working Abroad, 1979

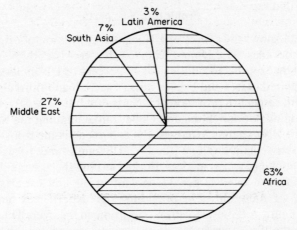

Source: *Communist Aid Activities in Non-Communist Less Developed Countries, 1979 and 1954–79: A Research Paper*, p. 21.

FIG. A.6. Destination of Communist Economic Technicians Working Abroad, 1979

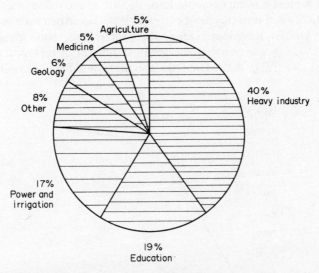

Source: *Communist Aid Activities in Non-Communist Less Developed Countries, 1979 and 1954–79: A Research Paper*, p. 3.

FIG. A.7. Fields of Employment of Soviet Overseas Technicians in non-Communist LDCs, 1979

Profile of UN Experts

Table A.1 shows the source of UN experts (by nation of origin) over the past three decades. The United Kingdom has consistently been the major source of UN experts, accounting for 12 percent of UN experts in 1980. In 1980 the United States and France ranked second and third closely behind the UK with respect to provision of UN experts. Interestingly, also in 1980, two developing nations, India and Chile, ranked among the top ten in the provision of UN experts. Although UN experts do come from a wide range of nations, three nations alone (the UK, US, and France) accounted for 31 percent of all UN experts in 1980. Earlier in 1960 these same three nations accounted for an even larger 37 percent of all UN experts. Thus, the dominance of these three in providing UN experts has more recently declined. Figure A.8 shows the trend over time in the overall number of UN experts. In the 1960s there was a dramatic increase, while in the 1970s there was only a modest growth in the provision of UN experts.

Table A.2, in contrast, shows where these experts serve and changes during the past two decades. The major shift has been away from the Middle East and toward Africa. As of 1980, 34 percent of UN experts were serving in Africa, while in 1960 only 19 percent were working in this critically important region with the most serious developmental problems.

Since countries with larger populations, such as the United States, United Kingdom, or India, could be expected to provide larger absolute numbers of advisers, we feel it is important to look also at the provision of experts on a per-capita basis. From this perspective in 1980, countries such as Belgium, Sweden, United Kingdom, Denmark, Switzerland, New Zealand, and Israel provide proportionately the greatest number of technical assistance personnel (see Table A.3). Data are also presented for developing nations

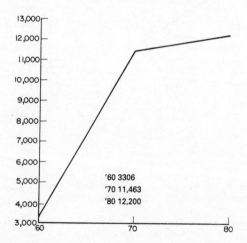

'60 3306
'70 11,463
'80 12,200

FIG. A.8. Trend Over Time in the Provision of UN Experts

TABLE A.1. *Source of UN Experts (by Nation of Origin)*
(percentage of Total UN Experts)

1960		1970		1980	
United Kingdom	14.8	United Kingdom	14.7	United Kingdom	12.0
United States	12.3	France	12.7	United States	10.2
France	9.4	United States	10.3	France	9.1
Netherlands	5.6	India	4.4	India	5.6
India	4.4	West Germany	3.7	West Germany	3.3
Canada	4.0	Canada	3.2	Canada	3.0
West Germany	3.7	Italy	2.8	Netherlands	2.8
Switzerland	2.9	Netherlands	2.7	Belgium	2.8
Italy	2.8	Czechoslovakia	2.4	Italy	2.6
Sweden	2.8	Sweden	2.1	Chile	2.4

Source: *Yearbook of the United Nations,* 1960, 1970, and 1980.

TABLE A.2. *Destination by Geographic Region of UN Experts Over Time*

Geographic region	1960	1970	1980
Asia and Pacific	30.2	22.2	25.9
Latin American and Caribbean	24.3	21.1	23.2
Africa	19.4	36.0	33.9
Middle East	17.3	9.2	8.5
Europe	6.4	6.8	4.9
Interregional	2.4	4.4	3.2
Other	.1	.0	.5

Source: Based on an analysis of raw data from *The Yearbook of the United Nations,* 1960, 1970, 1980.

TABLE A.3. *Top 20 Providers of UN Experts:*
Number of Experts per 1,000,000 Population

1960		1970		1980	
Norway	20.0	New Zealand	40.4	Belgium	32.9
Switzerland	17.0	Israel	38.6	Sweden	31.6
Denmark	17.1	Belgium	37.0	United Kingdom	25.1
Netherlands	15.7	Norway	34.0	Denmark	24.5
Sweden	12.0	Switzerland	30.8	Switzerland	24.5
New Zealand	11.3	Denmark	30.2	New Zealand	24.2
United Kingdom	9.0	United Kingdom	28.8	Israel	23.3
Australia	7.8	Sweden	28.8	Netherlands	23.2
Israel	7.6	France	27.2	Norway	21.2
Canada	7.0	Netherlands	23.0	France	19.7
Ireland	6.8	Australia	22.2	Australia	18.5
France	6.6	Czechoslovakia	18.0	Finland	17.3
Belgium	6.2	Ireland	16.9	Ireland	15.5
Finland	5.7	Canada	16.4	Canada	14.6
Greece	2.5	Yugoslavia	11.1	Austria	12.0
West Germany	2.2	Finland	10.9	Portugal	7.1
United States	2.2	Austria	8.9	Hungary	6.6
Austria	2.0	Hungary	7.5	Yugoslavia	5.8
Italy	1.8	Italy	5.6	Italy	5.4
Portugal	1.3	United States	5.4	United States	5.2

Source: See Table A.1.

TABLE A.4.   *Top 20 Providers of UN Experts Among Developing Nations: Number of Experts per 1,000,000 Population*

1960		1970		1980	
Lebanon	16.5	Lebanon	20.0	Chile	25.1
Jordan	13.5	Jordan	18.7	Trinidad	25.0
Costa Rica	13.3	Uruguay	17.1	Uruguay	21.8
Chile	10.4	Costa Rica	17.0	Jamaica	15.0
Haiti	4.8	Trinidad	16.7	Costa Rica	12.3
Ecuador	4.4	Chile	16.5	Lebanon	12.2
Bolivia	3.1	Haiti	12.0	Tunisia	11.1
Uruguay	2.8	Jamaica	10.5	Peru	9.7
Argentina	2.2	Panama	10.0	Bolivia	8.8
Cuba	1.8	Uganda	9.5	Benin	8.5
Peru	1.7	Bolivia	6.9	Argentina	8.2
Egypt	1.4	Argentina	6.8	Haiti	7.6
Paraguay	1.1	Syria	6.8	Sri Lanka	7.8
Colombia	1.1	Ecuador	5.7	Ecuador	7.8
Guatemala	1.1	Benin	5.0	Honduras	6.8
Sri Lanka	1.0	Sri Lanka	5.0	Singapore	6.7
Philippines	1.0	Colombia	4.8	Congo	6.3
Panama	1.0	Paraguay	4.8	Senegal	4.7
El Salvador	1.0	El Salvador	4.0	Colombia	4.7
Nicaragua	1.0	Togo	3.3	Syria	4.3

Source: See Table A.1.

on a per-capita basis. Among such countries Chile, Trinidad, Uruguay, Jamaica, and Costa Rica are the major providers of technical assistance experts (see Table A.4).

There is also the interesting question of which developing nations (on a per-capita basis) receive the most UN experts. Table A.5 presents these data for 1960, 1970, and 1980. Major recipients of UN experts in 1980 were Lesotho, Trinidad, Panama, Mauritania, Jamaica, Kuwait, Haiti, Congo, Costa Rica, and Somalia. These data suggest that some countries have clearly moved toward greater intellectual self-sufficiency. In 1960 Libya, Israel, Nicaragua, and Paraguay were major recipients of UN experts. In 1980 Israel had shifted to becoming a major provider of UN experts and Libya, Nicaragua, and Paraguay are no longer major recipients of UN experts. Soviet advisers, however, now have a significant presence in Libya.

During the past decade there has been considerable emphasis on technical cooperation among developing countries (TCDC). It is important to examine UN data on the provision of international experts, to see if the number of such technical assistance personnel from developing nations are in fact increasing. Figure A.9 presents the basic data. In 1960, 27 percent of experts were from developing countries. But then during the 'development decade' of the 1960s this percentage dropped to 22. In 1980, individuals from developing nations represented more than one of three UN experts, indicating considerable progress by the UN in implementing TCDC.

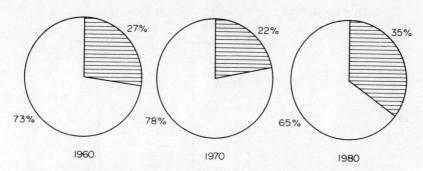

Note: The shaded area represents the percentage of UN experts from developing nations. Source: *Yearbook of the United Nations 1980*, United Nations, New York, 1983.

FIG. A.9. Percentage of UN Experts from Developing Nations, 1960–1980

TABLE A.5. *Top 20 Recipients of UN Experts: Number of Experts per 1,000,000 Population*

1960		1970		1980	
ibya	64.2	Liberia	56.4	Lesotho	50.7
iberia	31.0	Somalia	43.3	Trinidad	45.0
ebanon	23.1	Jamaica	40.5	Panama	37.7
araguay	19.4	Panama	40.0	Mauritania	36.6
olivia	17.8	Libya	39.5	Jamaica	35.0
rael	17.1	Togo	39.4	Kuwait	32.1
aos	15.5	Lebanon	38.3	Haiti	31.0
rdan	15.3	Tunisia	35.3	Congo	28.1
malia	14.5	Central African Republic	33.3	Costa Rica	27.2
onduras	12.1	Singapore	33.0	Somalia	26.6
ria	11.5	Zambia	32.4	Burundi	22.6
caragua	11.4	Lesotho	31.0	Singapore	21.7
nisia	11.0	Ivory Coast	30.0	Jordan	21.5
ngapore	10.0	Trinidad	28.9	Lebanon	21.1
nama	10.0	Burundi	27.5	Uruguay	20.3
ruguay	9.2	Jordan	27.4	Honduras	20.2
inidad	8.8	Senegal	27.2	Ecuador	19.5
uador	8.6	Mauritania	26.4	Central African Republic	19.1
go	8.6	Paraguay	26.1	Liberia	18.9
ile	8.2	Sierra Leone	25.0	Laos	18.9

urce: See Table A.1.

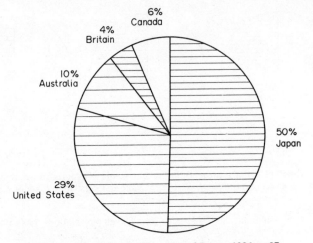

Source: *The Colombo Plan Annual Report 1986*, p. 87.

FIG. A.10. Geographic Origins of Colombo Plan Experts, 1985

Profile of Colombo Plan Experts

Experts are also provided to developing countries in the Asia–Pacific region under the Colombo Plan. During 1985 11,152 such experts were provided. As indicated in Figure A.11 Japan is the major source of such experts (accounting for 50 percent of the total) with the United States and Australia second and third respectively. The developing country receiving the greatest number of Colombo Plan experts is Indonesia (20 percent of the total), with Thailand and Bangladesh second and third respectively, as indicated in Fig. A.11.

Fortunately, the Colombo Plan keeps detailed data on the fields of expertise possessed by the technical assistance personnel financed under this program. Figure A.12 shows the breakdown by fields of expertise. The largest number of experts work in the area of agriculture (24 percent). Other major fields of expertise are public utilities, industry, education, health services, and economic planning and administration (cf. Fig. A.7). Over 90 percent of all Colombo Plan experts serve in these major fields.

Figure A.13 also shows the trend over time in the Colombo Plan financing of experts and volunteers. The 1977–85 period shows a substantial increase in funding for experts and volunteers of 296 percent. It is also interesting to note that the Colombo Plan spends twice as much on experts and volunteers as it does on students and trainees.

The Colombo Plan also finances experts for TCDC. Figure A.14 shows that India is the biggest provider of such experts, followed by South Korea and Pakistan. Figure A.15 shows the major recipients of TCDC experts

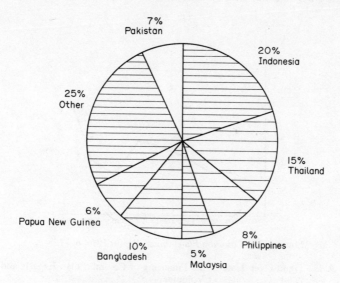

Source: *The Colombo Plan Annual Report 1986,* p. 18.

FIG. A.11. Destination of Colombo Plan Experts, 1985

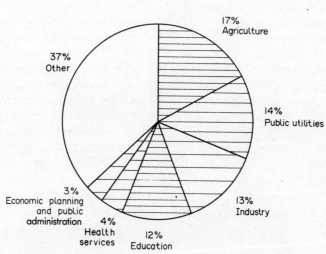

Source: *The Colombo Plan Annual Report 1986,* p. 87.

FIG. A.12. Colombo Plan Experts by Field of Expertise, 1985

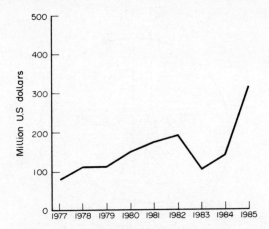

Source: *The Colombo Plan Annual Report 1986*, p. 77.

Fig. A.13. Trend Over Time in the Financing of Colombo Plan Experts and Volunteers

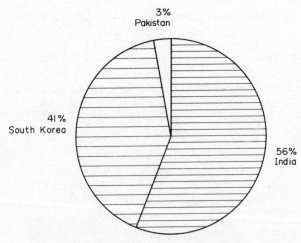

Source: *The Colombo Plan Annual Report 1986*, p. 25.

Fig. A.14. Geographic Origins of TCDC Experts Provided Under the Colombo Plan. 1985

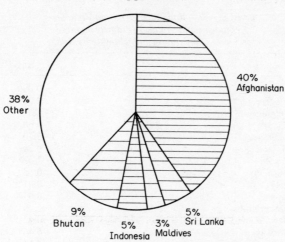

Source: *The Colombo Plan Annual Report 1986*, p. 25.

Fig. A.15. Major Recipients of Colombo Plan TCDC Experts, 1985

under the Colombo Plan in 1985. Major recipients of such TCDC experts are Afghanistan and Bhutan. The data on Colombo Plan TCDC are rather discouraging, however, in one respect. In 1985 TCDC experts represented only 0.8 percent of all Colombo Plan experts. Much more encouraging are data showing that the number of such experts increased 133 percent during the period 1983–5.

Indicator Reflecting Ratio of Fellowships Received to Experts Provided

There is considerable debate as to whether it is more effective to devote limited technical assistance funds to providing scholarships for nationals from developing nations or to financing experts to work in these countries.[4] This is the classic controversy referred to as the Peter the Great Approach (funding fellowships) versus the King of Siam Option (providing experts). Obviously, sound technical assistance involves a combination of the two types of knowledge and technology transfer. We now examine empirically the nature of this balance for various nations.

Table A.6 presents the results of our analysis for OECD donors. Among OECD donors, Australia, Austria, Germany, New Zealand, Finland, the UK, and Norway seem to favor the Peter the Great Approach. For every one of its experts sent abroad, Austria provides 10.9 fellowships for trainees and students. A number of other nations such as the United States, the Netherlands, Denmark, Sweden, and France in contrast provide greater numbers of publicly financed experts than fellowships.

TABLE A.6.   *Ratio of Experts and Volunteers*
to Students and Trainees (Publicly financed
technical co-operation and fellowships), 1985

Country	Ratio
Australia	0.08
Austria	0.06*
Belgium	1.41*
Canada	0.68
Denmark	2.10
Finland	0.24
France	2.68***
Germany	0.42
Italy	0.41
Japan	0.95
Netherlands	2.19
New Zealand	0.42
Norway	0.46
Sweden	4.64
Switzerland	0.91**
United Kingdom	0.39*
United States	1.44

Note: * Data are for 1984; ** Data are for 1983; *** Data are
for 1970.

Source: *Development Co-operation: Efforts and Policies of the
Members of the Development Assistance Committee 1986
Report;* OECD, Paris, 1987, p.243.

Using UN data on experts, we have also examined recipient nations to see
the balance between experts and UN fellowships received. Table A.7
presents the results of this analysis for the years 1960, 1970, and 1980. Saudi
Arabia has the highest ratio of UN experts to fellowships, 9.3. This is
somewhat misleading, however, since Saudi Arabia has sufficient funds of its

TABLE A.7.   *Ratio of Experts Received To Fellowships*
Received (United Nations)

1960		1970		1980	
Nepal	7.2	Algeria	3.4	Saudi Arabia	9.3
Trinidad	7.0	Zambia	2.3	Libya	8.0
El Salvador	5.5	Congo	2.0	Haiti	5.0
Cameroon	3.0	Tunisia	2.0	Nicaragua	5.0
Venezuela	3.0	Saudi Arabia	1.9	Dominican Republic	4.2
Liberia	2.8	Ivory Coast	1.9	Mozambique	3.0
Jamaica	2.7	Morocco	1.6	Honduras	2.6
Brazil	1.9	Afghanistan	1.6	Costa Rica	2.4
Morocco	1.9	Ethiopia	1.6	Trinidad	2.3
Ghana	1.9	Haiti	1.5	Laos	2.2

Source: See Table A.1.

own to finance fellowships for its nationals. Among non-oil-exporting countries, those nations receiving the most experts relative to fellowships are Haiti, Nicaragua, Dominican Republic, Mozambique, Honduras, Costa Rica, Trinidad, and Laos. These nations reflect the King of Siam pattern. Ironically, Thailand (formerly Siam) is not among them.

Profile of Experts and Volunteers Provided to a Developing Country, Thailand, as a Case Study

To provide a sense of the overall extent of technical assistance personnel working in a developing country, we present precise data on Thailand for a given year as a sample case. The basic data are presented in Tables A.8 and A.9. During 1981 Thailand received the services of 1,438 experts for a total

TABLE A.8. *List of Experts in Thailand Under Various Bilateral and Multilateral Auspices, 1981*

Auspices	Number of experts	Person-months	Average duration of assignment (months)
Japan	1,107	2,853	2.8
Australia	77	594	7.7
Germany	72	721	10.0
WHO	46	198	4.3
FAO	37	256	6.9
NGOs*	31	236	7.6
France	28	235	8.4
ILO	19	94	4.9
Israel	17	13	.8
Unesco	15	39	2.6
UN (DTCD)	13	95	7.3
United Kingdom	13	184	14.2
United States	12	95	7.9
Denmark	10	60	6.0
UNIDO	7	40	5.7
UN (ICAO)	6	25	4.2
Netherlands	5	60	12.0
UNDP (OPE)	4	6	1.5
UN (UNFDAC)	4	41	10.3
UNFPA	2	20	10.0
UNEP	1	.5	.5
UPU	1	1	1.0
Norway	1	12	12.0
Italy	1	12	12.0
World Bank	na	460	na
Canada	na	na	na
Totals	1,439	6,351	4.4

Note: *NGOs refers to non-governmental organizations such as the Ford Foundation, Rockefeller Foundation, and the Population Council.

Source: *Eighteenth Compendium of Development Assistance to Thailand 1981.*

TABLE A.9.   *List of Agencies Providing Volunteers*
Under Various Auspices in Thailand, 1981

Auspices

US Peace Corps
German Voluntary Service (GVS)
Japan Overseas Cooperation Volunteers (JOCV)
Canadian University Service Overseas (CUSO)
New Zealand Voluntary Service Abroad (VSA)
Voluntary Service Overseas (VSO), United Kingdom
International Executive Service Corps (IESC)
The Canadian Executive Service Overseas
Volunteer Development Corps (VDC)
The British Executive Service Overseas

Source: *Eighteenth Compendium of Development Assistance to Thailand, 1981.*

of 6,349 person-months (the equivalent of 529 person-years). Slightly over two-thirds of these experts were provided by a single country, Japan, under its bilateral assistance program. Australia, Germany, and WHO were the next-largest providers of experts to Thailand. With respect to total person-months of expertise provided, Thailand receives the most assistance from Japan, Germany, Australia, and the World Bank in that order respectively. The data suggest that assignments under bilateral assistance tend to be longer in duration (except for Japan) than those under UN or multilateral auspices. An average Unesco assignment in Thailand, for example, was 2.6 months, while experts from the UK served for an average of 14.2 months.

Table A.9 indicates the range of various agencies providing volunteers to Thailand. Unfortunately, data are not available with respect to the precise number of volunteers from each agency. The agencies as a whole, however, spent a total of $2.1 million on providing volunteers to Thailand in 1981. US Peace Corps expenditures of $1.4 million accounted for more than half of the total.

These data clearly indicate that Thailand does receive substantial outside expertise from a diverse range of sources, and that the bilateral type of assistance tends to dominate, primarily because of the prominent role of Japan's technical assistance.[5]

Statistical Models and Analyses Related to the Supply of, and Demand for, International Advisers and Consultants

An initial simple model test is to see if nations having received international advisers in the past have now become self-sufficient and no longer need advisers. To test this model we compute a simple correlation matrix for

TABLE A.10. *Correlation Matrix Showing Relations Between Demand for Advisers in 1960, 1970, and 1980*

	Demand in 1960	Demand in 1970	Demand in 1980
Demand in 1960	1.0	0.69	0.62
Demand in 1970	0.69	1.0	0.74
Demand in 1980	0.62	0.74	1.0

Note: All relationships are significant at the 0.01 level.

all countries receiving UN experts in 1960, 1970, and 1980. The correlation matrix is presented in Table A.10. A null hypothesis of no relationship in the demand for UN experts at different points in time clearly fails. The high correlations across decades suggest a persistence in the geographic patterns of the provision of UN experts. The persistence in the 1970s was slightly higher than in the 1960s.

The Supply of International Experts

The purpose of this model is to explain the supply of UN experts by various nations. For example, we hypothesize that a nation whose national language is an international one such as English or French will tend to supply more experts, other things being equal. Our basic supply function model includes the following variables:

Dependent variable: number of UN experts provided in 1980.
Independent variables:
Population of country, 1980 (+)
National language is an international one (+)
Income per capita, 1980 (+)
Former major colonial power (+)
Former minor colonial power (+)
Percentage of population in higher education, 1960 (+)

The plus signs indicate that we hypothesize a positive relationship between the independent variable and the supply of UN experts.

The two colonial power variables are included as dummies. There are two major reasons for including these historical variables. First, there are many former colonial servants who have years of development experience in areas such as Africa or Asia. Thus former major colonial powers such as England or France will have a larger potential pool of experienced advisers. Second, many nations such as the Ivory Coast or the Philippines retain close links with their former colonial powers.

The income per capita and population variables are rather straightforward. Other things being equal, we hypothesize that bigger and richer countries will supply more experts.

Our final explanatory variable reflects the extent to which a nation has invested in providing higher education to its population. We hypothesize that such nations will have a larger pool of qualified individuals available to serve as international experts. This variable is lagged two decades, since recent college graduates are unlikely to be engaged as experts immediately, but are more likely to be involved initially in volunteer roles.

Results

The hypothesized model has excellent explanatory power, accounting for 85 percent of the variance in the supply of UN experts (Table A.11). The dummy variable, former major colonial power, has the greatest explanatory power, followed by population and then percentage of population in higher education. Though income per capita has a sizeable simple correlation with supply of experts, that becomes insignificant statistically, once other relevant variables are included. Thus the wealth of a nation *per se* has little direct association with the extent of its provision of international experts. The case of the United Kingdom clearly illustrates this finding. Though many countries have now surpassed the UK in income per capita, it still remains the major supplier of UN international experts.

TABLE A.11.   *A Regression Model for Explaining the Supply of UN Experts, 1980*

Explanatory variable	Hypothesized sign	b	beta	t	r
Population, 1980 (in millions)	+	0.967	0.34	7.99**	0.42
National language is international	+	45.5	0.09	2.28*	0.18
Income per capita, 1980	+	0.004	0.07	1.28	0.42
Percentage of population in higher education, 1960	+	13.6	0.30	5.34**	0.56
Former major colonial power	+	1014	0.64	15.15**	0.72
Former minor colonial power	+	117	0.13	2.65**	0.29
Constant	...	− 47.46			

Note: Multiple regression statistics: $F(6,86) = 86.1$; $N = 93$; $R^2 = 0.85**$; $R = |0.41|$.
Notation: b = unstandardized regression coefficient,
       beta = standardized regression coefficient,
       t = t value for the regression coefficient,
       r = simple bivariate correlation,
       R^2 = coefficient of multiple determination (adjusted for small sample),
       $|R|$ = the determinant of the correlation matrix of independent variables, a measure
          of multicollinearity.
Plots of regression residuals indicate a pattern of randomness.
*$p < 0.05$; **$p < 0.01$.

The Demand for International Experts

The purpose of this model is to try to explain the demand for UN experts by various nations. For example, we hypothesize that the richer the developing country, the less need it will have for UN experts. Our basic demand function model includes the following variables:

Dependent variable: number of UN experts utilized in 1980.
Independent variables:
Number of UN experts utilized two decades earlier in 1960 (−)
Number of UN fellowships received in 1960 (−)
Percentage of population in higher education in 1960 (−)
Population in 1980 (+)
Income per capita, 1980 (−)
Former British colony (+)
Former French colony (+)
National language is an international one (+)
Quality of life in 1980 (−)

The plus signs indicate that we hypothesize a positive relationship between the independent variable and the demand for UN experts, and minus signs indicate an assumed negative relationship.

Basically, we are hypothesizing that the greatest demand for UN experts will be among poorer countries which were former French or British colonies. We are also hypothesizing that the least demand for UN experts today will be among nations which two decades earlier invested more heavily in their own human capital and received more technical assistance (UN fellowships and experts) to help develop their own indigenous capacities.

Results

Among the variables in our model, previous number of experts in 1960 has the greatest explanatory power. In other words the best predictor of a nation's demand for UN experts in 1980 is the number it had in 1960. The simple correlation is a high 0.71. This suggests that the notion of experts working themselves out of jobs is largely a myth. Intellectual dependence of this type seems to persist over time. This finding is rather consistent with the inevitable impermanence of technology. As developing nations catch up in one area of technology, such as civil engineering, they may lag behind in relatively new areas of technology, such as information science or biotechnology.

This variable, previous demand for experts 20 years earlier, is, however, dropped from our final multiple-variable demand model, because its presence leads to the technical problem of multicollinearity (an econometric problem arising when independent variables are too interrelated).

TABLE A.12.   *A Regression Model for Explaining the Demand for UN Experts, 1980*

Explanatory variable	Hypothesized sign	b	beta	t	r
Quality of life, 1980	−	−1.50	−0.05	0.36	−0.30
Number of UN fellowships, 1960	−	0.30	0.19	1.25	0.42
Percentage of population in higher education, 1960	−	−3.43	−0.24	1.57	−0.29
Population in 1980 (in millions)	+	0.28	0.38	2.53*	0.40
Income per capita, 1980	−	0.01	−0.26	1.75	−0.35
Former British colony	+	−7.35	−0.05	0.36	0.08
Former French colony	+	6.94	0.03	0.25	0.00
National language is international	+	−16.78	−0.11	0.85	−0.11
Constant	⋯	118.7			

Note: Multiple regression statistics: $F(8,47) = 4.2$; $N = 56$; $R^2 = 0.32$; $R = |0.13|$.
Notation: See Table A.11.

Table A.12 indicates our final demand model. This model is based on only those countries receiving UN experts. Rich industrial countries are excluded. Our demand model unfortunately has slightly less than half the explanatory power of our supply model. Since we are working with nearly the complete population of major developing countries, the statistical tests of significance presented are not particularly relevant, or necessary.

As in our supply model, population is a major predictor. The larger the country, the greater the number of experts utilized. A particularly interesting finding relates to the impact of prior investments in indigenous higher education. Those countries which 20 years earlier provided greater opportunities in higher education for their own citizens, had less demand for UN experts in 1980.

Contrary to our hypothesis, the more UN fellowships received 20 years earlier in 1960, the greater was the demand for UN experts in 1980. There are several possible explanations for this rather anomalous finding. First, UN fellows may develop professional and personal contacts which may facilitate the provision of future experts. Second, most UN technical assistance packages included funding for both fellowships and experts. Thus these two types of technical assistance are naturally interrelated, given the persistence in the demand for experts over the 20-year period under consideration.

With respect to quality of life and income per capita, relations are in the expected direction, but much weaker than anticipated. While there is a tendency for UN experts to be found in the poorer LCDs with a lower quality of life, the negative relations found are surprisingly small. In other words, a country's income per capita and level of quality of life are only weakly associated with its receipt of UN experts. There are two major explanations for these weak relationships. First, developing countries vary significantly in their absorptive capacity to utilize outside technical assistance and expertise.

In numerous cases richer LDCS may have more absorptive capacity than poorer nations. Second, there may be a tendency for experts to prefer more pleasant settings where considerable amenities exist. Countries such as Costa Rica, Ivory Coast, Malaysia, Brazil, Botswana, Kenya, Thailand, and Sri Lanka appear to be among favorite locales for experts, even though such countries may not have the greatest genuine needs with respect to quality-of-life improvements.

With respect to the colonial power variable, it is interesting that former French colonies are more likely to seek UN expertise than former British colonies.

Conclusion

During the past two decades, the number of individuals involved in international advising and consulting has increased rather dramatically. This is particularly true for nations such as Japan, the Netherlands, Australia, and Austria. There has also been an impressive internationalization of the advising and consulting process. In the early 1960s this process was dominated by the United Kingdom, United States, and France. Now in the 1980s a much wider range of nations are involved in the process of transferring technology and expertise via international advisers. As part of the movement to promote technical cooperation among developing countries (TCDC), India, China and Chile are now significant suppliers of international advisers and technicians. The majority of long-term experts provided by the Commonwealth Secretariat are from developing nations. Though TCDC has certainly grown, it has not increased as fast as many in the South would have liked.

With respect to destination, the major trend is an increasing emphasis on placing personnel in Africa. Given Africa's pressing development problems, particularly related to agriculture and water resource management, this trend is encouraging. Expertise provided to the Asia–Pacific region has in turn declined. In fact the Asia–Pacific region, with its impressive economic dynamism and technological innovations, is becoming a major new source of international advisers and consultants. Countries such as Japan and China are now major suppliers of international experts and advisers. China's assistance has largely been concentrated in African countries such as Tanzania, while Japan's assistance has focused primarily on the Asian region in nations such as Thailand.

In many respects Japan's history as regards outside advisers is exemplary. In its earlier stage of development Japan made highly selective use of outside experts from a wide range of nations. Our case study of W. Edwards Deming, 'the father of quality control in Japan' in Chapter 9, vividly illustrates this process. Having attained impressive developmental and technological success, Japan in recent decades has dramatically increased its own sharing of technical expertise with other nations.

In the decades ahead it is likely that other nations will follow the example of Japan and become net suppliers of international expertise. Some major candidates for this status are the Koreas, Brazil, Singapore, Malaysia, Thailand, and Mexico. Thus, as we approach the twenty-first century, our basic prediction is that the process of advising in developing countries will become even more diverse and international.

Notes

1. R. E. GOMORY, Technology development, *Science*, **220**, 579 (1983).
2. *Communist Aid to the Less Developed Countries of the Free World, 1976*, CIA, Washington, DC, 1977, p.8.
3. *Colombo Plan Annual Report, 1986*, Colombo Plan Bureau, Colombo, Sri Lanka, 1986, p.91.
4. J. S. COLEMAN, Professional training and institution building in the Thirld World, two Rockefeller Foundation experiences, in E. BARBER *et al.*, p.53.
5. A more recent document, *Twenty-Second Compendium of Development Assistance to Thailand 1985*, UNDP, Bangkok, 1985, provides detailed disaggregated data on experts in Thailand, their number and the types of projects on which they are working. Their institutional affiliations are also shown. These data suggest that the number of international experts working in Thailand has declined considerably since 1981, perhaps reflecting implementation of a Thai cabinet-level decision which requires use of *local* consultants and experts whenever available. The data also show that Japan and the UNDP remain the largest providers of international experts for Thailand. Of special value, the document generally specifies the costs of the expertise provided.

Standards of Professional Conduct and Practice for International Consultants and Advisers

These standards of professional conduct and practice signify voluntary assumption by members of the profession of international consulting and advising. These standards represent self-discipline and commitments above and beyond the requirements of the law. Their objective is to let the international community know that members of this profession intend to maintain a high level of ethics and public service. Members of this profession must accept the obligation to conduct their practice in a way that will be most beneficial to the public. They provide clients a basis for confidence that members will serve them in accordance with professional standards of competence, objectivity, integrity, and dedication.

Code of professional responsibility and practices

1. *Basic client responsibilities*
   1.1 We will at all times place the interests of clients ahead of our own and serve them with integrity, competence, and dedication.
   1.2 We will treat as confidential all information concerning the affairs of clients that we gather during the course of professional engagements; and we will not take personal, financial, or other advantages of material or inside information coming to our attention as a result of our professional relationship with clients; nor will we provide the basis on which others might take such advantage. Prior to any publication of material deriving from a consulting assignment, we will seek formal approval from the client and provide the client with a draft copy of the proposed publication.
   1.3 We will serve two or more competing clients on sensitive issues only with their prior knowledge.
   1.4 We will inform clients of any relationships, circumstances, or interests that might influence our judgments, objectivity of our services, or the quality of our work.

2. *Client arrangements*
   2.1 We will present our qualifications for serving a client solely in terms of our competence, experience, and professional standing. Qualifications will be described accurately and truthfully.
   2.2 We will accept only those engagements we are appropriately qualified to undertake.
   2.3 We will accept only those engagements which we believe will provide real benefits to clients and related populations. We will reject those engagements (regardless of how lucrative financially) which we perceive as having potentially adverse effects on human populations.
   2.4 We will not accept an engagement of such limited scope that we cannot serve the client effectively.
   2.5 We will carry out each assignment under the direction of a host country national who is responsible for its successful completion. We will dedicate our professional services to assist such individuals in carrying out their responsibilities. We will respect the host country national as our direct superior.

3. *Financial practices*
   3.1 We will charge reasonable fees which are commensurate with the nature of services performed and the responsibility assumed. Excessive charges abuse the professional relationship and discourage countries or agencies from utilizing the services of international consultants. Determination of the reasonableness of a fee requires consideration of many factors, including the nature of services performed; the time required; the consultant's relevant experience, ability, and reputation; the degree of responsibility assumed; the benefits that accrue to clients; and potential physical or health hazards involved.
   3.2 We will show flexibility in setting fees according to ability to pay.
   3.3 We will neither accept nor pay fees or commissions to others for client referrals. Nor will we under any circumstances accept fees, commissions, or other valuable considerations from individuals or organizations whose equipment, supplies, or services we might recommend in the course of our work with clients.
   3.4 We will not accept special payments for additional services rendered where such payments are prohibited by the organization engaging the consultant. Our standard fee is expected to cover such services without additional payments.
   3.5 We will not participate in black-market activities for private financial gain.
   3.6 We will respect the host country's monetary and foreign exchange regulations.
   3.7 We will avoid involvement in any type of illegal and/or corrupt

practices (with the exception of minor 'user fees' to obtain essential bureaucratic services).

3.8 We will endeavor, to the extent possible, to use local economic services and products.

3.9 We will not seek unnecessary extensions of consulting services for purposes of personal financial gain.

4. *Intellectual aspects*

4.1 We will share credit and recognize the primary role of host country nationals in successes achieved.

4.2 We will readily accept blame for our failures or ineffectiveness without bitterness or rancour.

4.3 In consultancies involving research, we will share all data and research results with host country clients. Such data and research will remain the 'intellectual property' of the host country which will have final authority with respect to approving the broader dissemination and distribution of research findings.

4.4 In consultancies involving evaluation, we will report honestly and reliably with respect to genuine program or project outcomes. We will not cover up failures or inadequacies. At the same time we will not look only for faults but try to ascertain all program benefits (intended or unintended) accruing from the project being evaluated.

4.5 We will seek to make our clients self-reliant and less dependent on our future services by acquainting client personnel with all relevant principles, methods, techniques, and technologies applied. In this way, improvements suggested or implemented may be properly managed and continued without outside assistance after completion of the engagement.

5.1 *Cultural practices*

5.1 We will strive to respect the local culture and customs and avoid violating cultural taboos.

5.2 We will strive to avoid extravagant and ostentatious luxury consumption.

5.3 We will show a commitment to study seriously and sensitively the local cultures and languages.

6. *Political–administrative practices*

6.1 We will not 'experiment with the lives of others.' We will not recommend innovations or changes which may have risks adversely affecting human populations, or the effects of which are yet uncertain.

6.2 We will not use human subjects in consultancies involving research without prior careful evaluation of intended and unintended impact on these subjects.

6.3 We will not try to impose our ideas or programs on others.

6.4 We will not use our authority or power to obtain sexual favors.

6.5 We will not participate in local partisan political activities such as rallies or fund-raising dinners.

6.6 We will not provide financial assistance to any local political group or organization.

6.7 We will strive to maintain a low profile and not attempt to bring undue publicity to our individual efforts or those of our organization.

Notes

Helpful to us in preparing our code of ethics were the sample codes of ethics included in Mr. Kubr's volume on the profession of management consulting previously cited. Also relevant is a carefully thought out code of ethics on North–South scholarly exchange developed at a special conference at the East–West Center in December 1985. That code has been published as part of the volume, G. SHIVE, S. GOPINATHAN, and W. CUMMINGS (editors), *North–South Scholarly Exchange: Access, Equity, and Collaboration*, Mansell, London, 1988. Another relevant code of ethics is that developed by the Association of Management Consulting Firms. It is available on request from ACME Inc., 230 Park Avenue, New York, New York 10169.

Bibliography

General Development Works with Implications for International Consulting

BAUER, P. T. and B. S. YAMEY, The Pearson Report: a review in T. J. BYERS (editor), *Foreign Resources and Economic Development*, Frank Case, London, 1972, pp.41–76.

CHAMBERS, R., Rural poverty unperceived: problems and remedies, *World Development*, **9**, 1–19 (1981).

CRITCHFIELD, R., Revolution of the village, *Human Behavior*, **1**, 18–26 (1979).

CRITCHFIELD, R., Science and the villager, *Foreign Affairs*, **61**, 14–41 (1982).

DORE, R., *The Diploma Disease: Education, Qualification and Development*, University of California Press, 1976.

FOSTER, G., *Traditional Societies and Technological Society*, Harper & Row, New York, 1973.

FRANK, L., The development game, *Granta*, **20**, 229–43 (1986).

GANT, G. F., *Development Administration: Concepts, Goals, Methods*, The University of Wisconsin Press, Madison, 1979.

GOODENOUGH, W. H., *Cooperation in Change: an Anthropological Approach to Community Development*, Sage, New York, 1963.

GOULET, D., *The Uncertain Promise: Value Conflicts in Technology Transfer*, IDOC, New York, 1977.

GRAN, G., *Development by People: Citizen Construction of a Just World*, Praeger, New York, 1983.

HAYDEN, B., The ethics of development: AID—a two-way process? Speech by Mr Bill Hayden, Minister of Foreign Affairs (Australia), at the 17th Waigani Seminar, The University of Papua New Guinea, Port Moresby, 1986.

HEILLEINER, G. K., *International Economic Disorder: Essays in North–South Relations*, University of Toronto Press, Toronto and Buffalo, 1980.

HILL, P., *Development Economics on Trial: the Anthropological Case for a Prosecution*, Cambridge University Press, New York, 1986.

JACKSON, SIR R., *A Study of the Capacity of the United Nations Development System*, United Nations, Geneva, 1969, two volumes, UN document DP/5, UN sales no. E.70.1.10.

KORSMEYER, P. and G. ROPES, *The Development Directory: A Guide to the U.S. International Development Community*, Editorial PKG, Madison, Connecticut, 1988.

KORTEN, D., Community organization and rural development,—a learning process approach, *Public Administration Review*, **40**, 480–511 (1980).

LEGER, R., People meeting other people: a challenge and a chance for a new interdependence and international cooperation, in A. MATTIS (editor), *A Society for International Development Prospectus 1984*, Duke University Press, Durham, North Carolina, 1983, pp.175–7.

MENSING, F., *Bridge Building between North and South: Applied Technology for the Third World*, Inter Nationes, Bonn, Germany, 1987.

MONTGOMERY, J. (editor), *International Dimensions of Land Reform*, Westview Press, Boulder, Colorado, and London, 1984.

NIEHOFF, A. H., *A Casebook of Social Change*, Aldine, Chicago, 1966.

RIBES, B. *et al.*, *Domination or Sharing? Endogenous Development and the Transfer of Technology*, Unesco Press, Paris, 1981.

ROBERTSON, A. F., *People and the State: an Anthropology of Planned Development*, Cambridge University Press, New York, 1984.

SOLO, R. A., *Organizing Science for Technology Transfer in Economic Development*, Michigan State University Press, East Lansing, Michigan, 1975.

SPICER, E. H., *Human Problems in Technological Change,* Russell Sage Foundation, New York, 1952.
STAVRIANOS, L., *Global Rift,* Morrow, New York, 1981.
WEERAMANTRY, C. G., *Equality and Freedom,* Hansa Publications, Colombo, Sri Lanka, 1976.

The Process of Advising, Consulting, and Sharing of Expertise: Roles and Expectations

Advisors and Counterparts, Technical Assistance Methodology Division, US Agency for International Development, Washington, DC, 1972.
ANDERSON, G. W. (editor), *Consult Australia,* 2nd edn, The Australian Professional Consultants Council, Sydney, 1980.
BAUM, H., The adviser as invited intruder, *Public Administration Review,* **42,** 546–52 (1982).
BENVENISTE, G. and W. F. ILCHMAN, *Agents of Change: Professionals in Developing Countries,* Praeger, New York, 1972.
BIDGOOD, R., *Consulting Overseas: A Guide for Professionals in Construction,* Northwood Publications, London, 1976.
BRUNER, J., The role of the researcher as an adviser to the educational policy maker, *Oxford Review of Education,* **1,** 3 (1978).
BRYNTSEV, A. S. and J. A. SAWE, Use of consultants and experts in the United Nations; note by the Secretary-General, Joint Inspection Union, General Assembly, United Nations, 30 July 1982 (A/37/358); (JIU/REP/8/8).
CAIDEN, G. E., International consultants and development administration: report on a meeting, *International Development Review,* **17,** 28 (1975).
CHAMBERS, R., Cognitive problems of experts in rural Africa, in J. C. STONE (editor), *Experts in Africa: Proceedings of a Colloquium at the University of Aberdeen, Aberdeen, 1985,* pp.96–102.
CLEVELAND, H. and G. J. MAGONE, *The Art of Overseasmanship,* Syracuse University Press, Syracuse, New York, 1957.
COCHRANE, G., The nonexpert side of the expert in advisory work, in *Development Anthropology,* Oxford University Press, New York, 1971, pp.65–79.
COGGINS, R., The development set, *Adult Education and Development,* **14,** (1976).
Conference on the role of the younger professional person in overseas development programs, held at the Princeton Inn, 24–26 September 1965, and sponsored by the Ford Foundation.
COOK, J. L., *The Advisor,* Dorrance, Philadelphia, 1973.
COULIBALY, M., Rôle des expertes dans les programmes de développement, in *Technical Assistance and Development,* The Hebrew University of Jerusalem, Truman Research Institute Publication no. 6, 1971, pp.94–101.
CURLE, A., *Educational Planning: the Adviser's Role,* International Institute for Educational Planning, no. 8 in Fundamentals of Educational Planning Series, Paris, 1968.
ESMAN, M. J., Development assistance in public administration: requiem or renewal, *Public Administration Review,* **40,** 430 (1980).
FRIEDMANN, J., Intention and reality: the American planner overseas, in J. FRIEDMANN (editor), *Urbanization, Planning, and National Development,* Sage, Beverly Hills, California, 1973, pp.287–98.
GOLDHAMER, H., *The Adviser,* Elsevier, New York, 1978.
GOULET, D., Development experts: the one-eyed giants, *World Development,* **8,** 481–9 (1980).
GREEN, E. C., Have degree will travel: a consulting job for AID in Africa, *Human Organization,* **40,** 92–4 (1981).
Guidelines for the Use of Consultants by World Bank Borrowers and by the World Bank as Executing Agency, World Bank, Washington, DC, 1981.
Guides to Team-Leaders in Technical Assistance Projects, US Agency for International Development, Bureau of Technical Assistance, Washington, DC, 1973.
GUTHRIE, G. M. and R. E. SPENCER, *American Professions and Overseas Technical Assistance,* Pennsylvania State University, University Park, Pennsylvania, 1965.
GUTTMANN, H. P., *The International Consultant,* McGraw-Hill, New York, 1976.

HAMNETT, I., The role of the anthropologist in local planning, *Journal of Development Studies,* **9**, 493–507 (1973).

HARARI, D., *The Role of the Technical Assistance Expert,* Development Centre Studies, OECD, Paris, 1974.

HARDIMAN, M. and J. MIDGELY, Foreign consultants and development projects: the need for an alternative approach, *Journal of Administration Overseas,* **17**, 232–44 (1978).

ILLICH, I., To hell with good intentions. Address delivered at the Conference on Inter-American projects, Cuernavaca, Mexico, 1968.

KELLEY, R. E., *Consulting: the Complete Guide to a Profitable Career,* rev. edn, Scribner, New York, 1986.

KLAUSNER, W. J., Foreign experts, in *Reflections on Thai Culture,* 2nd edn, Prachandra, Bangkok, 1983, pp.249–51.

KUBR, M., (editor), *Management Consulting: a Guide to the Profession,* International Labour Organization, Geneva, 1976.

LASKI, H. J., *The Limitations of the Expert,* Fabian Society, London, 1931.

LINTON, N., The role of the expatriate in developing countries, *International Development Review,* **12**, 24–7 (1970).

LUCE, D. and J. SOMMER, Big Adviser, in *Viet Nam—The Unheard Voices,* Cornell University Press, Ithaca, New York, 1969, pp.202–17.

Manual on the Use of Consultants in Developing Countries, United Nations, New York, 1968.

NIEHOFF, A. H. and C. M. ARENSBERG, *Introducing Social Change: a Manual for Americans Overseas,* Aldine, Chicago, Illinois, 1967.

PADDOCK, W. and E. PADDOCK, *We Don't Know How,* Ames, Iowa State University Press, 1973.

PEARSON, D. L., United States systematists in foreign countries, the new ugly American? *ASC Newsletter,* **14**, 1–6 (1986).

PINTO, R. F., Consultant orientations and client system perception: styles of cross-cultural consultation, in R. LIPPITT and G. LIPPITT (editors), *Systems Thinking—A Resource for Organization Diagnosis and Intervention,* International Consultants Foundation, Washington, DC, 1981, pp.57–73.

PLOWDEN, W. (editor), *Advising the Rulers,* Basil Blackwell, Oxford, 1987.

REINING, C. C., Expatriates in Africa. Paper presented at the 19th Annual Meeting of the African Studies Association, 3–6 November, Boston, Massachusetts, 1976.

RIMMER, P. J. and J. A. BLACK, Global financiers, consultants and contractors in the Southwest Pacific since 1970, *Pacific Viewpoint,* **24**, 112–39 (1983).

ROBERTS, G., Volunteers and neo-colonialism; an inquiry into the role of foreign volunteers in the Third World. Mimeo, US Peace Corps, Washington, DC, 1968?

SANDERS, I. T., American professionals overseas, *Bulletin of Atomic Scientists,* **22**, 40–5 (1966).

SCHWARZ, P., *Selecting Effective Leaders of Technical Assistance Teams,* Bureau for Technical Assistance, US Agency for International Development, Washington, DC, 1973.

SEERS, D., Why visiting economists fail, *Journal of Political Economy,* **70**, 325–38 (1962).

SMITH, D. and M. JESSIE, Barriers between expert and counterpart, *International Development Review,* **12**, 22–5 (1970).

SPITZBERG, I. J., *Exchange of Expertise: The Counterpart System in the New International Order,* Westview Press, Boulder, Colorado, 1978.

STONE, J. C., (editor), *Experts in Africa: Proceedings of a Colloquium at the University of Aberdeen, Aberdeen, 1980,* 1980.

TANHAM, G. K. *et al.,* *War Without Guns: American Civilians in Rural Vietnam,* Praeger, New York, 1966.

THURBER, C. E., Technical consultants, development administrators, and organization development, paper presented at annual SIETAR conference in Vancouver, British Columbia, 1981.

WINSLOW, A., The technical assistance expert, *International Development Review,* **4**, 19–24 (1962).

WOODS, J. L., Suggested framework for determining roles of international advisers/consultants, Note for Project Formulators no. 506, UNDP/DTCP, Bangkok, 1980.

YOUNG, C., *Consultancy in Overseas Development,* Overseas Development Institute, London, 1968.

Studies Related to Cross-cultural Communication and Adaptation

ARCHER, D., *How to Expand your Social I.Q.*, M. Evans, New York, 1980.

BASILE, J., *The Cultural Development of Managers, Executives, and Professionals* (translated from the French by B. ADLER), Helicon, Baltimore, Maryland, 1968.

BIRDWHISTELL, R., *Kinesics and Contexts*, University of Pennsylvania Press, Philadelphia, 1970.

BOCHNER, S., The mediating man and cultural diversity, in R. BRISLIN (editor), *Topics in Cultural Learning*, East–West Cultural Learning Institute, Honolulu, 1973, pp.23–37.

BRISLIN, R. W., *Cross-cultural Encounters: Face-to-Face Interactions*, Pergamon Press, New York, 1983.

BRISLIN, R. W. and P. PEDERSON, *Cross-cultural Orientation Programs*, Gardner Press, New York, 1976.

BRISLIN, R. W., K. CUSHNER, C. CHERRIE, and M. YONG, *Intercultural Interactions: A Practical Guide*, Sage, Beverly Hills, California, 1985.

CASINO, E. S., Consultants and competence in the development of cross-cultural contents, in *Handbook of Intercultural Training*, vol. 2, Pergamon Press, Elmsford, New York, 1983, pp.218–40.

CASSE, P., *Training for the Cross-Cultural Mind*, SIETAR, Washington, DC, 1980.

CLUTTERBUCK, D., Breaking through the cultural barriers, *International Management*, **35**, 41–2 (1980).

CONDON, J. and F. YOUSEF, *An Introduction to Intercultural Communication*, Bobbs-Merrill, Indianapolis, 1975.

COOPER, R. and N. COOPER, *Culture Shock! Thailand*, Times Books International, Singapore, 1982.

COPELAND, L. and L. GRIGGS, *Going International: How to Make Friends and Deal Effectively in the Global Marketplace*, Random House, New York, 1985.

CRAIG, J., *Culture Shock! What not to Do in Malaysia and Singapore*, Times Books International, Singapore, 1980.

DINGES, N. S., and W. S. MAYNARD, Intercultural aspects of organizational effectiveness, in D. LANDIS and R. W. BRISLIN (editors), *Handbook of Intercultural Training, Issues in Training Methodology*, vol.2, Pergamon Press, New York, 1982.

DRAINE, C., and B. HALL, *Culture Shock! Indonesia*, Times Books International, Singapore, 1986.

FIEG, J. P., *Guidelines for Thais and North Americans*, Intercultural Press, Chicago, Illinois, 1980.

FISHER, G., *International Negotiations: A Cross-Cultural Perspective*, Intercultural Press, Chicago, Illinois, 1982.

GLASER, W. A., Experts and counterparts in technical assistance, in K. KUMAR (editor), *Bonds without Bondage, Explorations in Transcultural Interactions*, University Press of Hawaii, Honolulu, 1979, pp.207–25.

HABERMAS, J., *Communication and the Evolution of Society* (translated from the German by T. McCARTHY), Beacon Press, Boston, Massachusetts, 1979.

HABERMAS, J., *Theory of Communicative Action* (translated from the German by T. McCARTHY), Beacon Press, Boston, Massachusetts, 1984.

HALL, E. T. and R. M. HALL, *Hidden Differences: Studies in Intercultural Communication*, Bungei Shunju, Tokyo, 1987.

HALL, E. T., *The Hidden Dimension*, Doubleday, New York, 1966.

HALL, E. T., *The Silent Language*, Anchor Press, Garden City, New York, 1973.

HAMMER, M. R., Behavioral dimensions of intercultural effectiveness: replication and extension, *International Journal of Intercultural Relations*, **11**, 65–88 (1987).

HOFSTEDE, G., *Cultural Pitfalls for Dutch Expatriates in Indonesia*, Deventer Landbouwers Vereniging Nji Sri, Deventer, the Netherlands, 1982.

HOOPES, D. G. and P. VENTURA (editors), *Intercultural Sourcebook: Cross-cultural Training Methodologies*, Intercultural Press, Chicago, Illinois, 1979.

IMAI, M., *Never Take Yes for an Answer: an Inside Look at Japanese Business for Foreign Businessmen*, Simul Press, Tokyo, 1982.

KAPP, R. A. (editor), *Communicating with China (P.R.C.)*. Intercultural Press, Chicago, Illinois, 1983.

KAWASAKI, I., *Japan Unmasked*, Tuttle, Rutland, Vermont, and Tokyo, 1969.

KONDRACKE, M., Ugly American redux, *New Republic*, **180**, 12–15 (1979).

LAURIE, J., America globally blind, deaf and dumb: a shocking report of our incompetence, through ignorance in dealing with other countries, Adelphi University, Garden City, New York, 1981.

LEBKICHER, R., G. RENTZ, M. SEINEKE et al., *The Aramco Enterprise: A Handbook for Employees of Arabian American Oil Company*, Aramco, Dhahran, Saudi Arabia, 1957.

LEE, C. K., Heart language, in *Proceedings of the International Conference on Thai Studies 3–6 July 1987*, Research School of Pacific Studies, ANU, Canberra, 1987, vol. 2, pp.149–93.

LIFTON, R. J., *Boundaries: Psychological Man in Revolution*, Random House, New York, 1969.

LIPPITT, G. L., and D. S. HOOPES, *Helping Across Cultures*, International Consultants Foundation, Washington, DC, 1978.

MARTIN, J. N. (editor), Special issue: theories and methods in cross-cultural orientation, *International Journal of Intercultural Relations (IJIR)*, **10**, 103–254 (1986).

PIET-PELON, N. J., and B. HORNBY, *In Another Dimension: A Guide for Women Who Live Overseas*, Intercultural Press, Yarmouth, Maine, 1985.

PYE, L., *Chinese Commercial Negotiating Style*, Oelgeschlager, Athenaum, Konigstein; Cambridge, Massachusetts, 1982.

REUBEN, B. R., L. R. ASHLING and D. J. KEALEY, *Cross-Cultural Effectiveness: Intercultural Communication State of the Art Review*, D. S. HOOPES (editor), SIETAR, Washington, DC, 1977.

SCHELL, O., *Watch Out for the Foreign Guests*, Pantheon, New York, 1980.

SINGER, M., *Intercultural Communication: A Perceptual Approach*, Prentice-Hall, Englewood Cliffs, New Jersey, 1987.

SIMON, P., *The Tongue-Tied American: Confronting the Foreign Language Crisis*, Continuum, New York, 1980.

WINFIELD, L., *Living Overseas*, Public Affairs Press, Washington, DC, 1962.

Studies Related to Methodology Employed

ARGYRIS, C., *Inner Contradictions of Rigorous Research*, Academic Press, New York, 1980.

BLACK, P. A., Participant observation and logical positivism in the social sciences: a note, *World Development*, **11**, 389–90 (1983).

Conference on evaluation of professional effectiveness in overseas technical assistance programs. Conference held in New York City and sponsored by the Carnegie Endowment of Peace, 28–29 January 1965.

The Evaluation of Technical Assistance, Organization for Economic Cooperation and Development, Paris, 1969.

FRY, G., S. CHANTAVANICH and A. CHANTAVANICH, Merging qualitative and quantitative research methods: a new research paradigm, *Anthropology and Education Quarterly*, **12**, 145–58 (1981).

GEERTZ, C., *Local Knowledge: Further Essays in Interpretative Anthropology*, Basic Books, New York, 1983.

INGERSOLL, J., Social analysis of development projects, a suggested approach for social soundness analysis, AID Development Studies Program, Washington, DC, 1977.

MYRDAL, G., *Objectivity in Social Research*, Arhabbey Press, Latrobe, Pennsylvania, 1969.

PETERS, H. W. and E. R. HENRY, Measuring successful performance overseas, *International Development Review*, **3**, 8–12 (1961).

ZIMNY, D., Polarity and political wisdom: the human science of Ernest Becker. Paper presented at the Western Social Science Association Annual Conference, Denver, Colorado, 26 April 1982.

200   *The International Education of the Development Consultant*

Related Novels and Literary Works

BURDICK, E., A role in Manila, in E. BURDICK (editor), *A Role in Manila: Fifteen Tales of War, Postwar, Peace, and Adventure*, New American Library, New York, 1966, pp.3–12.

BURGESS, A., *Malayan Trilogy*, Pan Books, London, 1964.

BURGESS, A., *A Devil of a State*, Ballantine Books, New York, 1968.

CHIANGKUN, W., As if it had never happened, in B. R. O'G. ANDERSON and R. MENDIONES (editors), *In the Mirror: Literature and Politics in Siam in the American Era*, Editions Duang Kamol, Bangkok, 1985.

DEJKUNJORN, V., Concerning *farang*, in H. P. Phillips (editor), *Modern Thai Literature*, University of Hawaii Press, Honolulu, 1987, pp.99–103.

DREWE, R., *A Cry in the Jungle Bar*, Collins, Sydney, 1979.

GREENE, G., *The Quiet American*, Viking Press, New York, 1956.

GREENE, G., *The Honorary Consul*, Pocket Books, New York, 1973.

HAU'OFA, E., Old wine in new bottles, in A. WENDT (editor), *Lali: a Pacific Anthology*, Longman Paul, Auckland, 1980, pp.225–230.

HAU'OFA, E., *Tales of the Tikongs*, Longman Paul, Auckland, 1983.

HAZZARD, S., *People in Glass Houses*, Penguin, Middlesex, England, 1983.

KEENLEYSIDE, T., *The Common Touch*, Doubleday and Co., Toronto, 1977.

LEDERER, W. J. and E. BURDICK, *The Ugly American*, W. W. Norton, New York, 1958.

LEWIS, T. and R. JUNGMAN (editors), *On Being Foreign: Culture Shock in Short Fiction, an International Anthology*, Intercultural Press, Yarmouth, Maine, 1986.

MULTATULI, *Max Havelaar, or, the Coffee Auctions of the Dutch Trading Company* (translated by R. EDWARDS), University of Massachusetts Press, 1982.

SRINAWK, K., The peasant and the white man, in *The Politician and Other Stories*, Oxford University Press, London, 1983, pp.61–71.

TWEEDIE, J., *Internal Affairs*, Penguin Books, Harmondsworth, 1987.

ULLMAN, J. R., *Windom's Way*, J. B. Lippincott, Philadelphia, Pennsylvania, and New York, 1952.

Biographical or Autobiographical Accounts of Professional Experience Abroad

BURNS, A., *Colonial Civil Servant*, Allen & Unwin, London, 1949.

CADY, J. F., *Contacts with Burma, 1935–1949: A Personal Account*, Southeast Asia Program, Ohio University, Center for International Studies, Athens, Ohio, 1983.

COATES, A., *Myself a Mandarin*, John Day, New York, 1969.

CURLE, A., *Planning for Education in Pakistan: A Personal Case Study*, Harvard University Press, Cambridge, Massachusetts, 1966.

CURRIE, L., *The Role of Economic Advisers in Developing Countries*, Greenwood Press, Westport, Connecticut, 1981.

DEMING, W. E., A view of how quality began in Japan, in *Quality, Productivity, and Competitive Position*, Center for Advanced Engineering Study, MIT, Cambridge, Massachusetts, 1982, pp.99–110.

DE VARIGNY, C., *Fourteen Years in the Sandwich Islands 1855–1868*, (translated from the French by A. L. KORN), University Press of Hawaii, Honolulu, 1981.

DOOLEY, T., *Dr. Tom Dooley's Three Great Books*, Farrer, Straus & Cudahy, New York, 1960.

EVANS, L. T. and J. D. B. MILLER (editors), *Policy and Practice: Essays in Honor of Sir John Crawford*, Australian National University Press, Sydney, 1987.

FAIRBANK, J. K., *Chinabound: A Fifty-Year Memoir*, Harper& Row, New York, 1982.

FOX, C. E., *Kakamora*, Hodder & Stoughton, London, 1962.

GALBRAITH, J. K., *A Life in our Times: Memoirs*, Houghton Mifflin, Boston, Massachusetts, 1981.

GARRETT, S., *Bangkok Journal: A Fulbright Year in Thailand*, Southern Illinois University Press, Carbondale, Illinois, 1986.

Bibliography 201

GUNSON, N., *Messengers of Grace: Evangelical Messengers in the South Seas 1797–1860*, Oxford University Press, Melbourne, 1978.

HEISER, V., *An American Doctor's Odyssey: Adventures in Forty-Five Countries*, Norton and Norton, New York, 1938.

LAMBERT, S. M., *A Yankee Doctor in Paradise*, Little, Brown & Co., Boston, Massachusetts, 1941.

LANGDON, R., Harry Maude: shy proconsul dedicated Pacific historian, in N. GUNSON (editor), *The Changing Pacific: Essays in Honour of H. E. Maude*, Oxford University Press, Melbourne, 1978, pp.1–21.

McCAY, C. G. R., *Samoana: a Personal Story of the Samoan Islands*, A. H. and A. W. Reed, Wellington, New Zealand, 1968.

MANGIN, W., Thoughts on twenty-four years of work in Peru: the Vicos Project and me, in G. FOSTER *et al.* (editors), *Long-Term Field Research in Social Anthropology*, Academic Press, New York, 1979, pp.65–84.

MEIER, G. and D. SEERS (editors), *Pioneers in Development*, Oxford University Press, New York, 1984.

OGURA, T., *Can Japanese Agriculture Survive?* Agricultural Policy Research Center, Tokyo, 1982.

PENFIELD, W., *The Difficult Art of Giving: The Epic of Alan Gregg*, Little, Brown & Co., Boston, Massachusetts, 1967.

SCHUMACHER, E. F., *Good Work*, Harper & Row, New York, 1979.

SEAGRAVE, G. S., *Burma Surgeon*, Norton and Norton, New York, 1943.

SEAGRAVE, G. S., *My Hospital in the Hills*, W. W. Norton, New York, 1955.

SHEN, T. H. (editor), Summary of the comments on Mr. W. I. Ladejinsky's Report on Rural Conditions in Taiwan. Mimeo, December (1951).

THOMSEN, M., *Living Poor: a Peace Corps Chronicle*, University of Washington Press, Seattle, Washington, and London, 1969.

WALINSKY, L. J., *The Selected Papers of Wolf Ladejinsky, Agrarian Reform as Unfinished Business*, Oxford University Press, New York, 1977.

WILLIS, B., *A Yanqui in Patagonia*, Stanford University Press, Stanford, California, 1947.

WOOD, B., *E. F. Schumacher: His Life and Times*, J. Cape, London, 1984.

WOOD, W. A. R., *Consul in Paradise: Sixty-Nine Years in Siam*, Souvenir Press, London; The Ryerson Press, Toronto, 1965.

Studies of Technical and Development Assistance

ADAB Business Kit: A Guide to the Opportunities for Commercial Involvement in Australia's Official Development Assistance Program, ADAB, Canberra, 1987.

ADAMS, M., *Voluntary Service Overseas: the Story of the First Ten Years*, Faber & Faber, London, 1968.

Aid from OPEC Countries, OECD, Paris, 1983.

ALLEN, P., The technical assistance industry in Africa: a case for nationalization, *International Development Review*, **12**, 9–16 (1970).

ALLEN, R., United Nations technical assistance: Soviet and East European Participation, *International Organization*, **11**, 620–7 (1957).

ARNOLD, G., *Aid in Africa*, Kogan Page, London; Nichols Publications, New York, 1979.

ARNOLD, S., *Implementing Development Assistance*, Westview Press, Boulder, Colorado, 1982.

ARNOVE, R. F. (editor), *Philanthropy and Cultural Imperialism: The Foundations at Home and Abroad*, Indiana University Press, Bloomington, Indiana, 1982.

Australia's Overseas Bilateral Aid Program 1986–1987, Australian Government Publishing Service, Canberra, 1986.

BARTKE, W., *China's Economic Aid*, C. Hurst, London, 1975.

BINGHAM, J., *Shirt-Sleeve Diplomacy: Point 4 in Action*, John Day, New York, 1954.

BOCK, E., *Fifty Years of Technical Assistance: Some Administrative Experiences of U.S. Voluntary Agencies*, Public Administration Clearing House, Chicago, Illinois, 1954.

BOORSTEIN, E., *The Economic Transformation of Cuba*, Monthly Review Press, New York, 1968.

BOXER, A. H., *Experts in Asia: An Inquiry into Australian Technical Assistance*, Australian National University Press, Canberra, 1969.

BROWN, E. R., Rockefeller medicine in China: professionalism and imperialism, in R. ARNOVE (editor), *Philanthropy and Cultural Imperialism*, Indiana University Press, Bloomington, Indiana, 1982, pp.123–46.

BULLOCK, M. B., *An American Transplant: The Rockefeller Foundation and Peking Union Medical College*, University of California Press, Berkeley, California, 1980.

BYRES, T. J., The white man's burden in neo-colonial settings, in T. J. BYRES (editor), *Foreign Resources and Economic Development*, Frank Cass, London, 1972, pp.79–116.

CHANDRASEKHAR, S., *American Aid and India's Economic Development*, Praeger, New York, 1965.

CUNNINGHAM, G., *The Management of Aid Agencies*, Croom Helm in association with the Overseas Development Institute, London, 1974.

Development Cooperation and the World Economy: Cooperation Between the Netherlands and Developing Countries, Development Cooperation Information Department, the Hague, 1980.

ELDRIDGE, P. J., *The Politics of Foreign Aid in India*, Weidenfeld & Nicolson, London, 1969.

ELDRIDGE, P. J., *Indonesia and Australia: the Politics of Aid and Development since 1966*, Australian National University Development Studies Centre, Canberra, 1979.

FAALAND, J., *Aid and Influence: The Case of Bangladesh*, St Martin's Press, New York, 1981.

FOSDICK, R. B., *The Story of the Rockefeller Foundation*, Harper & Row, New York, 1951.

GOLDMAN, M. I., *Soviet Foreign Aid*, Praeger, New York, 1967.

GORDENKER, L., *International Aid and National Decisions: Development Programs in Malawi, Tanzania, and Zambia*, Princeton University Press, Princeton, New Jersey, 1976.

A Guide to Japan's Aid, Association for Promotion of International Cooperation, Tokyo, 1982.

HARRAR, J. G., *The Agricultural Program of the Rockefeller Foundation*, Rockefeller Foundation, New York, 1956.

HARRAR, J. G., *Strategy toward the Conquest of Hunger*, Rockefeller Foundation, New York, 1967.

HASEGAWA, S., *Japanese Foreign Aid: Policy and Practice*, Praeger, New York, 1975.

HAZZARD, S., *Defeat of an Ideal: a Study of the Self-destruction of the United Nations*, Little, Brown & Co., Boston, Massachusetts, 1973.

HILLS, R. C., *Technical Assistance Towards Improving the Underlying Framework*, Australian National University, Occasional Paper no. 14, Development Studies Centre, Canberra, 1979.

KAMRANY, N. M., *Peaceful Competition in Afghanistan: American and Soviet Models for Economic Aid*, Communications Service Corporation, Washington, DC, 1979.

KIN'ICHIRO, T., Japanese Peace Corps turns technical, *Japan Quarterly*, **32**, 312–15 (1985).

KOMAROV, E. N., *Indo-Soviet Cooperation: Historical Background and Present-Day Development*, Allied Publishers, Bombay, 1976.

LARKIN, B. D., *China and Africa 1949–1979: The Foreign Policy of the People's Republic of China*, University of California Press, Berkeley, California, 1971.

LASKY, V., *The Ugly Russian*, Trident Press, New York, 1965.

LAUFER, L., *Israel and the Developing Countries: New Approaches to Cooperation*, The Twentieth Century Fund, New York, 1967.

LEDERER, W. J., *A Nation of Sheep*, W. W. Norton, New York, 1961.

LETHEM, F. and L. COOPER, *Managing Project-related Technical Assistance*, World Bank, Washington, DC, Management and Development Series, no. 13, 1983.

LIM, J. and C. TAN (editors), *Southeast Asian Perceptions of Foreign Assistance*, Institute of Asian Studies, Bangkok, 1977.

LINDHOLM, S., *Appointment with the Third World*, Almquist & Wiksell, The Dag Hammarskjold Foundation, Stockholm, 1974.

McNABB, S. and J. SOMSAK, What has 3 heads and preys on rural populations? (or bureaucratic politics and Hill Tribe education), *Adult Education and Development*, **22**, 135–42 (1984).

McWHINNEY, B. and D. GODFREY, *Man Deserves Man: CUSO in Developing Countries*, Ryerson Press, Toronto, 1968.

MADDISON, A., *Foreign Skills and Technical Assistance in Economic Development*, OECD, Paris, 1965.

MIHALY, E. B., *Foreign Aid and Politics in Nepal: A Case Study*, Oxford University Press, London, 1965.

MONTGOMERY, J., *The Politics of Foreign Aid*, Praeger, New York, 1965.

MORRIS, R. C., *Overseas Volunteer Programs*, Lexington Books, Lexington, Massachusetts, 1973.

NAIRN, R., *International Aid to Thailand: The New Colonialism*, Yale University Press, New Haven, Connecticut, 1966.

NURBY, B., AID education efforts: a critique, *Journal of Developing Areas*, **3**, 490 (1969).

OSSWALD, K., K. ULRICH and R. WERNER, *Frankreich's Entwicklungshilfe: Politik auf Lange Sicht?* Westdeutscher Verlag, Köln and Opladen, 1967.

PHILLIPS, R. W. *et al.*, Causes of success and failure in technical assistance projects, *International Development Review*, **1**, 22–7 (1959).

RAFSON, H. J., The role of the professional society in international development, *International Development Review*, **8**, 45–6 (1966).

RAWAT, P. C., *Indo-Nepal Economic Relations*, National Publishing House, Delhi, 1974.

RICE, G. T., *The Bold Experiment, JFK's Peace Corps*, University of Notre Dame Press, Notre Dame, Quebec, 1985.

RIX, A., Projects, surveys, and consultants, in A. RIX (editor), *Japan's Economic Aid: Policy-Making and Politics*, St Martin's Press, New York, 1980, pp.191–220.

SELIM, H. M., *Development Assistance Policies and the Performance of Aid Agencies: Studies in the Performance of DAC, OPEC, the Regional Development Banks and the World Bank Groups*, Macmillan, London, 1983.

SLACK, J., The grey Peace Corps, *Business in Thailand*, **15**, 55–9 (1984).

SOMMER, J., *Beyond Charity: U.S. Voluntary Aid for a Changing Third World*, Overseas Development Council, Washington, DC, 1977.

SPERLING, J., *The Human Dimension of Technical Assistance: The German Experience in Rourkela, India* (translated from the German by G. ON), Cornell University Press, Ithaca, New York, 1969.

STANISLAUS, M. S., *Soviet Economic Aid to India*, N. V. Publications, New Delhi, 1975.

SUFRIN, S. C., *Technical Assistance—Theory and Guidelines*, Syracuse University Press, Syracuse, New York, 1966.

SUTTON, F. X., Philanthropy, patronage, politics, *Daedalus: Journal of the American Academy of Arts and Sciences*, **116**, 41–91 (1987).

SWIFT, R. and R. CLARKE, *Ties that Bind: Canada and the Third World*, Between the Lines, Toronto, 1982.

TANDON, Y., (editor), *Technical Assistance Administration in East Africa*, Almquist & Wiksell, The Dag Hammarskjold Foundation, Stockholm, 1973.

Technical Assistance and Development, Proceedings of the Truman International Conference on Technical Assistance and Development Held at the Harry S. Truman Research Institute, The Hebrew University of Jerusalem, 1970.

Technical Assistance and the Needs of Developing Countries, OECD, Paris, 1968.

Technical Cooperation Among Developing Countries: What India can Offer, Indian Council of Agricultural Research, New Delhi, 1980.

TENDLER, J., *Inside Foreign Aid*, Johns Hopkins University Press, Baltimore, Maryland, 1975.

TEXTOR, R. B., *Cultural Frontiers of the Peace Corps*, MIT Press, Cambridge, Massachusetts, 1968.

THOMPSON, K. W., *Foreign Assistance: A View from the Private Sector*, University of Notre Dame Press, Notre Dame, Quebec, 1972.

WARNE, W. E., *Mission for Peace: Point 4 in Iran*, The Bobbs-Merrill Co., Indianapolis and New York, 1956.

WATERS, A. R., African development and foreign aid, *Publications in Comparative Research*, **2**, 1–10 (1984).

WHITE, J., Experts and advisers, in *German Aid*, Overseas Development Institute, London, 1965, pp.165–71.

WYSE, P., *Canadian Foreign Aid in the 1970s: an Organizational Audit*, Center for Developing-Area Studies, McGill University, Occasional Monograph Series, no. 16, Montreal, Canada, 1983.

Empirical Studies of International Consultants, Advisers, and Overseas Personnel and their Effectiveness

ALEXANDER, Y., *International Technical Assistance Experts: A Case Study of the U.N. Experience*, Praeger, New York, 1966.

BASS, B., The American advisor abroad, *Journal of Applied Behavioral Science*, **7**, 285–308 (1971).

BROWN, I., British financial advisers in Siam in the reign of King Chulalongkorn, *Modern Asian Studies*, **12**, 193–215 (1978)

BYRNES, F. C., *Americans in Technical Assistance: A Study of Attitudes and Responses to Their Role Abroad*, Praeger, New York, 1965.

CLEVELAND, H., G. MANGONE and J. C. ADAMS, *The Overseas Americans*, McGraw-Hill, New York, 1960.

DOBYNES, H. F., P. L. DOUGHTY and A. R. HOLMBERG, *Peace Corps Program Impact in the Peruvian Andes: Final Report*, Cornell Peru Project, Department of Anthropology, Cornell University, Ithaca, New York, 1966?.

DONALDSON, P. J., Foreign Intervention in medical education: a case study, *International Journal of Health Services*, **6**, 251–70 (1976).

GONZALES, R. and A. NEGANDHI, *The United States Overseas Executive: His Orientation and Career Patterns*, Graduate School of Business Administration, Michigan State University, East Lansing, Michigan, 1967.

HAWES, F. and D. J. KEALEY, *Canadians in Development: an Empirical Study of Adaptation and Effectiveness on Overseas Assignments*, Canadian International Development Agency, Ottawa, 1979.

MINKLER, M., Consultants or colleagues—role of United States population advisors in India, *Population Development Review*, **3**, 403–19 (1977).

NUNMONDA, T., The first American advisers in Thailand, *Journal of the Siam Society*, **62**, 121–48 (1974).

SANDERS, I. T., Satisfactions and problems of overseas work as reported by United States academic professionals. Address presented at public meeting of the Seminar on Institutional Structures and Cultural Values as Related to Agricultural Development, at Washington State University, 29 October 1965.

SIGGEL, E., Technical transfer to developing countries through consulting engineers: a model and empirical observations from Canada, *Developing Economies*, **24**, 229–50 (1986).

Examples of Technical Assistance Projects Abroad

BONGSADAT, M., Reflections on the city planning development of Bangkok: the past, present, and possible future, in *Proceedings of the International Conference on Thai Studies 3–7 July*, vol. 3, Research School of Pacific Studies, ANU, Canberra, 1987.

CASE, H. L. and R. A. BUNNELL, *The University of the Philippines: External Assistance and Development*, Institute for International Studies in Education, College of Education, Michigan State University, East Lansing, Michigan, 1970.

FOX, R. D., Spirulina: the alga that can end malnutrition, *The Futurist*, **19**, 30–5 (1985).

FREIRE, P., The people speak their word: learning to read and write in Saõ Tomé and Príncipe, *Harvard Educational Review*, **51**, 27–30 (1981).

FRY, G. and R. KAEWDAENG, Budgeting for greater equity: a normative regression analysis, *International Journal of Policy Analysis and Information Systems*, **6**, 115–31 (1982).

HAYDEN, H., *Moturiki: a Pilot Project in Community Development*, Oxford University Press, London, 1954.

HOXENG, J., *Let Jorge Do It: An Approach to Rural Nonformal Education*, Center for International Education, School of Education, University of Massachusetts, Amherst, Massachusetts, 1973.

KARNJANAPRAKORN, C., L. MCKIBBEN and W. THOMPSON, *NIDA: A Case Study in Institution Development*, International Development Research Center, Indiana University, Bloomington, Indiana, 1974.

LEMARCHAND, R., *The World Bank in Rwanda—The Case of the Office de Valorisation Agricole et Pastorale du Matara*, International Development Institute, Indiana University, Bloomington, Indiana, 1982.

LOVE, R. N., Pacific island livestock development: South Pacific in L. J. GOODMAN and R. N. LOVE (editors), *Management of Development Projects: An International Case Study Approach*, Pergamon Press, New York, 1979, pp.14–51.
TEAF, H. F. and P. G. FRANCK (editors), *Hands Across Frontiers: Case Studies in Technical Cooperation*, Cornell University Press, Ithaca, New York, 1955.
WOLCOTT, H., A Malay village that progress chose: Sungai Lui and the Institute of Cultural Affairs, *Human Organization*, **42**, 72–81 (1983).

Education and Training Dimensions

BARBER, E., P.ALTBACH and B. MYERS (editors), *Bridges to Knowledge: Foreign Students in Comparative Perspective*, University of Chicago Press, Chicago, Illinois, 1984.
BOURAS, L., Training, an essential condition for the data processing development in developing countries: the role of cooperation, in *Computers in Education*, North Holland, Amsterdam, Proceedings of the IFIP TC-3 Conference on Computers in Education, 27–31 July 1981, in Lausanne, Switzerland, pp.583–7.
COX, A. and K. MATHIASEN III, *United Nations Institute for Training and Research*, Brookings Institution, Brookings Staff Paper, Washington, DC, 1964.
FRY, G., The economic and political impact of study abroad, in E. BARBER, P. ALTBACH and R. MYERS (editors), *Bridges to Knowledge: Foreign Students in Comparative Perspective*, University of Chicago Press, Chicago, Illinois, 1984, pp.55–72.
KERRIGAN, J. and J. LUKE, *Management Training Strategies for Developing Countries*, Lynne Rienner, Boulder, Colorado, 1987.
MITCHELL, J. et al., *A Ten Point Training Program: Report on the Task Force on Training and Orientation for AID*, International Cooperation Agency, Washington, DC, 1961.
SANDERS, I. T., *Interprofessional Training Goals for Technical Assistance Personnel Abroad: Report*, Council on Social Work Education, New York, 1959.
SAYRE, W. S. and C. E. THURBER, *Training for Specialized Mission Personnel*, Public Administration Service, Chicago, Illinois, 1952.
THURBER, C. E., The problem of training Americans for service abroad in U.S. government technical programs. Unpublished Ph.D. dissertation, Stanford University, *Dissertation Abstracts*, **22**, 1704 (1961).
THURBER, C. E. and E. W. WEIDNER, *Technical Assistance in Training Administrators: Lessons from American Experience*, Institute of Training for Public Service, Indiana University, Bloomington, Indiana, 1962.
TRAIL, T. F., *Education of Development Technicians: A Guide to Training Programs*, Praeger, New York, 1968.
The training of trainers, *IIEP Newsletter*, **5**, 1–2 (1987).
WENGERT, E. S., Can we train for overseasmanship? *Public Administration Review*, **18**, 136–9 (1958).

The University and Technical Assistance

ADAMS, R. and C. CUMBERLAND, *United States University Cooperation in Latin America: A Study Based on Selected Programs in Bolivia, Chile, Peru, and Mexico*, Michigan State University, East Lansing, Michigan, 1960.
ADAMS, W. and J. A. GARRETY, *Is the World Our Campus?* Michigan State University, East Lansing, Michigan, 1960.
BOCK, D., Technical assistance abroad, in *Beyond the Ivory Tower: Social Responsibilities of the Modern University*, Harvard University Press, Cambridge, Massachusetts, 1982, pp.195–213.
CASSE, P., Technical assistance for the Third World: the role of Western universities, *The Bridge*, **5**, 25–6 (1980).

EDUCATION AND WORLD AFFAIRS, *The Professional School and World Affairs: a Report*, University of New Mexico Press, Albuquerque, New Mexico, 1968.

FRIEDMAN, B. D., Needed: a national policy toward universities of the underdeveloped world, *Public Administration Review*, **28**, 39–43 (1968).

GARDNER, J. W., *Aid and the Universities: a Report to the Administrator of the Agency for International Development*, Education and World Affairs, New York, 1964.

GOPINATHAN, S. and G. A. SHIVE, Scholarly access: opportunities and problems in North-South academic relations, *Comparative Education Review*, **31**, 490–508 (1987).

GOODWIN, C. D. and M. NACHT, *Fondness and Frustration: The Impact of American Higher Education on Foreign Students with Special Reference to the Case of Brazil*, Institute of International Education, New York, IIE Research Report no. 5, 1984.

GUNTER, M. M., Academe in the Third World: the experience of a Fulbright lecturer, *International Studies Notes*, **9**, 4–8 (1982).

LEE, K. H. and J. P. TAN, The international flow of third level LDC students to DCs: determinants and implications, Education Department, World Bank, Washington, DC, 1984.

McCAUGHEY, R., *International Studies and Academic Enterprise: A Chapter in the Enclosure of American Learning*, Columbia University Press, New York, 1984.

SANDERS, I. T. and J. C. WARD, *Bridges to Understanding: International Programs of American Colleges and Universities*, McGraw-Hill, New York, 1970.

SHIVE, G., S. GOPINATHAN and W. K. CUMMINGS (editors), *North–South Scholarly Exchange: Access, Equity and Collaboration*, Mansell, London, 1988.

SMUCKLER, R. (editor), *International Role of the Universities in the Eighties*, International Studies and Programs, Michigan State University (Proceedings of the Michigan State University International Year Conference, 25–27 April), East Lansing, Michigan, 1982.

SNYDER, H., The Michigan State University—aid project with the National Economic Development Board, 1964–68, Center for Studies in Education and Development, Harvard Graduate School of Education, Cambridge, 1979.

STREETEN, P., Reflections on the role of universities in developing countries, *World Development*, **16**, 639–40 (1988).

THOMPSON, K. W. *et al.*, Higher education and national development: one model for technical assistance, in *Education and Development Reconsidered*, vol.2 (document prepared for a conference at the Villa Serbelloni, Bellagio, Italy, 3–5 May), 1972.

International Management and Organizational Theory

AITKIN, T., *The Multinational Man: The Role of the Manager Abroad*, Wiley, New York, 1973.

BASS, L. W., *Management by Task Forces: A Manual on the Operation of Interdisciplinary Teams*, Lomond Books, Mt. Airy, Maryland, 1975.

CHESANOV, N., *The World-Class Executive: How to Do Business like a Pro Around the World*, Rawson Associates, New York, 1985.

FAYERWEATHER, J., *The Executive Overseas: Administrative Attitudes and Relationships in a Foreign Culture*, Syracuse University Press, Syracuse, New York, 1959.

HOFSTEDE, G., *Culture's Consequences: International Differences in Work-related Values*, abridged edn, Sage Publications, Beverly Hills, California, 1980.

ILLMAN, P., *Selecting and Developing Overseas Managers*, Amacon, New York, 1976.

KLITGAARD, R., *Controlling Corruption*, University of California Press, Berkeley, California, 1988.

KOBRIN, S. J., *International Expertise in American Business*, IIE, New York, IIE Research Report no. 6, 1984.

LYONS, N., *The Sony Vision*, Crown Publishers, New York, 1976.

MAISONROUGE, J. G., The education of a modern international manager, *Journal of International Business Studies*, **14**, 14–46 (1983).

MARCH, J. and J. P. OLSEN, *Ambiguity and Choice in Organizations*, Universitetsforlaget, Bergen, Norway, 1979.

MORAN, T., *Managing Cultural Differences*, 2nd edn, Gulf, Houston, Texas, 1987.

NSEKELA, A., Educating the international manager: some issues in the African context, *World Development*, **8**, 193–204 (1980).

PARSONS, T., Professions, in D. SILLS (editor), *International Encyclopedia of the Social Sciences*, Macmillan and the Free Press, New York, 1968, pp.536–47.

TORRE, M., *The Selection of Personnel for International Service*, World Federation for Mental Health, Geneva and New York, 1963.

Statistical Data on International Advisers, Consultants, and Technical Personnel

BOYNES, W. (editor), *TAICH Directory 1978: US Non-Profit Organizations in Development Assistance Abroad*, American Council of Voluntary Agencies for Foreign Service, 1978.

The Colombo Plan Annual Report 1986, Colombo Plan Bureau, Colombo, Sri Lanka, 1986.

The Colombo Plan for Co-operative Economic Development in South and South-East Asia: The Special Topic, New Dimensions of International Technical Co-operation of the 24th Consultative Committee Meeting Singapore 26 Nov–5 Dec 1974, Colombo Plan Bureau, Colombo, Sri Lanka, 1975.

Communist Aid Activities in Non-Communist Less Developed Countries, 1979 and 1954–79: A Research Paper, National Foreign Assessment Center, Central Intelligence Agency, Washington, DC, 1980, Document ER 80-103180.

Development Cooperation: Efforts and Policies of the Members of the Development Assistance Committee, Organization for Economic Cooperation and Development, Paris, 1987.

Directory of Non-Government Organizations of OECD Member Countries Active in Development Co-operation, Development Centre, Paris, 1981.

Eighteenth Compendium of Development Assistance to Thailand 1981, Development Assistance Group for Thailand and Srianant Press, Bangkok, 1981.

Japan International Cooperation Agency Annual Report 1983, Japan International Cooperation Agency (JICA), Tokyo, 1984.

Programme Budget for the Biennium 1982–1983. Use of Experts and Consultants in the United Nations: Report of the Secretary-General, United Nations, New York, 8 November 1982, A/C.5/37/27.

Report of the Colombo Plan Council for the Year 1 July 1981 to 30 June 1982, Colombo Plan Bureau, Colombo, Sri Lanka, 1982.

Report of the Commonwealth Secretary-General 1983, Commonwealth Secretariat, Marlborough House, London, 1983.

RIMMER, P. J., *Consultancy Services: Supply to Southeast Asia from Australia*, ASEAN–Australia Joint Research Project, ASEAN–Australia Economic papers, no. 7, Kuala Lumpur, Malaysia; Canberra, Australia, 1984.

Statistical Abstract of the United States 1987, US Bureau of the Census, US Department of Commerce, Washington, DC, 1987.

Twenty-Second Compendium of Development Assistance to Thailand 1985, UNDP, Bangkok, 1985.

Yearbook of the United Nations 1980, United Nations, New York, 1983.

Yearbook of the United Nations 1982, Department of Public Information, United Nations, New York, 1986.

Studies of Linkages to Power and Action

BENVENISTE, G., *The Politics of Expertise*, 2nd edn, Boyd and Fraser, San Francisco, California, 1977.

CALLIERERS, F., *On the Manner of Negotiating with Princes*, (translated from the French by A. F. WHYTE), Houghton Mifflin, Boston, Massachusetts, 1919.

HABERMAS, J., *Legitimation Crisis*, (translated from the German by T. MCARTHY), Beacon Press, Boston, Massachusetts, 1973.

KETUDAT, S. and G. FRY, Relations between educational research, policy, and planning, *International Review of Education,* **27**, 141–52 (1981).

Ross, L. A., Collaborative research for more effective foreign assistance, *World Development,* **16**, 231–6 (1988).

WILDAVSKY, A., *Speaking Truth to Power: The Art and Craft of Policy Analysis,* Little Brown & Co., Boston, Massachusetts, 1979.

INDEX